CU00688756

Africa in International Polit

Africa has long been considered marginal to the world in both economic and political terms. This important volume seeks to rectify this, arguing that there has been a continual flow of both ideas and goods between Africa, Europe, Asia and later the Americas. Indeed, Africa has never existed apart from world politics, but has been unavoidably entangled in the ebb and flow of events and changing configurations of power.

Africa in International Politics examines and compares external involvement in the continent, exploring the foreign policies of major states and international organisations towards it. Drawing on critical approaches from International Relations, International Political Economy and Security Studies, the book sets out a framework for understanding Africa's place in world politics and provides detailed analyses of the major external states and international organisations currently influencing African politics. At the same time, Africa is viewed as a player in its own right whose behaviour and agency acts to define, in many cases, the policies and even identities of external agents.

This book provides the first comprehensive, critical and up-to-date analysis of the policies of the major external actors towards Africa after the Cold War. The chapters focus on the policies of the United States, the UK, France, China, Russia, Japan and Canada, as well as the European Union, international financial institutions and United Nations peacekeeping.

Ian Taylor is a Senior Lecturer in African Politics at the University of Botswana and Visiting Research Fellow in the Department of Political Science, University of Stellenbosch, South Africa.

Paul Williams is a Lecturer in Security Studies at the University of Birmingham, UK.

Routledge Advances in International Relations and Global Politics

Africa in International Politics

External involvement on the continent

**Edited by Ian Taylor
and Paul Williams**

Routledge
Taylor & Francis Group

LONDON AND NEW YORK

First published 2004
by Routledge
2 Park Square, Milton Park, Abingdon, Oxon, OX14 4RN

Simultaneously published in the USA and Canada
by Routledge
270 Madison Ave, New York NY 10016

Routledge is an imprint of the Taylor & Francis Group

Transferred to Digital Printing 2006

Typeset in Times by Taylor & Francis Books Ltd

British Library Cataloguing in Publication Data
A catalogue record for this book is available from the British Library

Library of Congress Cataloging in Publication Data
Africa in international politics : external involvement on the continent/
edited by Ian Taylor and Paul Williams.
    p. cm.
Includes bibliographical references and index.
1. Africa–Foreign relations–1960– I. Taylor, Ian, 1969–
II. Williams, Paul, 1975–
    DT30.5.A3536 2004
    327.6
                                                    2003017310

ISBN 0–415–31858–0 (hbk)
ISBN 0–415–35836–1 (pbk)

Contents

Tables

Contributors

Adekeye Adebajo is Director of the Africa Program at the International Peace Academy in New York and Adjunct Professor at Columbia University's School of International and Public Affairs, USA. He served on United Nations missions in South Africa, Western Sahara and Iraq. He is author of *Building Peace in West Africa: Liberia, Sierra Leone, and Guinea-Bissau* (Lynne Rienner, 2002) and *Liberia's Civil War: Nigeria, ECOMOG, and Regional Security in West Africa* (Lynne Rienner, 2002), and co-editor of *Managing Armed Conflicts in the Twenty-First Century* (Frank Cass, 2000).

David Black is Chair of the Department of International Development Studies and Associate Professor of Political Science at Dalhousie University in Halifax, Canada. His current research includes human rights in the foreign policies of South Africa and Canada; Canadian policy towards Africa; and sport and world politics. He is co-editor of *Bridging the Rift: The New South Africa in Africa* (Westview, 1997), and co-author of *Rugby and the South African Nation* (Manchester University Press, 1999).

Scarlett Cornelissen is a Lecturer in the Department of Political Science at the University of Stellenbosch, South Africa. Her research interests are in international relations; the political economy of tourism; development theory and global tourism. She has published articles on Japan's relations with Africa and identity politics in the Western Cape in South Africa.

James J. Hentz is Associate Professor in the Department of International Studies and Political Science, Virginia Military Institute, USA, where he teaches national security, international relations and African political and economic development. He is the co-editor of *New and Critical Security and Regionalism: Beyond the Nation State* (Ashgate, 2003). His book *South Africa and the Logic of Cooperation in Southern Africa* is forthcoming (Indiana University Press). Dr Hentz was a visiting Fulbright Scholar at the Miklós Zrínyi National Defence University, Budapest, Hungary, in the spring of 2003.

Stephen R. Hurt is a Lecturer in International Relations at Oxford Brookes University. His research area is international political economy with a particular interest in development and southern Africa. He has published articles on European development policy in *Third World Quarterly* and *International Relations.*

Daniela Kroslak recently received a PhD from the University of Wales, Aberystwyth, focusing on the role and responsibility of the French government in the Rwandan genocide. She spent six months at the Norwegian Institute of International Affairs (NUPI) in 2002 where she was employed as a researcher on the programme *Training for Peace.* Her research interests include ethics in international relations; genocide; French African politics; issues of peace and security; and, in particular, conflict in the Great Lakes and West African regions.

Vladimir Shubin is Deputy Director of the Institute for African Studies, Russian Academy of Sciences. Before joining academia he was involved in political and practical support of African liberation movements, in particular as Secretary of the Soviet Afro-Asian Solidarity Committee and Head of the African Section of the CPSU International Department. He is the author of (in English) *ANC: A View from Moscow* (Bellville, 1999), *Social Democracy and Southern Africa* (Moscow, 1989, under a pen name, Vladimir Bushin) and various articles and chapters.

Ian Taylor is a Senior Lecturer in the Department of Political and Administrative Studies, University of Botswana and Visiting Research Fellow, University of Stellenbosch, South Africa. He is the author of *Stuck in Middle GEAR: South Africa's Post-Apartheid Foreign Relations* (Praeger, 2001), and co-editor of *South Africa's Multilateral Diplomacy and Global Change: The Limits of Reform* (Ashgate, 2001) and *Regionalism and Uneven Development in Southern Africa: The Case of the Maputo Development Corridor* (Ashgate, 2003). His research interests lie in the international relations of Africa; regionalism in Africa; the political economy of Botswana, South Africa and Zimbabwe; Botswana and South Africa's foreign policy; and Chinese policy towards Africa.

Caroline Thomas is Professor of Global Politics at Southampton University, UK. She has researched and published widely on South/North political, economic and security relations. Her books include *Global Governance, Development and Human Security* (Pluto, 2001), *Globalisation and the South* (co-edited, Macmillan, 1998), *Globalisation, Human Security and the African Experience* (co-edited, Lynne Rienner, 1999) and *Global Trade and Global Social Issues* (co-edited, Routledge, 1999). Currently she is working on the impact of current IFI policies on development opportunities in the South.

Paul Williams is a Lecturer in the Department of Political Science and International Studies at the University of Birmingham, UK. He is co-author of *Understanding Peacekeeping* (Polity/Blackwell, 2004) and co-editor of *Peace Operations and Global Order* (Frank Cass, 2004). He is currently writing a book on contemporary British foreign policy.

Acknowledgements

This volume sprang from conversations that the editors had between themselves and with some of the contributors as to the contemporary relationship between Africa and the outside world. Tired of the cliché that Africa was the 'hopeless continent', we wanted to explore what roles the major external actors – states, international organizations and corporations – played in and on the continent. In trying to draw out just how these external actors have helped perpetuate – as well as change – some of the features of contemporary African politics, we have been challenged and enthused by our collaborators and contributors. In particular, we would like to express our thanks to David Black for pushing us to broaden the focus of this book, and also to Shaun Breslin, Julie Gilson and Jürgen Haacke for exchanging ideas and commenting on various chapters. Thanks also go to the team at Routledge who have been encouraging – as well as patient – and have supported this project from the start.

Introduction

Understanding Africa's place in world politics

Ian Taylor and Paul Williams

Writing on the cusp of the new millennium, Jean-François Bayart correctly noted that, 'More than ever, the discourse on Africa's marginality is a nonsense' (2000: 267). Understood from the perspective of the *longue durée*, there has been a continual flow of both ideas and goods between Africa, Europe, Asia, and later the Americas. Africa has never existed apart from world politics but has been unavoidably entangled in the ebb and flow of events and changing configurations of power. This recognition highlights the sterility of attempts to define a rigid relationship between Africa and a somehow separate international system. In practice, Africa cannot enjoy 'a relationship' with world politics because 'Africa is in no sense extraneous to the world'; the two are organically intertwined (Bayart 2000: 234). To start any enquiry from the assumption of Africa's marginality from world politics thus misses the point; the continent has in fact been dialectically linked, both shaping and being shaped by international processes and structures.

Arguably the reason that the majority of commentaries talk confidently of Africa's economic marginalization and its political decay is a product of the inadequacies of dominant tools of social scientific analysis that renders 'much of what happens in Africa invisible to outsiders' (Bayart 2000: 229). In particular, many analyses of Africa's place in world politics suffer from an inability to conceptualize processes, events and structures that fall within the realm of what is usually considered private, illegal or – worse – mundane and apolitical. Rectifying these inadequacies would require, according to Bayart, paying close attention not only to what transpires within government structures, but also at 'the trading-post, the business-place, the plantation, the mine, the school, the hospital, and the Christian mission-station' (2000: 246). Obviously, a single volume cannot hope to be comprehensive in its coverage but it should remain sensitive to the multiple dimensions and sites of Africa's interaction with the world.

Africa's current predicament does not lack scholarly interest, but the bulk of contemporary studies on Africa have focused upon how the continent is in 'crisis', or succumbing to war, militarism, famine, poverty, natural catastrophes, corruption, disease, criminality, environmental degradation and crises of governance (see Zartman 1995; Ayittey 1998; Reno 1998; Bayart *et al.* 1999; Van de Walle 2001; MacLean *et al.* 2001; Schwab 2001; Zack-Williams *et al.* 2002; de Waal 2002b). This does not, however, mean that the continent should be written off as 'hopeless' (*The Economist* 13 May 2000). Rather, Africans, through a dialectic of structural pressures and their own political agency, have continually interacted with the world in ways that encompass notions of progress, order and justice although these concepts are defined in ways that do not necessarily resonate with dominant liberal approaches (Chabal and Daloz 1999). Moreover, the politics of resistance to these dominant approaches is very much alive in Africa (Harrison 2002). Realistic interpretations of the continent's position in world politics thus lie somewhere between the fatalism inherent in Afro-pessimism and the some-what utopian dreams of Afro-optimists. Both extremes do a disservice to the study of Africa. The point is that analyses need to remain sensitive to both the contingent aspects of Africa's interaction with the world and those steadier rhythms that constitute forces of continuity.

The scholarly literature addressing Africa's place in world politics has tended to focus upon the foreign policies that (relatively powerful) African states have employed in their dealings with the outside world (see Akinrade and Sesay 1998; Oyebade and Alao 1998; Lumumba-Kasongo 1999; Wright 1999; Khadiagala and Lyons 2001; Pinkney 2001; Adar and Ajulu 2002). Broadly speaking, these studies suffer from three significant limitations.

First, although some of these studies have recognized the increasing inter-connections between certain actors and processes in world politics, commonly (although often misleadingly) discussed under the umbrella term of 'globalization', they have concentrated on analysing the policies African states have adopted towards the outside world rather than on the policies external powers have adopted towards Africa (e.g. Harbeson and Rothchild 1995). This has been an omission in the literature for some time (see Shaw and Aluko 1984; Onwuka and Shaw 1989; Adedeji 1993). One of the few exceptions to this is Clapham's (1996) excellent study which focused on the ways in which the wider international system helped shape Africa, particu-larly forms of state power on the continent. This volume aims to complement Clapham's earlier efforts.

However, by largely confining themselves to examining the international relations of African states, most previous studies have told only one part of the story of Africa's place in world politics. After all, although talk of Western disengagement from Africa has assumed the status of orthodoxy, Western governments 'have not renounced their self-proclaimed right to influence the course of events' on the continent (Bayart 2000: 239). Indeed, discourses of globalization and interdependence, and fear of drugs, disease and disorder emerging from a Conradian heart of darkness, have encour-aged Western leaders to try and ensure that Africa's political trajectory fits with their visions of a well-managed and stable world economy. It is there-fore not surprising that since 1989 Africa has become a laboratory for many multilateral schemes, including those designed to achieve debt relief, economic development, security sector reform, crisis management and peacekeeping capabilities, and, of course, 'good governance'.

Second, many of these studies have employed conceptual frameworks that remain state-centric in both their ontology and approach (e.g. Lumumba-Kasongo 1999; Wright 1999). They have, with few exceptions (such as Harbeson and Rothchild 2000), failed to pay due attention to the important roles played by non-state actors in Africa's relations with the outside world, especially the international financial institutions (IFIs), development and humanitarian NGOs and transnational corporations. Tracing, let alone analysing, such interactions is beyond the task of a single volume. But while providing a comprehensive empirical survey and analysis would require a monumental effort, sketching a conceptual framework whereby such phenomena are not rendered invisible or perpetually consigned to the status of anomaly is possible. Indeed, recent research has made some important steps forward on this issue (see pp. 5–6).

Finally, many, although not all, of these studies have not contextualized Africa's current position within the broader context of (ongoing) structural changes within the global political economy. As a result of these limitations, the majority of studies exploring Africa's place in world politics tell only part of an admittedly complex tale. That is why a study of Africa's place in world politics from an outsider's perspective is vitally needed. Our intention, therefore, is to offer another part of the story of Africa's place in world politics. We do this by analysing the factors shaping how certain key external actors have interacted with Africa after the Cold War. But which outsiders should take centre stage in any such study? In the current era of contemporary globalization there have been obvious transformations in the state system. Non-state actors such as transnational corporations, diasporic communities and even criminal networks all flourish alongside and 'beneath' the more readily observable state-to-state interaction that has been the staple fodder of the discipline of International Relations. However, it is important not to throw the baby out with the bath water. The notion advanced by some that Africa simply maintains 'the fiction of Westphalia' and that states do not exist beyond paper declarations is plainly wrong (Swatuk 2001: 175). Despite such assertions, the society of states and the international organizations that its members have established continue to provide one important context for understanding African affairs. However, the society of states exists alongside and in a reciprocal relationship with a global political economy that exhibits alternative, non-state forms of authority (see Strange 1996; Barnett 2001) and where actors engaged in commerce and/or advocacy increasingly bypass political boundaries. Sophisticated analyses of Africa's place in world politics need to understand how these two contexts, the society of states and the global political economy, influence the continent's affairs. Analysts thus face a choice about how best to organize their thoughts on this issue.

Rather than try and adopt a distinctly 'political' or 'economic' approach, our contributors reflect upon the ways in which the society of states relates to the global political economy on issues relevant to African affairs. This position acknowledges that states have both shaped and are being shaped by the processes commonly known as globalization (see Clark 1997, 1999), although African states have had few opportunities to shape rather than react to these processes. Our intention in this volume is to focus upon those external actors (primarily states and international organizations but also corporations and NGOs) which have been significantly engaged (politically, economically and socially) with African affairs after the Cold War.

Geoeconomics: a neo-liberal global political economy?

Since at least the early 1980s, important changes have occurred within the global economy that have formed the structural backdrop for the way in which outsiders have interacted with Africa (see Drucker 1986; Dicken 1986). The dominant modes of thought and action within the global economy, commonly described as neo-liberal, have set the parameters within which debates about how the major external powers should interact with Africa have been conducted. Virtually all aspects of contemporary (state) policy have been heavily influenced by neo-liberal discourse, including trade, aid, investment, good government and governance, development, state-building, crisis management and peacekeeping, and human rights. In short, neo-liberalism has become the predominant ideology legitimating various policies (especially privatization and de-regulation) and delegitimizing others (such as centralized provision of basic welfare, and increased public expenditure and taxation). The desire to develop high levels of centralized and privatized social control thus lies at the heart of the neo-liberal project.

Today, the neo-liberal project operates in a context where it is possible to talk of the transnationalization of capital, where local, regional and global markets are increasingly organically connected. This has facilitated (and been facilitated by) an internationalized ownership of capital and its relatively unimpeded transit between various corporations and territories. These developments have been made easier by technological advancements which impact upon contemporary configurations of power and allow non-state entities to assume greater levels of political authority (see Barnett 2001). Often referred to by neo-liberals as 'globalization', this scenario has witnessed states relinquishing (often voluntarily) most of their ability to plan and regulate their national social and economic policies. As Timothy Shaw (1994: 18) has pointed out, these developments require analysts interested in explaining foreign and/or strategic policies 'to begin by recognising and evaluating transformations in the global political economy, especially in the South'.

In Africa, the power of the neo-liberal discourse was most obviously reflected in two developments. First came the structural adjustment programmes, initiated after the World Bank's Berg Report of 1981. While these programmes have spawned a massive literature (most of it highly critical), they served to buttress the political aspirations of dominant groups and reduce inherently political questions of social inequality and the role of the state to technical, bureaucratic procedures.

The second development has been the increasing re-privatization of external interaction with Africa (see Clapham 1996). This privatization can be identified in several spheres:

In security provision and the management of risks   The period since 1989 has witnessed the increasing privatization of the instruments of military power and violence and the concomitant erosion of the state's monopoly to wield such power legitimately. Arguably the most obvious manifestation of this trend in Africa has been the re-proliferation of so-called private security companies such as Executive Outcomes and Sandline International Ltd (Musah and Feyemi 2000; Muthien and Taylor 2002) and the more long-standing phenomenon of the military–commercial complex (de Waal 2002b: 123–5).

In commercial transactions and the extraction of the continent's natural resources   Today, private corporations are re-emerging as a significant means through which to extract Africa's resources (both human and physical). In many ways this is a return to the days of the British South Africa Company, *La Compagnie du Congo pour le Commerce et l'Industrie* and the *Deutsche Kolonialgesellschaft für Südwest-Afrika*. Decolonization may have occurred but this has not meant that external powers no longer have commercial interests in Africa. Indeed, as the US-led 'war on terrorism' continues, Africa's pockets of oil (notably in the Sudan, Nigeria and Angola) and the discovery of new offshore deposits along the Gulf of Guinea are likely to assume a greater degree of prominence in the world's corridors of power. Extra-African actors have constructed numerous transnational networks linking African localities to commercial centres such as Geneva, Brussels, Lisbon, London, Paris and Washington. According to one analysis, these networks can be understood as part of a broader phenomenon of transboundary formations that

> link global, regional, national, and local forces through structures, networks, and discourses that have wide-ranging impact, both benign and malign, on Africa, as well as on the international community itself. Above all, they play a major role in creating, transforming, and destroying forms of order and authority.
>
> (Latham *et al.* 2001: 5)

In many ways, such formations have simply developed the type of commercial activities that have existed for years between, for example, central Africa and Europe (see MacGaffey and Bazenguissa-Ganga 2000; Bayart 2000; Taylor 2003). However, until recently, the majority of these transactions did not appear on the formal economic radar screens of social scientists or were lumped together as illegitimate and/or criminal (Nordstrum 2001).

In relation to governance, administration and political authority   It is no secret that many African governments have never been able to broadcast their power and exercise effective control over large areas of 'their' territory (see Herbst 2000). Such realities of course point us in the direction of asking what exactly we mean by 'the state' in many parts of Africa. In these areas, informal (in orthodox parlance, non-state) forms of authority and governance have always thrived. But in certain African states, the erosion of the government's administrative capacity, even within the respective major cities, has encouraged the further 'delegitimization of public authority' and served as 'a precursor to its confiscation by private actors' (Bayart *et al.* 1999: 96). This is reflected in a whole gamut of private activities, ranging from neighbourhood patrols, vigilantism and localized judicial/court systems, to the employment of technologically advanced security equipment, private security personnel and gated communities. In such a scenario, the provision of security bears a direct correlation to one's ability to pay for such services.

In relation to knowledge about contemporary Africa   The push and pull of market forces within many of the states discussed in this volume has left their mass media obsessed with issues of fashion, lifestyle and entertainment. News about international affairs has, in comparison, assumed a smaller and smaller portion of media output. Consequently, and because most of the information collected by governments remains unavailable to their publics, even common knowledge of Africa is increasingly contained within the reports of private organizations such as the International Crisis Group, Amnesty International, Global Witness or Human Rights Watch, and periodicals such as *Africa Confidential* and *Africa Research Bulletin*. African news is out there, but only if one makes an effort to find it. In a different but related sense, the increasing trend towards the enforcement of intellectual property rights has meant that, for example, the scientific knowledge necessary to combat the scourge of disease on the African continent is also often contained exclusively within private organizations.

Geopolitics: getting beyond the Cold War?

During the Cold War, diplomatic, economic and military support was often given to individual African leaders who allied themselves (sometimes interchangeably) with either the United States or the Soviet Union. These alliances of convenience ensured a steady flow of resources from the superpowers to their respective allies. Little attention was paid to the ways in which these resources helped fuel corruption, patrimonialism and militaristic systems of governance. During the Cold War, the rules of the political game were understood by both patrons and clients alike: the superpowers sought geostrategic advantage and rhetorical support for their cause, while African leaders skilfully utilized the resources that came with supporting one side or the other, often to fend off political opponents at home. Superpower rivalry thus temporarily magnified Africa's geostrategic value and enhanced the influence that African states could wield within the United Nations (UN) system, the Commonwealth and several other international forums. But it also created a political climate that left virtually no room to address, let alone resolve, the political problems left behind by colonialism, such as the introduction of capitalist logic into virtually every social sphere (magnified after the Berlin Wall was brought down), the ideological dominance of the sovereign state as *the* legitimate form of political community, the institution of private property rights and the militarization of systems of governance.

Given the symbiotic nature of the relationship between many African leaders and the Cold War contest, it was hardly surprising that the end of the latter provoked a crisis in the former. As quickly as the Berlin Wall was toppled, those African leaders who had played the Cold War game most skilfully found themselves in a precarious domestic as well as international position as their continent's geostrategic 'value' plummeted, their primary source of external resources evaporated, and the nature of their domestic societies was placed under increasing levels of international scrutiny. It was under these pressures that many African states 'discovered' the imperatives of democracy and good governance.

The winding down of the Cold War and the collapse of the Soviet Union had other effects on the continent. Within the UN, for instance, African states lost one-third of the numerical advantage they had previously enjoyed. Approximately twenty new member states have been admitted to the UN since 1990, only two of which are African (Namibia and Eritrea). The others hail from the former republics of the Soviet Union, a disintegrated Yugoslavia, a divided Czechoslovakia and an embattled East Timor. These developments have not just affected the size and influence of voting blocs within the UN system: they also signalled a shift in the priorities of the major Western powers away from Africa. China, on the other hand, has increasingly sought to court African states after 1989 as a way to fend off Western criticism of its human rights record and establish its credentials as leader of the developing world bloc (see Chapter 4).

In particular, the end of the Cold War turned the West's old adversaries east of the Iron Curtain into Africa's main rivals for Western attention and resources. Since 1989, Western aid and investment have been increasingly channelled to former members of the Warsaw Pact rather than into Africa. In addition, the perceived triumph of 'market socialism' in China, and to a lesser extent Vietnam, has generated a new magnet for Western corporate resources. Western interest in eastern Europe and Asia have thus come partly at the expense of those African states that offered their support during the Cold War. During the 1990s, arguments that Western aid to Africa could be rationalized to domestic audiences in terms of enlightened self-interest became increasingly difficult to make in the face of mounting evidence of corruption, militarism and, by implication, bad governance. Without the spectre of communism on the horizon, Western chancelleries began to curtail their diplomatic representation on the continent and allocated Africa less and less money for foreign aid. Thus, just as the end of the Cold War deprived Western governments of the foreign policy equivalent of a 'magnetic north', so it deprived many African states of the lynchpin to their own international relations.

And yet the growing fascination with globalization and interdependence within Western governments, combined with the aftershock of the terrorist assault on America in September 2001, persuaded some leaders to argue for a return to earlier notions that foreign aid should be used explicitly as an instrument of enlightened self-interest. The aftermath of '9–11' stimulated a renewed debate – reminiscent of those surrounding the Marshall Plan in the aftermath of the Second World War – about the potential 'boomerang effect' of allowing large sections of the world's population to miss out on the benefits of economic development and democratic forms of governance. Within the European Union (EU), part of the response to these events was to channel more resources into international development programmes and to pay more attention to preventing (or at least responding to) collapsed and failing states, both within Africa and beyond (see Chapter 8). In the US, on the other hand, the response was more militaristic. This focused on first assessing America's own vulnerabilities from what successive administrations called 'rogue' or 'axis of evil' states, and then demonstrating that US (military) power was sufficient to topple these regimes if required. Other contending visions of what Africa was – or could be – to the US were trumped (see Chapter 1).

Finally, during the Cold War many African leaders, rather than seeking legitimacy from their people through representative democracy, relied on authoritarian or patrimonial forms of rule backed by foreign resources and powers. The end of the Cold War has made such political strategies more difficult or, at the very least, it has forced Africa's strongmen to look for alternative sources of external support. The increased difficulty of maintaining authoritarian or patrimonial rule without access to significant external resources can partly explain the wave of 'democratization' that occurred in Africa during the late 1980s and early 1990s. African elites certainly knew how to play the game in order to ensure a steady flow of resources from outside. The idea that many of these cases of democratization resulted, in large part, from a crisis of patrimonialism also helps explain why the emergence of multi-party liberal democracy has failed to incorporate, either economically or ideologically, precisely the most alienated segments of many African societies, namely youth, rural communities and women (see Bayart 2000: 227; Abrahamsen 2000). One might argue they were never meant to (Chabal 2002).

Structural changes in the global economy and the end of the Cold War have thus left Africa virtually invisible in economic terms but highly visible as a region suffering from violent conflict, famine, disease, poverty, environmental degradation and corruption. It is for this reason that some commentators have identified the continent as 'hopeless' or as one of the primary sources of a 'coming anarchy' (Kaplan 1994). Partly because of the frequency and importance attached to these negative images of Africa in the collective imagination of the major external powers, the continent has moved from being viewed as deserving charitable attention to being seen as a source of risk and danger. In an attempt to contain such risks from seeping out beyond Africa's borders, some of the major external powers, notably the G-7/8 states, and some key African states (notably Nigeria, South Africa, Senegal and Algeria) have proposed a New Partnership for Africa's Development (NEPAD). While the NEPAD has already generated controversy (see Taylor and Nel 2002; Chabal 2002; de Waal 2002a), it is important that the initiative originates from African states themselves rather than external donors.

Overview of the book

Which external powers to focus on and which to ignore is obviously a controversial issue. This volume is structured around states but hopes to avoid being either statist (investing supreme moral and political legitimacy within states) or state-centric (ignoring non-state dimensions of world politics) in its analyses. Chapters 1–5 explore the Africa policies of the five permanent members of the UN Security Council, namely the US, Britain, France, China and Russia. Chapters 6 and 7 explore the Africa policies of two states that have, for a variety of reasons including their membership of the G-7, been important external actors on the continent, namely Japan and Canada. Finally, Chapters 8–10 analyse how the major international organizations, namely the EU, the IFIs and the UN, have sought – to varying degrees – to promote peace, prosperity and democracy on the continent.

While the post-Cold War era has witnessed unprecedented levels of US power, this does not necessarily mean we are living within an American Empire. In our opinion, the Gramscian notion of hegemony more accurately describes the current position of the US government within the society of states and the global economy (see Gramsci 1971). The US, in other words, does not simply control political outcomes in Africa. Indeed, compared to the former European imperial states, it has paid the continent relatively little attention. During the Clinton years, for instance, the first term was largely characterized by responding to disasters and disengagement, and during the second term Africa ranked last in the five regional listings in the National Security Strategy. Nevertheless, and contrary to the Clinton administration's post-Somalia dictum of 'no US boots on African soil', between 1990 and 2000 US troops conducted twelve evacuation operations in seven African states, and seven humanitarian operations in five states (Frazer 2003: 290).

What attention the current administration of George W. Bush has devoted to Africa has been primarily framed by the principles of political realism. As in the Clinton years, this has involved building strong links with Africa's leading powers (especially Nigeria and South Africa); promoting US trade and investment, especially in oil-producing states; and emphasizing that Africans needed to 'do more for themselves' (Schraeder 2001). The prospects for the latter have been complicated by an inability to agree on what exactly 'African solutions to African problems' means in practical terms. In the aftermath of the 11 September terrorist attacks, however, Africa's current and future potential as a source of terrorism and oil has gained increasing attention from US foreign-policy-makers, not least because African oil is perceived to be much easier to 'manage' politically than that from the Middle East (Ellis and Killingray 2002). This rather interestingly dovetails with China's own policies towards Africa whereby oil is a major component and stimulus (see Chapter 4). More recently still, the September 2002 US National Security Strategy identified South Africa, Nigeria, Kenya and Ethiopia as 'anchors' for US engagement with the continent.

As Hentz argues in Chapter 1, a sophisticated understanding of US foreign policy towards Africa after the Cold War requires an analysis of the interrelationships between three ideological traditions: *realpolitik* (primarily concerned with geopolitics), Hamiltonianism (primarily concerned with geoeconomics), and Meliorism (primarily concerned with humanitarianism). Each of these traditions has supportive domestic constituencies within the US. After the Berlin Wall was toppled, a political opportunity opened up for US foreign policy towards Africa to embrace a more Meliorist approach. However, with the brief and problematic exception of Somalia in the early 1990s, both the Clinton and George W. Bush administrations have generally neglected Africa's genocides, wars, famines and epidemics. The policy frameworks adopted by the US, such as the African Growth and Opportunity Act, the African Crisis Response Initiative, the African Center for Strategic Studies and the various versions of the Heavily Indebted Poor Countries initiative, have failed to significantly improve the lives of ordinary Africans, although certain states and their elites have benefited from them.

Unlike the US, Britain's relationship with Africa after the Cold War continues to bear the imprint of its imperial past. Britain continued to enjoy very close ties to some anglophone and Commonwealth states in Africa, most notably South Africa. But under successive Conservative governments (1979–97) it significantly downgraded its presence on the continent as other areas of the world, notably central and eastern Europe and east Asia, assumed a higher priority in its foreign policy. As former British Secretary of Defence Malcolm Rifkind (1996: 633) put it, after the Cold War, 'Africa's voice risk[ed] becoming lost in the clamour of regions competing for attention'. According to Williams (in Chapter 2), the New Labour government elected into office in May 1997 has devoted greater resources and attention to African affairs than its Conservative predecessors, but the strategic objectives of Britain's Africa policy have remained consistently expressed: the promotion of peace, prosperity and democracy on the continent.

For Williams, Britain's post-Cold War Africa policy has been shaped by several important contextual factors, most notably the low priority accorded to African affairs, the selective nature of Britain's official interests on the continent, the unwillingness to move beyond an imperial spheres of influence approach, the British state's close collaboration with its transnational corporations, and the 'coups and catastrophes' approach that characterizes the little media attention given to events on the continent. In terms of promoting peace, prosperity and democracy on the continent, Britain has a mixed record. Notable failure to respond effectively to genocide in Rwanda has only been partially offset by the recent commitment invested in Sierra Leone. In relation to prosperity, successive British governments have defined this as being synonymous with the adoption of free market economies and the concept of 'good governance' as defined by the IFIs. The form of liberal democracy promoted by the British in Africa is also seen as being compatible with market economies, and often privileges the importance of civil and political rights over economic, social and cultural ones. In sum, despite some potentially encouraging developments in Sierra Leone, Williams contends that Britain's Africa policy has remained one of damage limitation.

Like Britain, as Kroslak demonstrates in Chapter 3, France's African policy has been marked by a contradictory process of reform and continuity since the early 1990s. France has traditionally claimed a special relationship with Africa, although it has drawn criticism for bearing all the characteristics of paternalistic neo-colonialism. The links between France and Africa have been highly personalized, perhaps more so than any other external actor. The French Presidency has played a key role in this relationship with the continent emerging as the President's favourite fiefdom. Essentially, France's African policy remains dominated and managed by a small, tightly knit community of politicians, diplomats and businessmen surrounding the President. This has been the traditional way of conducting Franco-African relations.

This means of policy-making has weathered the reformist impulses that emerged after the Rwanda debacle, the crisis in Zaire and the rebellions in the Central African Republic, all of which encouraged the new generation of leaders, such as Alain Juppé and Lionel Jospin, to overhaul France's links with the continent. However, as Kroslak points out, such impulses did not penetrate very deeply. The return of the conservatives to power has meant that 'business as usual' once again characterizes France's African policies, particularly under the Gaullist Jacques Chirac, with his all too discernible posturing of *la grandeur de la France*. As a result, the tentative moves towards developing a more multilateral African policy, even so far as involving *la perfide Albion*, have borne little fruit.

Like many other actors on the continent, France's ties with Africa reflect a reciprocal relationship, driven primarily in France's case by the desire to be seen as a global player and the wish to export a broader francophone project. The projection of French identity and cultural values overseas is an integral part of Paris's African policies, with what is in essence a cultural and linguistic crusade being pursued with an almost paranoid eye ever watchful for 'English' encroachment. In this sense, France needs Africa for its own image just as much as Africa needs France for material and political support.

Relative to the US, Britain and France, China's relations with Africa have not attracted a great deal of international media attention, yet this does not mean China has been inactive on the continent. According to Taylor (in Chapter 4), China's links with Africa are motivated by a number of clear goals. As a general foundation, the crisis in China's international relations after the Tiananmen Square incident in June 1989 prompted Beijing to rethink its links with both the developing world and with the West. In Taylor's opinion, the Chinese government concluded that the Third World – including Africa – was a more reliable and, crucially, non-critical ally of China than the West. Consequently, after 1989 Beijing made a concerted effort to rebuild and develop links to the African continent. Much of this is based on China's desire to take advantage of Africa's considerable numerical standing in the UN in order to prevent criticism of its human rights record *and* to ensure that the 'renegade province' of Taiwan remains an unrecognized international outcast. The expansion of Chinese trade in the 1990s and its concomitant increasing appearance in Africa have helped facilitate these policy aspirations: China is no longer a far-off country with ideological pretensions, it is now an active investor and trader with a significant physical presence in Africa. However, bereft of any meaningful civil society that might moderate Beijing's activities in Africa (unlike in most of the other permanent members of the UN Security Council), there is a danger that the more negative aspects of Chinese policy in Africa may, as Taylor suggests, not promote peace or development.

Russia, on the other hand, retains only a shadow of its former diplomatic and commercial presence on the continent. Compared to the Cold War era, Russia's contact with Africa has dramatically declined. This has been a direct consequence of the collapse of the Soviet Union, which left many Russians preoccupied with domestic issues, especially mitigating the many disastrous effects of the transition towards a market economy. Moscow's influence on the African continent has thus been significantly reduced. During the Cold War, African states had a special role to play as what Shubin in Chapter 5 calls the 'detachments of the world struggle against imperialism'. Today, however, few Russian elites are eager to establish close relations with Africa, preferring instead to cultivate their relationship with western European countries. Russia's relative neglect of Africa was thus highly likely. Africa (and Africans in Russia) even became a scapegoat for some of Russia's ills, the argument being that Soviet assistance to Africa was partly responsible for the economic problems that helped bring about the disintegration of the Union.

However, Shubin argues that there has been a change in Russian foreign policy towards Africa in recent years. Under the presidency of Vladimir Putin, Russia is looking to move beyond its recently subdued role in world politics by developing a more pro-active foreign policy. This has included a refurbished interest in Africa, particularly with regard to promoting peace on the continent, and also promoting economic relations. Taking seriously what it sees as its 'special responsibility' as a permanent member of the UN Security Council, Russia now asserts that there is no ideological context to its links with Africa, only trade and economic aspirations. Interestingly, Shubin also highlights a quite widespread negative portrayal of Africa and Africans, especially in Russia's mass media outlets. He suggests these developments need to be understood within the context of a post-Soviet social breakdown and the concomitant need for scapegoats. Russia's African community has consequently faced discrimination, if not outright violence, and Shubin deals with such a situation as part of an overall treatment of the domestic aspects of Moscow's ties with Africa and Africans.

Having been denied a foreign policy of its own for many years after 1945, Japan's ties to Africa have only developed relatively recently. Nevertheless, they are now extensive. Although in September 1994 an African country, Rwanda, became the site for the first deployment of Japanese soldiers in a foreign mission since the end of the Second World War, Japan's Africa policy has had little impact in the military security sphere. Instead, commerce forms the centrepiece of Japan's Africa policy, especially its complicated and extensive aid programme. However, Africa has not been the passive recipient of Japan's policy. Rather, the developing relationship between Japan and Africa, while partly the result of changing Japanese interests and fortunes, can also be read as the outcome of political shifts within Africa over the past two decades. Specifically, the emergence of new power coalitions centred around key African leaders – such as Thabo Mbeki of South Africa and Olusegun Obasanjo of Nigeria – has meant that Japan has been engaged with what are essentially African initiatives rather than simply imposing any agenda from the outside.

As Cornelissen argues in Chapter 6, it is true that aid constitutes a core factor in the relationship between Japan and Africa. But a significant element of Japan's activities on the continent is built upon a notion of a common destiny, an identity that can be encapsulated in the concept of an 'Afro-Asia bloc'. Just as China often tries to advance what it sees as its developing world credentials, policy-makers in Tokyo have also been keen to promote Japan as a non-Western country with a 'special relationship' with Africa. However, as Cornelissen points out, beneath this rhetoric Japan's Africa policy is in practice largely self-serving, using Japan's presence in Africa as a means to attain Tokyo's international objectives, and focused predominantly upon South Africa.

It seems clear that, like China, Japan pursues much of its Africa policy with a view to cultivating a supportive constituency at the UN. However, while China advances this strategy as a means of avoiding censure for its human rights record and to protect itself from 'interference' by other actors, Tokyo has seen a hypothetical 'Africa bloc' as an important potential ally in promoting Japan's bid to secure a permanent seat in the UN Security Council. As Cornelissen notes, Japan was elected as a non-permanent member of the Security Council seven times largely on the basis of receiving a substantial number of votes from the 'Afro-Asian bloc'. But this raises questions about the sincerity and depth of Japan's links with Africa. After all, Japan has effectively utilized its multilateral development policy prominence as a lobbying instrument for votes. If such votes were not forthcoming, would Tokyo retain such an interest in Africa? A further imperative for Japanese policy-makers is to ensure that their concentration of aid, trade and investment with South Africa does not jeopardize their ability to cultivate political support from other African states within the UN.

For Canada's part, Ottawa has played a number of leading roles on the African continent. At first glance this is somewhat surprising given that the country has never traditionally had any role in Africa – Canadian troops being sent to support the imperial power during the Boer War notwithstanding. In addition, Afro-Canadian commerce is relatively weak and Canada's geographic distance from the continent (in realist terms meaning that there is no compelling 'national interest' for Canada to involve itself in Africa) means that the motives for Canadian engagement with Africa emerge from other factors. Nevertheless, unlike in other G-7 states such as Britain or the US, Canadian engagement with the continent has resonated in the Canadian mass media and attracted widespread support from the country's attentive public. Canada has also become the base for an array of active advocacy networks, Partnership Africa Canada being but one example.

It appears, as Black notes in Chapter 7, that much of Canada's activism in Africa derives from the powerful self-image that Canadians have about their country: as one of peace-broker, concerned international citizen and repository of liberal values. This has translated into Canada maintaining a persistent – albeit somewhat inconstant – role in agenda-setting and institutional innovation. Yet such aspirations are hidebound by the restricted amount of resources that Canadian policy-makers seem willing to disburse in the pursuit of such projects. In addition, Canadian efforts are occasionally undermined by the lack of what Black calls 'followership' for its initiatives.

Nevertheless, Ottawa is engaged in Africa across a variety of dimensions, be it multilateralism, the promotion of 'human security', development assistance or a vibrant debate regarding corporate social responsibility. It seems that, unlike other G-7 states involved in Africa, Canadian policy-makers have to answer almost continually to careful observers of their Africa policies. As a result, Canada has arguably one of the most consistently positive records of promoting peace and development on the continent – although the purchase of such policies is undermined (and undermanned) by diminishing resources and the lack of 'power' that Canada possesses relative to other actors. However, Canada's engagement with Africa has not been wholly benevolent. As Black asserts, Canada's role has also been largely consistent with Western hegemonic aspirations on the continent, particularly with regard to the reconfiguration of Africa's polities and economies.

These seven powerful states have also been deeply involved with the development of the major international organizations that continue to influence African affairs. With regard to the European Union, since the end of the Cold War the organization's agenda has increasingly revolved around developments in its own continent and has become preoccupied with questions concerning the nature of the Union and its relationship with potential candidates for membership, particularly those to its east. Although never particularly high on the EU's collective agenda, Africa has slipped even further down the list of priorities. Indeed, EU–Africa relations have for some time been largely subsumed within the broader category of EU external relations with African, Caribbean and Pacific (ACP) states.

Both before and after the Cold War, EU–Africa relations have been dominated by issues of political economy, specifically trade, aid and development cooperation. As Hurt argues in Chapter 8, in many respects the terms of trade between the EU and African states have been getting steadily worse for the latter since the original negotiations which led to the Lomé Convention. Levels of aid have fallen and increasingly intrusive conditions have been attached to much of what remains. Hurt highlights the appearance of several morbid symptoms that are increasingly influencing the EU–Africa relationship. First, the EU's discourse of 'partnership' concerning issues of trade and development cooperation is not convincing, the reality being that African states do not have control over their own development policies. As far as most Europeans are concerned this is not seen as a major problem for states governed by authoritarian regimes, but it is a far more serious issue for African leaders who genuinely hold a popular mandate. Second, the EU has increasingly justified its own arguments with reference to the need to follow World Trade Organization regulations. Hurt suggests the EU has portrayed these regulations in far more rigid terms than is necessary. In sum, Hurt illustrates how the concessions originally granted by the EU to African states are being eroded, the number and scope of conditionalities are growing, and neo-liberal modes of thinking have become more firmly entrenched on both sides of the relationship as indicated in the greater role being accorded to private sector actors. The implementation of the Cotonou Agreement, which entered into force on 1 April 2003, has reinforced these trends for the next two decades.

In traditional political terms, since 1993 the EU has engaged with African affairs through its fledgling Common Foreign and Security Policy (CFSP). Apart from the adoption of a variety of common positions on events in Nigeria, the Great Lakes and South Africa's transition from white minority rule, the CFSP has been conspicuous by the absence of concrete activities undertaken under its rubric. Nevertheless, the EU has been engaged in a variety of conflict prevention measures in Africa dating back to the 1970s, and after the Cold War has taken a stand on the question of democratic governance, imposing sanctions regimes against several states, including Togo and Zimbabwe. Since the European rapid reaction force was declared hypothetically operational in December 2001, speculation has emerged that this could add a new dimension to EU–Africa relations. Most analysts have concluded that, for the foreseeable future, it seems likely that most military activities on the African continent conducted by European troops will be in their national rather than an EU capacity. That said, at the time of writing the French-led multinational force deployed to the Ituri district of the Democratic Republic of the Congo between June and September 2003 may signal a change of direction.

Like the EU, the IFIs have also adopted a variety of strategies and initiatives that seek to generate the appearance of significant changes in policy. Since the end of the Cold War, the IFIs have dramatically increased both the scope of their activities and the extent of their involvement in their clients' internal affairs (Williams 2000). They have also engaged in a series of attempts to reinvent their tarnished image on the continent and elsewhere by claiming to reject the harsh economic neo-liberalism that characterized the structural adjustment policies of the 1980s (Abrahamsen 2000; Thomas 2000). In part, the IFIs' broader and more intrusive agenda was a result of the negative consequences and failings of their earlier structural adjustment policies. As Clapham (1996: 176, 251) observed, not only had a variety of African states formally accepted adjustment packages while simultaneously 'failing to implement their least desirable provisions' but also one of their many unintended consequences was to reduce African states 'to a point at which personal networks rather than effective institutions provided the best road to survival'.

However, as Thomas argues in Chapter 9, the claims made by the IFIs that they are focusing upon pro-poor growth and helping to build lasting democracy in Africa are 'more cosmetic than substantive'. Thomas explores the extent to which African states have been given a voice within the IFIs after the Cold War in two ways. First, she finds that, as member states of the IFIs, African states have virtually no significant voice within their decision-making processes. For example, African interests at the IFIs are currently championed by only two, horrendously overburdened, African Executive Directors and the G-24 states from Africa, Asia and Latin America. In response to complaints about issues of representation, the IFIs have consistently avoided making structural changes to their decision-making mechanisms and instead interpreted these complaints as requiring them to develop more sensitive 'listening skills'. Second, in their position as clients of the IFIs, Thomas argues that African states have had virtually no say in the design and application of a variety of IFI programmes. Although the IFIs have recently adopted a new set of strategies based on the stated objectives of promoting pro-poor growth by designing country-specific Poverty Reduction Strategy Papers and enhancing the degree of local 'ownership' of the programmes, Thomas persuasively highlights the ways in which the IFIs have maintained 'the sole authority to give the stamp of approval to an entire *national* development strategy'. In short, African states still do not 'own' their national development strategies in any meaningful sense. The IFIs thus continue to promote neo-liberal economic principles in the face of overwhelming evidence of their negative social, political and even economic consequences. UN peacekeeping personnel have been at the forefront of those outsiders who have dealt with these negative consequences at the sharp end.

Despite some noticeable successes, as in Namibia, Mozambique, Cambodia and Macedonia, during the 1990s UN peacekeeping attracted most attention for its big three failures in Somalia, Rwanda and Bosnia-Herzegovina. The dominant powers within the Security Council have also been criticized for promoting a form of 'market democracy' as the centrepiece of their peace-building strategies after violent conflict has subsided (see Paris 1997, 2002). As Adebajo highlights in his analysis of UN peacekeeping in Africa in Chapter 10, after an initial period of relative euphoria in the immediate aftermath of the Cold War, the UN Security Council became reluctant to engage in further peacekeeping operations on the continent after the debacle in Somalia. Rwanda was the first casualty of the new rules of peacekeeping adopted by the US in Presidential Decision Directive 25. After this US-led withdrawal of the major powers from peacekeeping in Africa, it was left to the continent's own regional organizations to take the lead: for example, ECOWAS in Sierra Leone, Guinea-Bissau and the Ivory Coast, and SADC in Lesotho and the Democratic Republic of the Congo (DRC). However, none of these cases of regional-led intervention proved entirely satisfactory. The UN Security Council reappeared on the continent right at the end of the 1990s when it deployed peacekeeping operations to Sierra Leone, the DRC and later to supervise the end of the war between Ethiopia and Eritrea in 2000.

For Adebajo, the record of post-Cold War UN peacekeeping in Africa highlights a number of lessons relevant to Africa's place in world politics. First, he suggests that Western donors need to demonstrate a similar level of commitment to resolving African conflicts as they have done in Bosnia, Kosovo and East Timor. To date, Africa's conflicts have suffered from a lack of constructive engagement from powerful Western states. Second, there remains a pressing need to establish an appropriate division of labour between the UN and Africa's fledgling security organizations, which need to be greatly strengthened if they are to improve upon their current track record. Third, Adebajo calls for future UN operations to take a far more robust approach to dealing with 'spoilers' such as Jonas Savimbi in Angola or Foday Sankoh in Sierra Leone.

Concluding remarks

To return to our initial starting point, Africa is not marginalized from world politics and external actors continue to play a highly visible role in the continent, even if the international mass media only concentrates sporadically on the occasions when death and disaster temporarily guarantee viewing or readership figures. The motives behind this engagement remain complex and diverse and have been articulated by a variety of actors, including corporate councils, advocacy and solidarity networks, humanitarian organizations, private individuals and state officials constructing 'national interests'. The way in which such channels of influence converge and diverge provides a rich tapestry for this volume to explore. Who benefits and who loses out from these patterns of engagement is of vital concern. Indeed, the compelling motive for this book was to investigate whether the major external players on the continent are actually promoting peace, prosperity and development – as their glossy publications proclaim – or whether their policies are in some cases encouraging war, poverty and underdevelopment for significant numbers of Africans. The verdict, as the chapters in the volume discuss, is mixed.

In the same way that the Afro-pessimism/Afro-optimism dichotomy is unhelpful, so too must analysts be wary of relying upon the concept of neo-colonialism to explain the entirety of external involvement in Africa. African agency most certainly exists, whether our focus is on state elites craftily negotiating their relationships with creditors and diplomats or informal commercial networks of African traders and merchants in Paris, Brazzaville or Lagos. Contrary to some accounts there is little credible evidence of an international conspiracy to 'keep Africa down'. Rather, an eclectic mix of factors push and pull Africa and the rest of the world together, with motives for outside engagement ranging from crude profit-seeking and resource extraction to genuine humanitarian concerns to help alleviate some of the continent's crises.

Yet arguably one of the most enduring motives is the way in which engaging with 'Africa' provides an opportunity for external actors to define and re-define their own identity and self-image. As several of the contributors to this volume argue, Africa and its peoples serve as a means through which national and institutional self-images are developed and defined. Examples of this trend are apparent in the concerns of successive French governments about French civilization and the role Africa plays in maintaining its virulence; recent British attempts to save rather than conquer Sierra Leone; the persistent American claim to be making the continent (if not the world) safe for liberalism, capitalism and democracy; while Russia's withdrawal from Africa after the disintegration of the Soviet Union reflects its own ongoing struggle to regain its great-power status. In Asia, both China and Japan seem to observe in Africa a potential 'kindred spirit', one not quite Western enough to rule out various positions of solidarity and shared identity. For Japan this notion of a shared self-image with Africa appears to be driven by primarily selfish motives but is no less real for that. For China's part, its self-image as a former great power moving to claim its 'rightful place' in world politics needs African support in order to fulfil this objective. The growing corporate presence in Africa, as well as the burgeoning Chinese diaspora scattered throughout the continent, also projects this self-image. Similarly, Canada's self-image as a good international citizen demands that Ottawa play a constructive role on the continent. Whether this can involve more than being the humane face of Western capitalism on the continent remains to be seen.

The same trend can also be detected in relation to the EU, the IFIs and the UN. The founding documents of both the IFIs and the UN proclaim their intent to promote a liberal international order. This has compelled these institutions to engage with Africa, which has in many ways remained the most illiberal and underdeveloped of the world's continents. As far as the EU is concerned, the imperial legacy of several of its member states has ensured it retains a persistent presence in African affairs. However, in its external relations, the EU has lumped Africa together with other developing states in the Caribbean and Pacific. Moreover, as the Union enlarges to incorporate new member states with few historical ties to or little commercial interest in Africa, and themselves beset by problems of restructuring and rebuilding, it is doubtful that Africa will climb dramatically up the EU's list of priorities. Arguably, especially after 11 September 2001, the desire of EU states to contain the 'risks' and 'threats' (primarily in the form of immigrants and terrorists) that may emanate from African crises appears to offer the most urgent reason for lifting Africa higher up their agenda.

In sum, it appears that in order to understand Africa's place in world politics we must look not just at Africa but also at how outsiders perceive their own identity and relationship to the continent.

References

Abrahamsen, R. (2000) *Disciplining Democracy: Development Discourse and Good Governance in Africa*, London: Zed Books.

Adar, K. and R. Ajulu (2002) *Globalisation and Emerging Trends in African States' Foreign Policy-Making Process*, Aldershot: Ashgate.

Adedeji, A. (ed.) (1993) *Africa within the World: Beyond Dispossession and Dependence*, London: Zed Books.

Akinrade, S. and A. Sesay (eds) (1998) *Africa in the Post-Cold War International System*, London: Pinter.

Ayittey, G. (1998) *Africa in Chaos*, Basingstoke: Macmillan.

Barnett, M. (2001) 'Authority, Intervention and the Outer Limits of International Relations Theory' in T. Callaghy, R. Kassimir and R. Latham (eds) *Intervention and Transnationalism in Africa: Global–Local Networks of Power*, Cambridge: Cambridge University Press, pp. 47–65.

Bayart, J.-F. (2000) 'Africa in the World: A History of Extraversion', *African Affairs*, 99: 217–67.

Bayart, J.-F., S. Ellis and B. Hibou (1999) *The Criminalisation of the State in Africa*, Oxford: James Currey.

Chabal, P. (2002) 'The Quest for Good Government and Development in Africa: Is NEPAD the Answer?', *International Affairs*, 78: 447–62.

Chabal, P. and J.-P. Daloz (1999) *Africa Works: Disorder as Political Instrument*, Oxford: James Currey.

Clapham, C. (1996) *Africa and the International System: The Politics of State Survival*, Cambridge: Cambridge University Press.

Clark, I. (1997) *Globalization and Fragmentation: International Relations in the Twentieth Century*, Oxford: Oxford University Press.

—— (1999) *Globalization and International Relations Theory*, Oxford: Oxford University Press.

de Waal, A. (2002a) 'What's New in the "New Partnership for Africa's Development"?', *International Affairs*, 78: 463–75.

—— (ed.) (2002b) *Demilitarizing the Mind: African Agendas for Peace and Security*, Trenton, NJ: Africa World Press.

Dicken, P. (1986) *Global Shift: The Internationalisation of Economic Activity*, London: Chapman.

Drucker, P. (1986) 'The Changed World Economy', *Foreign Affairs*, 64: 768–91.

Ellis, S. and D. Killingray (2002) 'Africa after 11 September 2001', *African Affairs*, 101: 5–8.

Frazer, J. E. (2003) 'The United States' in M. Baregu and C. Landsberg (eds) *From Cape to Congo: Southern Africa's Evolving Security Challenges*, Boulder, CO: Lynne Rienner, pp. 275–99.

Gramsci, A. (1971) *Selections from the Prison Notebooks*, London: Lawrence and Wishart.

Harbeson, J. and D. Rothchild (eds) (1995) *Africa in World Politics: Post-Cold War Challenges*, Boulder: Westview Press.

—— (eds) (2000) *Africa in World Politics: The African State System in Flux*, Boulder: Westview Press.

Harrison, G. (2002) *Issues in the Contemporary Politics of Sub-Saharan Africa: The Dynamics of Struggle and Resistance*, Basingstoke: Palgrave.

Herbst, J. (2000) *States and Power in Africa: Comparative Lessons in Authority and Control*, Princeton: Princeton University Press.

Kaplan, L. (1994) 'The Coming Anarchy', *Atlantic Monthly*, February, pp. 44–76.

Khadiagala, G. and T. Lyons (eds) (2001) *African Foreign Policies: Power and Process*, Boulder: Lynne Rienner.

Latham, R., R. Kassimir and T. Callaghy (2001) 'Introduction: Transboundary Formations, Intervention, Order, and Authority' in T. Callaghy, R. Kassimir and R. Latham (eds) *Intervention and Transnationalism in Africa: Global–Local Networks of Power*, Cambridge: Cambridge University Press, pp. 1–20.

Lumumba-Kasongo, T. (1999) *The Dynamics of Economic and Political Relations between Africa and Foreign Powers*, Westport: Praeger.

MacGaffey, J. and R. Bazenguissa-Ganga (2000) *Congo–Paris: Transnational Traders on the Margins of the Law*, Oxford: James Currey.

MacLean, S., F. Quadir and T. Shaw (eds) (2001) *Crises of Governance in Asia and Africa*, Aldershot: Ashgate.

Mshomba, R. (2000) *Africa in the Global Economy*, Boulder: Lynne Rienner.

Musah, A.-F. and J. 'K. Feyemi (eds) (2000) *Mercenaries: An African Security Dilemma*, London: Pluto Press.

Muthien, B. and I. Taylor (2002) 'The Return of the Dogs of War? The Privatization of Security in Africa' in T. Biersteker and R. Hall (eds) *The Emergence of Private Authority in Global Governance*, Cambridge: Cambridge University Press, pp. 183–99.

Nordstrum, C. (2001) 'Out of the Shadows' in T. Callaghy, R. Kassimir and R. Latham (eds) *Intervention and Transnationalism in Africa: Global–Local Networks of Power*, Cambridge: Cambridge University Press, pp. 216–39.

Onwuka, R. and T. Shaw (eds) (1989) *Africa in World Politics*, London: Macmillan.

Oyebade, A. and A. Alao (eds) (1998) *Africa after the Cold War: The Changing Perspectives on Security*, Trenton: Africa World Press.

Paris, R. (1997) 'Peacebuilding and the Limits of Liberal Internationalism', *International Security*, 22, 2: 54–89.

—— (2002) 'International Peacebuilding and the "Mission Civilisatrice"', *Review of International Studies*, 28, 4: 637–56.

Pinkney, R. (2001) *The International Politics of East Africa*, Manchester: Manchester University Press.

Reno, W. (1998) *Warlord Politics and African States*, Boulder: Lynne Rienner.

Rifkind, M. (1996) 'Africa – Time to Take Another Look', speech to the Royal Institute of International Affairs, 28 November, cited in RUSI, *Documents on British Foreign and Security Policy: Vol. I: 1995–1997*, London: TSO, 1998, pp. 629–36.

Schraeder, P. J. (2001) ' "Forget the Rhetoric and Boost the Geopolitics": Emerging Trends in the Bush Administration's Policy towards Africa, 2001', *African Affairs*, 100: 387–404.

Schwab, P. (2001) *Africa: A Continent Self-Destructs*, Basingstoke: Palgrave.

Shaw, T. (1994) 'The South in the New World (Dis)Order: Towards a Political Economy of Third World Foreign Policy in the 1990s', *Third World Quarterly*, 15: 17–30.

Shaw, T. and O. Aluko (1984) *The Political Economy of African Foreign Policy*, Aldershot: Gower Press.

Strange, S. (1996) *The Retreat of the State: The Diffusion of Power in the World Economy*, Cambridge: Cambridge University Press.

Swatuk, L. (2001) 'The Brothers Grim: Modernity and "International" Relations in Southern Africa' in K. Dunn and T. Shaw (eds) (2001) *Africa's Challenge to International Relations Theory*, Basingstoke: Palgrave, pp. 163–83.

Taylor, I. (2003) 'Conflict in Central Africa: Clandestine Networks and Regional/Global Configurations', *Review of African Political Economy*, 30, 95: 45–55.

Taylor, I. and P. Nel (2002) ' "Getting the Rhetoric Right", Getting the Strategy Wrong: "New Africa", Globalisation and the Confines of Elite Reformism', *Third World Quarterly*, 23, 1: 163–80.

Thomas, C. (2000) *Global Governance, Development and Human Security*, London: Pluto Press.

Van de Walle, N. (2001) *African Economies and the Politics of Permanent Crisis, 1979–1999*, Cambridge: Cambridge University Press.

Williams, D. (2000) 'Aid and Sovereignty: Quasi-states and the International Financial Institutions', *Review of International Studies*, 26, 4: 568–72.

Wright, S. (ed.) (1999) *African Foreign Policies*, Boulder: Westview Press.

Zack-Williams, T., D. Frost and A. Thomson (eds) (2002) *Africa in Crisis: New Challenges and Possibilities*, London: Pluto Press.

Zartman, I. W. (1995) *Collapsed States: The Disintegration and Restoration of Legitimate Authority*, Boulder: Lynne Rienner.

1   The contending currents in United States involvement in sub-Saharan Africa

James J. Hentz

When in the course of a presidential debate with Vice President Albert Gore, George W. Bush was questioned about United States' foreign policy towards Africa, he responded that we do not have any vital interests there. This royal we, of course, meant a splinter of the US foreign policy establishment ensconced in the world-view of a particular branch of the Republican Party. However, in general, Africa is well down the list of American priorities.

This does not mean that the US has ignored Africa. President John F. Kennedy and his Assistant Secretary of State for African Affairs, Mennan Williams, for instance, were considered very 'pro-Africa', and President Ronald Reagan's Assistant Secretary of State for Africa, Chester Crocker, spent almost eight full years trying to cobble together a peace in Angola. In 1994, the Clinton White House hosted a conference on Africa and later dispatched Jesse Jackson to broker a (widely disputed) peace agreement in war-ravaged Sierra Leone. President Clinton himself made a rare presidential visit to the continent, which included his famous *mea culpa* for doing less to stop the 1994 genocide in Rwanda. Secretary of State Colin Powell, the first African-American to hold that post, visited Africa in 2002 and again in 2003 with George W. Bush.

The 2002 visit by an American luminary is revealing and foreshadows the theme of this chapter. *The Washington Post* on 19 September 2002 stated: 'Africa, the neglected stepchild of American diplomacy, is rising in strategic importance to Washington policy makers, and one word sums up the reason – oil.' Powell visited oil exporters Angola and Gabon, and in September 2002 Gabon became eligible for assistance under the African Growth and Opportunity Act (AGOA) (signed into law as Title 1 of the US Trade and Development Act on 18 May 2000). This followed the lifting of long-standing sanctions against The Gambia six months earlier, which had prevented the country from benefiting from any US bilateral assistance. Nigeria's oil also remains important: according to a source at the American Institute of Advanced Strategic and Political Studies, the US is hoping to double its oil imports from Nigeria from 900,000 barrels per day to around 1.8 million barrels daily in the next five years (*This Day* (Lagos), 6 July 2002). By the end of the century, Africa is expected to supply as much as 25 per cent of US oil imports. Finally, there are also reports of interest in a US naval base in the Gulf of Guinea and on the southern tip of South Africa.

Why the sudden interest? In the wake of 11 September the US–Saudi Arabian relationship in particular and US–Arab relations in general have become increasingly strained. While during the Cold War the US viewed Africa mainly as a Cold War battleground, oil has changed American perceptions of Africa's importance. However, while Africa's importance, or lack of it, to the US has almost always been defined by exogenous factors, it has been so within competing master narratives of US foreign policy. These might be summarized as: *realpolitik* (or geopolitics), Hamiltonianism (or geoeconomics) and Meliorism (essentially, humanitarianism).

The *realpolitik* school emerges from what Mead calls 'continental realism' (2001: 34–55). This approach resurrects the foreign policy approach of Metternich and Bismarck and in the American context was typified by Henry Kissinger and by the overall philosophy of the Ronald Reagan presidency. The heart of this approach is a balance-of-power game where 'a pawn is advanced here, a rook sacrificed there; here a feint, there an advance, there a strategic retreat' (Mead 2001: 39).

The Hamiltonian tradition – geoeconomics – in American foreign policy focuses on the promotion of a global order through the creation of an international legal and financial order (Mead 2001: 127). Critics say that this is basically a system that creates an integrated world market that promotes American interests. The creation of the international financial institutions (IFIs), in particular the World Bank and the International Monetary Fund (IMF), and the General Agreement on Tariffs and Trade (GATT), in the immediate years following the end of World War II are classic examples of Hamiltonianism. From this perspective, economic stability is considered the lynchpin of security (see Chapter 9).

Finally, global Meliorism is described by Walter McDougall as 'the socio-economic and politico-cultural expression of an American mission to make the world a better place' (1997: 173). Although it is intrinsic to Wilsonianism, Wilson's vision was much more circumscribed. In McDougall's words, 'after all, Wilson just hoped to make the world safe for democracy ... Global Meliorism [is] economic, cultural, and political' (1997: 175).

The pull of these different currents can vary depending on the times. The Hamiltonian tradition has been the longest and strongest and can also be considered the default option. The Meliorist, associated with American exceptionalism, also has a long history, but a relatively weak pull on US foreign policy, and has often been subsumed on the one hand by Hamiltonianism, through tied aid, or on the other by *realpolitik*, through aid for 'friendly' dictators. The *realpolitik* current is often overwhelming and destructive but, due to the relative neglect of Africa as a major part of American foreign policy, has not particularly been a consistently strong current in American relations with the continent. US foreign policy for Angola during the Cold War is an interesting case in point. In an ironic twist, the Cuban troops supporting the MPLA

(Popular Movement for the Liberation of Angola) government against the US-backed UNITA (National Union for the Total Independence of Angola) rebels helped to protect the interests of US oil companies against rebel attacks.

This chapter explores these three themes in US foreign policy towards Africa. The constant theme across the Cold War and immediate post-Cold War period was that American policy in Africa was framed by specific US interests and/or was delegated to others to manage. To some extent, this was a legacy of the colonial era: colonial powers only secured their relatively short-run interests, rather than the security of the African countries (Howe 2001: 29) and the US allowed Europe to 'watch over' Africa. In particular, Washington tended to follow the British lead in anglophone Africa. As Assistant Secretary of State for Africa Herbert Cohen (2003) described it:

> Ever since the late 1950s, when most of the African colonies were in the final stages of the independence process, the United States has attempted to play a secondary role to that of the Europeans. During President Eisenhower's second term (1957–1961), the National Security Council proposed a division of labour for the developing world. The Europeans would be responsible for Africa, while the United States would play the dominant role in Latin America, its own backyard.

Certainly, at points and at particular places during the Cold War, American policy was driven by its geopolitical chess game with the Soviet Union. In addition, to a large extent the US farmed out much of its policy-making to the IFIs, and continued to do so well into the post-Cold War era. As Cohen (2003) states, after the Cold War 'the United States reverted to its original low profile by relying on the World Bank and the IMF to bear the major responsibility for leading the Africans towards market economies and private-sector-led growth'.

But in the immediate post-Cold War era, US policy lost the rudder provided by its geopolitical chess match with the Soviets. In general, Washington – at least until 11 September 2001 – struggled with the strategic lacuna created by the Soviet collapse. In the contemporary period the question regarding what drives American foreign policy in sub-Saharan Africa has re-emerged with a vengeance.

The currents driving and directing America's Africa policy have obvious domestic constituencies in the US. The Hamiltonian current is driven by the material interests of US transnational business, and to some extent the IFIs. The *realpolitik* school is situated in the bureaucracies of the American foreign policy machine: the Department of State, the Department of Defense, the Central Intelligence Agency, the National Security Council, etc. The Meliorist approach draws its strength from NGOs concerned with Africa and with grass-root groups looking out for Africa's 'interests'. Such groups are most likely to have strong transnational ties and are often linked to the African-American community.

Obviously, as in all analytical categories, the borders between and among the three are not so clear in the real world. Not all government bureaucracies operate from the same page. For instance, the Department of Commerce arguably belongs to the Hamiltonian tradition. Its mission is to promote US commerce and it has traditionally battled with the Department of Defense over policy. Certainly, the IFIs have often been the handmaiden of US geopolitical interest, for instance in Zaire. But in the case of the World Bank's claim to promote development and poverty reduction, that institution might be considered part of the Meliorist tradition. Nonetheless, these three different and often opposing currents pull the US in different directions: each has a distinct political undercurrent and each treats Africa differently.

With the end of the Cold War, which of these currents would direct US foreign policy for sub-Saharan Africa was an open question. From one perspective, the lack of a 'grand strategy' after the Cold War, at least up until 11 September, opened the gates for more particularistic interests to influence US foreign policy and for non-state actors like the media to shape those interests. That is, for interests outside the formal policy-making apparatus of the government to have a strong influence, whether it be an undertow for Hamiltonianism or for Meliorism. In fact, foreign policy experts in the US warned that in lieu of an overarching guiding principle, special interests would drive overall global American foreign policy, and that there was a risk that some of the most powerful of these would be 'hyphenated Americans': i.e. ethnic groups with close ties to their homelands.

The strongest proponent for the Meliorist approach should logically be the African Diaspora, but it does not appear to have leveraged its political power to influence US policy towards the continent. This is not to say it has been silent: the Congressional Black Caucus has played an important role in foreign policy towards Africa, for instance in the sanctions campaign against apartheid South Africa. But, with some exceptions, other actors – corporations, NGOs and academics – have played much more important roles. For instance, the Ford Foundation was probably more instrumental in the sanctions campaign against apartheid South Africa. Thus it might be said that no group within the US has really gained purchase of American foreign policy for Africa in the same way other groups have for their ancestral homelands.

It seems clear that the African Diaspora in America will not drive American policy. In a speech to the Nigerian Institute of International Affairs commemorating African-American History Month, the US Ambassador to Nigeria, Howard F. Jeter, told his audience that the Diaspora stands as a 'political and economic resource that can benefit us all if properly understood and utilized' (US Department of State 2003). He noted that the African-American community is expected to reach 45 million by 2020, and today (2003) has a collective purchasing power of about US$450 billion per annum. But the speech reflected the paralysis of the

Africa Diaspora as Jeter (ibid.) remarked that he did not 'want to talk about the Diaspora as a historical reality. There is little of historic value I could say that you do not already know. I'd rather discuss the Diaspora in the future tense – as a dynamic community.' He was forced to use the future tense because the African Diaspora has not been a force in influencing American policy towards Africa. As Jeter put it,

> Is Africa using the African-American community as a primary political constituency in the United States? The answer is a resounding 'NO'. Are African-Americans really encouraged to do business with Africa – I don't think so. These are just a few of the questions that must be asked and answered in mapping out this strategy.
>
> (ibid.)

The lack of a strong – and effective – interest by the African Diaspora does not mean Africa does not have an American constituency; Assistant Secretary of State for Africa Herman Cohen (under George H. Bush), for instance, noted the importance of the Americo-Liberian lobby (Cohen 2000: 131). But it does mean that it is more difficult to escape the relatively lowly status accorded it in American policy.

Instead of an ethnic constituency, America's Africa policy is largely driven by the bureaucrats. Keller and Rothchild noted that in the mid-1990s the influence of bureaucrats in US foreign policy for Africa was on the rise (1996: 195). Peter Schraeder noted a similar pattern, labelling it 'bureaucratic instrumentalism' (1994: 196). There is a Catch-22, with a caveat, here. If the bureaucracy is largely driven by geopolitical concerns – of which there are few for the US in sub-Saharan Africa – one would expect disengagement to be the norm. In fact, for much of the post-Cold War this is what happened. The caveat is the so-called 'CNN effect', defined by Piers Robinson as 'instances when media coverage come to play a significant role in persuading policy makers to pursue a particular policy' (2002: 37). The CNN effect is strongest in periods when the policy-making elite lack certainty or direction. Finally, Howe argues that humanitarian NGOs in close relationship with the media helped influence states such as the US to intervene in humanitarian crises (2001: 105).

The Cold War era

The Cold War era emerged alongside and was influenced by the colonial era. After all, the decade of Africa – the 1960s – was also one of the most dangerous of the Cold War. In the waning days of colonial rule, the European powers sought – to varying degrees – to sow the seeds of democracy in the soon-to-be-independent states, but it did not take hold. Instead of democratic Weberian states, sub-Saharan Africa became populated by what Jackson labelled 'quasi states' (1990). In Cooper's words, the modern manifestation of this is 'the weakness of bonds between the state and the people within its territory and the reliance of state rulers on the very idea of the state, on resources deriving solely from its position within a global structure of sovereignties' (2001: 43).

The geopolitical machinations of the US, the Soviet Union and, to some extent, China at once promoted these quasi states and perpetuated this status. Super-power support made it possible for these states to use scarce foreign exchange for weapons purposes (Howe 2001: 77). There was also an understanding between the Soviet Union and the US that their respective client states would not be allowed to invade neighbouring countries (Howe 2001: 78). The result was that weakened states developed with a great potential for spill-over into neighbouring states, thus producing regional contagion.

Yet part of the problem was American attitudes to the post-colonial state in Africa. These countries were often considered as simply strange creations of colonialism and its denouement, and even though these artificial states gained international legitimacy by participating in world forums such as the UN their status as 'real' states – and that is how the bilateralism of US foreign policy approached Africa – was largely due to external guarantees rather than effective governance or domestic legitimacy. The worth of individual states was firmly embedded in their importance in the US strategic game with the Soviet Union. As Copson noted, 'the US typically justified its aid to Africa, whether economic or military, by stressing the strategic importance of the countries getting the aid' (1994: 104). Thus, such as it was, the Meliorist approach during the Cold War was embedded in the geopolitical struggle with the Soviet Union: during the heady days of the Cold War, US aid became indistinguishable from its geopolitical game. In 1973, 22 per cent of US bilateral aid was for political and strategic purposes, and 78 per cent for development. In 1985, it was almost reversed: 67 per cent was for political and strategic purposes and 33 per cent for development (Spero and Hart 2003: 204).

Angola is a case in point. In March 1975, a civil war broke out and the US supported the National Front for the Liberation of Angola (FNLA) as a counter to the MPLA. After the FNLA fell apart, the US switched to supporting UNITA. The US refused to support the *de jure* MPLA government and what ensued was a quarter-century civil war. At the peak of US (clandestine) involvement, President Ronald Reagan labelled UNITA's guerrilla leader, Jonas Savimbi, a 'combatant for liberty' (in Kambwa *et al.* 1999: 68). In 1981, the US announced a policy of 'constructive engagement' that led to the 1998 New York Accords and the subsequent exit from Angola of Cuban and South African forces aligned, respectively, with the MPLA and UNITA. But this did not end the civil war, it only ended the direct involvement of extra-continental actors and redefined the conflict matrix.

Certainly, during the Cold War US geopolitical interests in Africa were narrow in scope, but the commitment where it existed was deep. On the other hand, its geoeconomic interests, at least as indirectly represented by IFI activity in the continent, were broad, but quite shallow. More often than not, economic relations served geopolitical objectives. Out of all this, the Meliorist current was the weakest of the three.

The post-Cold War era

American foreign policy towards Africa in the post-Cold War era has witnessed the continuation of Cold War themes. However, the dynamic relationship between the *realpolitik*, Hamiltonianism and Meliorist currents may lead to new directions in US foreign policy for Africa. Interestingly, with the toppling of the Berlin Wall, the diminishing geopolitical – even the geoeconomic – importance of Africa, together with the CNN effect, may have strengthened the Meliorist current. Each will be examined in turn.

The geopolitical imperative has all but disappeared and the IFIs continue to act as surrogates for US interests in general and for the Hamiltonian tradition in particular. There are some questions concerning the US promotion of democracy in Africa. As Cox *et al.* (2000: 5) assert, it has become a much more prominent part of US foreign policy. For instance, in December 1990 the US Agency for International Development announced the 'Democracy Initiative' (Clough 1992: 58). But the promotion of democracy is difficult to separate from its Hamiltonian moorings. Capitalism needs stability, and America's post-Cold War promotion of democracy is part of a larger plan to promote a stable, peaceful and prosperous international order (Cox *et al.* 2000: 10–11). From the African perspective, Ottaway wrote that the 'new leaders' of Eritrea, Ethiopia and Uganda were themselves more interested in the reconstruction of the state and the economy – stability – than in democratization (1999: 11). The US for its part lauded the success of these new leaders.

The American argument that Africa needs to take responsibility for itself with the concomitant encouragement of regional arrangements to promote security, or for peacekeeping missions, is really a resurrection of the Nixon Doctrine, which as the US sought to withdraw from Vietnam argued that Asians should fight their own wars, although with US equipment and support. For instance, the Africa Crisis Responsibility Initiative (ACRI), which was formally announced on 10 October 1996, was a way to upgrade substandard African armies. Congressman Donald Payne in a hearing on the ACRI stated:

> I think that since the US has made it a policy issue of not sending US troops into harm's way unless it is a very, very unique [sic] situation – and I don't see Africa ever getting up to that level of the bar – I think then the next best thing would be that we ought to be able to train troops to be proficient in attempting to avoid the types of problems that we saw in the past.

> (US Government 2001)

As Howe relates, the first assumption underlying the ACRI was that African states and regions would have primary responsibility for their security (2001: 248). Operation Focus Relief under Bill Clinton, for instance, spent $50 million to train and equip units from Nigeria, Ghana and Senegal for deployment to Sierra Leone.

A similar logic explains American support for the privatization of security in Africa. In 1997 the Defense Intelligence Agency held a workshop entitled 'Privatization of National Security in Sub-Saharan Africa' which supported the notion of private militaries operating in Africa (Reno 2001: 210). In 1999, the US Agency for International Development (USAID) contracted for seven employees of the American security firm Military Professional Resources Inc. (MPRI) to present to the Obasanjo government of Nigeria a way to professionalize his army (Howe 2001: 220).

American disengagement was also reflected in the fact that nine of its twenty-one missions for overseas aid that were to be closed down in 1999 were in Africa (Martin and Schumann 1998: 25). Consequently, USAID was accused of picking 'winners' (Rothchild and Sisk 1996: 288). In Africa, the level of assistance declined in step with the continent's diminished geopolitical importance. US state-to-state/bilateral aid to Africa went from a peak of US$2.4 billion in 1985 to US$1.2 billion in 1990, and this did not go any higher for the rest of the 1990s (Reno 2001: 200).

At the same time, the IFIs continue to be an important proxy for US interests in Africa (see Chapter 9). African private debt at 35 per cent of its total is, unlike Latin America, relatively small, and Africa, therefore, is particularly susceptible to IFI influence. More importantly, Treasury Secretary Robert Rubin listed a renewed US commitment to using the IFIs as instruments to develop the Third World as a priority of Clinton's second term. The Clinton administration's *A Comprehensive Trade and Development Policy for the Countries of Africa: Executive Summary* (US Government 1997) notes that, as of 1996, twenty-three African states had reform programmes in effect with the IMF, and thirty-one participated in World Bank-led Special Programmes of Assistance. The *Executive Summary* adds, 'if obstacles that hinder investment are removed, benefits will accrue to both the US investors and the African nations' (1997: 3).

But sub-Saharan Africa has remained the orphan of international interest and investment. In general, as Arnold states, 'although the population [of southern Africa] is estimated to exceed 100 million, individual markets are relatively small, and they consequently do not presently attract significant domestic or foreign investment' (1992: 152). It is easy to understand why. Africa's return on investment fell from 30.7 per cent in the 1960s to 2.5 per cent in the 1980s (Callaghy 1996: 8), and during the 1990s sub-Saharan Africa's share of global investment decreased from 12 per cent in 1985 to just under 3 per cent in 1994. To put Africa in comparative perspective, the amount of external financing done in 1991 through bonds for South Asia was $1.9 billion, for Africa zero (Callaghy 1996: 9). As the new millennium started, the *realpolitik* current was weak; the Hamiltonian current was constant but weakened by its failures in Africa.

Of course, if the *realpolitik* and Hamiltonian currents weaken, the pull of Meliorism could become relatively more powerful. Raymond Copson (1994: 115) states:

> Clearly, however, US motivations were also in part humanitarian – an outgrowth of the deep concern felt among many Americans over war and famine in Africa. This concern was inspired by media reports and articulated by interested individuals, church organizations, relief agencies, and lobbies for the hungry and refugees. Congressional hearings and legislative proposals aimed at promoting peace and helping the victims of war made public concern over Africa's wars and their consequences clear to policy makers.

Outside the formal halls of government, the Meliorist tradition had already succeeded in moving US policy towards Africa. The sanctions campaign against South Africa is an important example. First, the Reagan administration was forced to abandon its 'Tar Baby' option of relying on apartheid South Africa for the promotion of US interests in southern Africa. Second, even before the recalcitrant American government employed sanctions, private groups such as powerful universities and transnational corporations began to disinvest from South Africa. In other parts of Africa, Uganda's National Resistance Army (NRA) used its external wing in New York to prompt a US Congressional hearing in 1982 on the human rights violations of the Obote government (Ngoga 1998: 97). Herman Cohen chronicles US involvement in seven African countries during his service as George H. Bush's Under Secretary of State for Africa: Ethiopia, Sudan, Angola, Liberia, Rwanda, Mozambique and Somalia. With the exception of Angola, each case had a powerful humanitarian pull on US policy. And in most cases, the US media (the CNN effect) pushed the humanitarian cause (Cohen 2000).

Somalia and its aftermath is an example of the ebb and flow of Meliorism, and reflective of its shallow currents in US foreign policy. In late 1992 President George Bush announced Operation Restore Hope (under UN Security Council Resolution 704), an effort to protect relief supplies in Somalia. Herman Cohen claims that this was a case of humanitarian outrage defeating bureaucratic resistance in Washington (2000: 208). At the time it was the most expensive humanitarian operation ever undertaken (Ahmed 1999: 248), though Compagnon argues that it was largely a show for public opinion (1998: 87). The result was a chronicled disaster for the US epitomized in October 1993 when eighteen US soldiers were killed and seventy-three wounded in Mogadishu. The US movie industry memorialized the deaths of US soldiers in the film *Black Hawk Down*. The aftermath of the failure of the most expensive humanitarian effort, six months after the debacle, was the April 1994 genocide in Rwanda. The CNN effect indeed has its dark side.

In her account of US policy-making during the Rwanda genocide, Samantha Power chronicles a period of paralysis (2001). The most poignant symbol of US interaction was the refusal of the Clinton administration to use the word 'genocide', because under the 1948 Genocide Convention it would necessitate action. The details of Power's account illuminate, or darken, the themes addressed above, and offer an introduction to the next section. First, Congress was largely inactive and the Congressional Black Caucus unwilling to act (Power 2001). Second, policy was driven by the Rwanda Interagency Working Group, which was dominated by key mid-level bureaucrats at the Department of Defense and the White House. They chose to do nothing, and in fact the 'Pentagon Chop' stopped any form of intervention (Power 2001). Finally, the most knowledgeable group, Human Rights Watch, lacked a grass-roots base from which to mobilize a large part of US society (Power 2001).

In whose interests?

The end of the Cold War has created a bifurcation in policy towards Africa. First, and particularly in the wake of 11 September, there is a 'new' strategic interest. Second, destabilization – latent in Cold War policy in Africa and ravaging the continent today – has created a whole range of new concerns, typically considered 'humanitarian'. The Hamiltonian tradition remains the default option while the opposed poles of *realpolitik* and Meliorism are pulling US foreign policy for sub-Saharan Africa in diametrically different directions. With these new issues comes a range of interested parties. Thus, ironically, while the US government, as one collective actor, may be losing interest, other actors have become more interested.

In the early years of this millennium, Africa's place in US policy remains the same as always – distant and marginalized. The relative strengths of the three currents, *realpolitik*, Hamiltonianism and Meliorism, determine whether it can take a new course. This, in turn, depends on the subcutaneous forces and undertows of each of these currents. It is important to look at each of these forces.

Realpolitik

As noted above, sub-Saharan Africa's geopolitical importance has waned. However, this may not last, as Africa is rich in four key resources: oil, minerals, gems and timber (Klare 2001: 217). The minerals sector includes such strategic resources as platinum, cobalt, bauxite and manganese. A rejuvenated strategic interest would mean that American national security bureaucracies could be re-engaged. As Assistant Secretary of State for Africa Susan Rice (Clinton administration) stated:

There was a time not long ago when Africa was the exclusive domain of one understaffed bureau at Foggy Bottom ... But now virtually every government agency is building the capacity to implement new programmes that support our policy of comprehensive engagement with Africa.

(Klare 2001: 219)

But there has been little substance to back up these words.

The most concrete commitment the US has made to African security is the ACRI. The genesis of the ACRI is the failure of the US-proposed African Crisis Response Force (ACRF). Among other reasons, many Africans were concerned with the foreign creation of the force and wondered whether it was merely an instrument of US strategic interests in Africa (Howe 2001: 250). The ACRI is designed to build military capacity within selected units of national militaries. They would act in concert with other military units when requested by the UN, OAU or regional bodies, but the US would determine membership. From an African perspective, the ACRI's insistence on determining the criteria for military assistance smacks of 'neo-colonialism'. As Howe concludes, because of its foreign roots it is a flawed initiative (2001: 275). In fact, the United States' two most important African partners, Nigeria and South Africa, did not participate.

Hamiltonianism

The ACRI is primarily about military security, but insomuch as it is about stability and establishing order it could also be considered a component of the Hamiltonian current. As Kapstein argues, the building of a liberal world economy has been a consistent American objective since the end of World War II (1994: 79). The Africa Growth and Opportunity Act (AGOA) is the embodiment of the Hamiltonian tradition. In essence, it is meant to pick up where the IFIs failed – bring Africa into the international economic fold. As the US Department of Commerce describes it:

The Act offers tangible incentives for African countries to continue their efforts to open their economies and build free markets. President Bush signed amendments to AGOA, also known as AGOA II, into law on August 6, 2002 as Sec. 3108 of the Trade Act of 2002. AGOA II substantially expands preferential access for imports from beneficiary sub-Saharan African countries.

AGOA provides reforming African countries with the most liberal access to the US market available to any country or region with which the United States does not have a Free Trade Agreement. It supports US business by encouraging reform of Africa's economic and commercial regimes, which will build stronger markets and more effective partners for US firms.

(www.agoa.gov/About_AGOA/about_agoa.html)

The domestic response to AGOA has been strong, ranging across American and international civil society.

The Association of Concerned Africa Scholars, however, argued that AGOA had conditionalities similar to those imposed by the IFIs on African countries. They furthermore criticized the bill's use of the NAFTA model of regional economic integration (Hentz 2000). Other domestic activists also weighed in. However, the driving force behind AGOA was American business, and in particular the Corporate Council on Africa (CCA). In its own words, 'CCA is involved with AGOA at every level, from our AGOA Steering Committee to our involvement in the past two AGOA Forums, to the State Department's flagship AGOA grant – the AGOA Professional Development Programme' (www.africacncl.org/agoa/default.asp). Most importantly, the CCA not only strongly supported AGOA, but CCA chairs the AGOA Steering Committee, a body appointed by the White House, with open meetings once a month to discuss key AGOA-related trade issues.

Non-governmental international groups have also been given a voice. The first AGOA–NGO Forum took place from 13 to 15 January 2003 at the Indira Gandhi Centre for Indian Culture in Phoenix, Mauritius. One hundred and fifty participants attended the event. The AGOA–NGO forum made a series of recommendations but the first on the list is revealing, forming a bridge to the Meliorist tradition: 'AGOA [shall] be not restricted to trade but be made an integrated package that also caters for human development in terms of better access to education, health care, sanitary conditions, etc.' (www.agoa.mu/speech/speech14.htm).

Meliorists in the US made similar points. For instance, the Lutheran Office for Governmental Affairs (1998) stated that

> in the last two years, Washington's debate about Africa has centred on the Africa Growth and Opportunity Act and presidential initiatives along the same line. Despite token endorsements of aid, debt relief and human rights inserted into later versions of the bill, its principal backers continued to present it as a 'paradigm shift' from aid to trade and investment.

Congresswoman Maxine Walters summarized the opposition's feeling about AGOA when she said that she

> had hoped [that what] would emerge would be an Africa trade and aid bill that would act as an important first step towards a comprehensive economic approach with the continent of Africa. African nations should be treated as equals in trade while continuing to receive the vital aid needed for sustainable development. What we now face is an omnibus trade bill, which appears to be a 'Christmas tree' for multinational corporations. This new bill shows little regard for the importance of leaving the ownership of Africa in the hands of Africans.
>
> (*Public Citizen*, 30 July 1998)

What had annoyed Walters was the Senate Finance Committee's stripping of the Africa bill of important provisions that dealt with debt relief. However, even though there was widespread dissent and lobbying *vis-à-vis* AGOA, it became law, promoting a Hamiltonian strategy for sub-Saharan Africa, and backed by American business.

Meliorism

Both the *realpolitik* and Hamiltonian currents in US foreign policy for sub-Saharan Africa do have elements of Meliorism. In fact, as Howe argues, military engagement in Africa after the Cold War was driven largely by a moral imperative (2001: 104). In the immediate years after the Cold War the 'moral' argument seemed strong: in 1991 Congress increased development aid by 25 per cent (Copson 1994: 170). The following year, however, Congress failed to boost aid because of, among other reasons, concerns within the Democratic Party that their support for foreign assistance would hurt their chances for re-election (ibid.). So not only was the Meliorist current lacking strong domestic support, but domestic political currents pulled in the opposite direction.

This is where the Heavily Indebted Poor Countries (HIPC) initiative becomes interesting. The HIPC initiative does, of course, have geopolitical and geoeconomic elements. For instance, it is a way for the US to support client states in an era of severe budgetary constraints (Callaghy 2001: 139). Debt relief was also necessary for many countries to be able to buy American products. Nonetheless, it is the best example of the Meliorist tradition in US foreign policy, and the most successful case of broad pro-Africa lobbying.

By the early 1990s, it had become clear that Africa's debt problem was more about insolvency than it was about liquidity. By 1996, the IFIs had designated forty-one of its members as HIPCs; thirty-three were from sub-Saharan Africa (Callaghy 2001: 120). Endless trips to the IMF did not solve the debt problem of these states. In fact, the problem was worsening. Thus in September 1996 the IMF and the World Bank launched an initiative for debt relief for highly indebted poor countries at the international economic summit in Cologne. In June 1999, the G-7 approved the enhanced HIPC programme.

The HIPC initiative is supposed to be about poverty: the goal of the programme is to reduce debt in order to attack chronic poverty. The enabling legislation, the Debt Relief for Poverty Reduction Act of 1999, stated that the initiative was 'to require the United States to take action to provide bilateral debt relief, and improve provision of multilateral debt relief, in order to give a fresh start to poor countries'. Each country that qualifies for debt relief under the HIPC initiative must produce a Poverty Reduction Strategy Paper (PRSP), which describes a country's macroeconomic, structural and social policies and programmes, that are meant to promote growth and reduce poverty, as well as associated external financing needs (see Chapter 9). Governments, through a participatory process involving civil society and development partners including the World Bank and the IMF, prepare the PRSPs.

The HIPC initiative was no more sudden than the Third Word Debt crisis that hit the US headlines with the Mexican financial crisis of 1982. The Western states that make up the Paris Club, which is in charge of rescheduling public debt, had been incrementally proposing more flexible terms for the severely indebted countries. One might trace the trajectory of this through the Toronto Terms of 1988, the London Terms of 1991, the Naples Terms of 1994, and the Lyons terms of 1996 (Callaghy 2001: 125). According to Callaghy, although seemingly not the engine behind the HIPC initiative, the US *did* actively lobby in favour of it with its G-7 partners (2001: 131). Domestic groups and NGOs with transnational linkages also actively and successfully lined up behind the HIPC initiative. The important point to build on here is that non-state actors, most forcefully NGOs, led the charge. Thus, even as Hamilitonian and geopolitical logics partially captured the HIPC initiative, it is set apart from those traditions by its strongest constituency and it has a different undercurrent.

Within the US, the National Black Caucus of Locally Elected Officials (NBC–LEO) adopted a resolution calling for active debt cancellation and relief for African countries. The resolution urged full appropriation of President Clinton's request for funding of the Cologne Initiative, and an international effort of the G-7 industrialized states to bring debt relief to highly indebted poor countries. Of course, many of the same groups have lobbied for African interests in other areas, particularly against AGOA. But the playing field in the debate over the HIPC initiative was more open, broader and therefore more level. Certainly, the HIPC initiative in the US is supported – albeit not uncritically – by the Jubilee USA Network which began as Jubilee 2000/USA in 1997 and includes over sixty organizations including labour, churches, religious communities and institutions, AIDS activists, trade campaigners and over 9,000 individuals. This extensive network is imbedded in transnational coalitions.

Indeed, NGOs played a central role in launching the HIPC debt initiative. In fact, Callaghy credits the Catholic Church and its debt-focused NGOs for convincing IMF chief Michel Camdessus to champion the cause (2001: 133). Oxfam and Eurodad also played central roles. Therefore, unlike the ACRI and AGOA, the HIPC initiative was not tightly held within the US administrative or political ambit, and because it is an international effort it has had a strong transnational following that goes beyond simply the state to include other actors of import.

Conclusion

The end of the Cold War has brought new challenges for US foreign policy towards sub-Saharan Africa. The argument presented in this chapter is that three currents of varying strengths across different eras have directed US foreign policy in the continent: *realpolitik*, Hamiltonianism and Meliorism. In the first two, the drivers respectively of the Cold War era and the imme- diate post-Cold War era, Africa was merely an object of US foreign policy. Decisions were subordinate to other designs, whether it was the contain- ment of communism or the spread of neo-liberalism. The undertows of these currents were sourced mostly in the foreign policy establishment of the American state. More recently, however, Washington has seemingly opened up to other policy influences, including both the corporate and non-governmental sector. The tradition of Meliorism has gathered strength as its undercurrent of support has deepened within the US and broadened through the confluence of transnational civil societies.

However, as strong as this current has become, as witnessed by the rela- tive success of the HIPC initiative, we must be aware of the potential of *realpolitik*. This is not to argue that the HIPC initiative is an unchallenged success. The most common criticism is that eligibility is dependent on a country's commitment to following economic policy prescriptions dictated by the World Bank and IMF. Second, while a step in the right direction, the initiative has not been bold enough. Six years after the introduction of HIPC, African countries are still forced to spend almost $15 billion each year repaying external debts, and even by the World Bank's own measure, thirty-one of the forty-two HIPC countries are not on track for reaching 'sustainable' debt levels through this process (Africa Action 2002). But the greatest threat to humanitarian initiatives is the rising tide of the influence of *realpolitik*.

In a hearing before the House of Representatives Subcommittee on Africa entitled, ominously, 'Africa and the War on Terrorism', US foreign policy once again risks being subsumed by a stance that sees Africa primarily as a threat rather than an opportunity. Edward Royce, Chairman of the Subcommittee, began the proceedings by stating:

> The Bush Administration has recognised Africa's centrality to the war on terrorism. National Security Advisor Condoleeza Rice, while speaking on October 30 to over 100 African ministers gathered in Washington for the African Growth and Opportunity Act Forum, said this: 'Africa's history and geography give it a pivotal role in the war on terrorism. Nevertheless, some Africans have expressed concerns that US attention and resources devoted to Africa will be shorted in favour of the Middle East and South Asia. This should not be the case under any circumstances. Africa is critical to our war on terrorism'.
>
> (US Government 2001)

There is an ironic twist to this statement. In the immediate aftermath of 11 September African voices expressed fears that the continent would be sidelined in the US-led 'war against terrorism'. However, it appears that, instead, US foreign policy has 'promoted' Africa to the status of being a part of its *realpolitik* strategy. The problem now is not that Africa will be ignored, but rather that what attention it gets will be framed by the American 'war against terrorism'. The bombing of US embassies in Dar-es-Salaam and Nairobi, precursors to 11 September we now know, pointed to Africa. Little, however, changed. The testimony by Susan Rice, former Assistant Secretary of State for Africa, reflected the tone of the hearings with comments such as 'the fact that some of Islam's most radical and anti-American adherents are increasingly active from South Africa to Sudan, from Nigeria to Algeria, ought to be of great concern to us' (US Government 2001). This concern is real, but while she understands that these issues go deeper than *realpolitik*, without the strong undercurrent of both the Hamiltonian and Meliorist traditions Africa risks becoming again a sidelined spectator *vis-à-vis* American foreign policy. The same can be said for the promotion of democracy. In the past, the need to co-operate on global and regional issues dealing with security pushed democracy to the background (Gordan 1997: 159). In the present, the 'war against terror' may subsume all other currents, democracy and human rights included.

References

Africa Action (2002) 'Critique of HIPC Initiative', http://www.africaaction.org/action/hipc0206.htm

Africa Fund (2000) 8 June, http://www.theafricafund.org/

Ahmed, I. (1999) 'Understanding Conflict in Somalia and Somaliland' in A. Adedeji (ed.) *Comprehending and Mastering African Conflicts*, New York: Zed Books, pp. 236–56.

Arnold, M. (1992) 'Engaging South Africa', *Foreign Policy*, 87: 139–57.

Callaghy, T. (1993) 'Political Passions and Economic Interests' in T. Callaghy and J. Ravenhill (eds) *Hemmed In: Responses to Africa's Economic Decline*, New York: Columbia University Press, pp. 463–519.

—— (1996) 'Africa Falling off the Map', *Current History*, 93: 31–5.

—— (2001) 'Networks and Governance in Africa: Innovation in the Debt Game' in T. Callaghy, R. Kassimir and R. Latham (eds) *Intervention and Transnationalism in Africa*, New York: Cambridge University Press, pp. 115–48.

Clough, M. (1992) *Free at Last? U.S. Policy toward Africa and the End of the Cold War*, New York: Council of Foreign Relations Press.

Cohen, H. (2000) *Intervening in Africa: Superpower Peacemaking in a Troubled Continent*, New York: St Martin's Press.

—— (2003) 'The United States and Africa: Nonvital Interests Also Require Attention' *American Foreign Policy Interests*, New York, 7 April, http://allafrica.com/stories/200304070607.html

Compagnon, D. (1998) 'Somali Armed Units: The Interplay of Political Entrepreneurship and Clan-Based Factions' in C. Clapham (ed.) *African Guerrillas*, Bloomington: Indiana University Press, pp. 73–90.

Cooper, F. (2001) 'Networks, Moral Discourse, and History' in T. Callaghy, R. Kassimir and R. Latham (eds) *Intervention and Transnationalism in Africa*, New York: Cambridge University Press, pp. 23–46.

Copson, R. (1994) *Africa's Wars and Prospects for Peace*, New York: M.E. Sharpe.

Cox, M., G. J. Ikenberry and T. Inoguchi (2000) 'Introduction' in M. Cox, G. J. Ikenberry and T. Inoguchi (eds) *American Democracy Promotion: Impulses, Strategies, and Impacts*, New York: Oxford University Press, pp. 1–17.

Gordan, D. (1997) 'On Promoting Democracy in Africa: The International Dimension' in M. Ottaway (ed.) *Democracy in Africa: The Hard Road Ahead*, Boulder: Lynne Rienner, pp. 153–64.

Grieco, J. and G. J. Ikenberry (2002) *State Power and World Markets*, New York: W.W. Norton.

Hentz, J. (2000) 'Redesigning US Foreign Policy: Regionalism, Economic Development and Instability in Southern Africa' in T. Shaw and K. Dunn (eds) *Africa's Challenge to International Relations Theory*, New York: Macmillan Press, pp. 185–203.

Howe, H. (2001) *Ambiguous Order: Military Forces in African States*, Boulder: Lynne Rienner.

Jackson, R. H. (1990) *Quasi-States: Sovereignty, International Relations and the Third World*, New York: Cambridge University Press.

Kambwa, A., D. Casimiro, N. Pedro and L. Hgonda (1999) 'Angola' in Adebayo Adedeji (ed.) *Comprehending and Mastering African Conflicts: The Search for Sustainable Peace and Good Governance*, London: Zed Books, pp. 55–79.

Kapstein, E. (1994) *Governing the Global Economy: International Finance and the State*, Cambridge: Harvard University Press.

Keller, E. and Rothchild, D. (1996) *Africa in the New International Order*, Boulder: Lynne Rienner.

Klare, M. (2001) *Resource Wars: The New Landscape of Global Conflict*, New York: Henry Holt.

Lutheran Office for Governmental Affairs (1998) 'Questions on Africa Policy for the 106th Congress', Washington Office on Africa (WOA), 16 October.

McDougall, W. A. (1997) *Promised Land, The American Encounter with the World since 1776*, New York: Houghton Mifflin.

Martin, H. and H. Schumann (1998) *The Global Trap*, New York: Zed Books.

Mbembe, A. (2001) *On the Post Colony*, Berkeley: University of California Press.

Mead, W. R. (2001) *Special Providence: American Foreign Policy and How It Changed the World*, New York: Alfred A. Knopf.

Ngoga, P. (1998) 'Uganda: The National Resistance Army' in C. Clapham (ed.) *African Guerrillas*, Bloomington: Indiana University Press, pp. 91–106.

Ottaway, M. (1999) *Africa's New Leaders: Democracy or State Reconstruction?*, Washington, DC: Carnegie Endowment for International Peace.

Power, S. (2001) 'Bystanders to Genocide: Why the United States Let the Genocide Happen', *Atlantic Monthly*, September, http://theatlantic.com/issues/2001/09/kelly/htm

Reno, W. (2001) 'How Sovereignty Matters: International Markets and the Political Economy of Local Politics in Weak States' in T. Callaghy, R. Kassimir and R. Latham (eds) *Intervention and Transnationalism in Africa*, New York: Cambridge University Press, pp. 197–215.

Robinson, Piers (2002) *The CNN Effect – The Myth of News, Foreign Policy and Intervention*, London: Routledge.

Rothchild, D. and T. Sisk (1996) 'US–Africa Policy: Promoting Conflict Management in Uncertain Times' in R. Lieber and K. Oye (eds) *Eagle Adrift: American Foreign Policy at the End of the Century*, New York: Longman, pp. 271–94.

Schraeder, P. (1994) *United States Foreign Policy toward Africa,* New York: Cambridge University Press.

Spero, J. and J. Hart (2003) *The Politics of International Economic Relations,* Belmont, CA: Thompson-Wadsworth.

US Department of State International Information Programs (2003) *Africa Diaspora is Vital 'Link' between Africa and West,* http://usinfo.state.gov/regional/af/usafr/a3022101.htm

US Government (1997) *A Comprehensive Trade and Development Policy for the Countries of Africa: A Report Submitted by the President of the United States to the Congress,* http://www.ustr.gov/reports/africa/1997/index.html

—— (2001) *Hearings before the Subcommittee on Africa of the Committee on International Relations, House of Representatives, 107th Cong., 1ˢᵗ sess.* Serial No. 107–20, http://www.house.gov/international-relations

2 Britain and Africa after the Cold War

Beyond damage limitation?[1]

Paul Williams

Ever since Britain's retreat from colonialism in Africa got underway in earnest the primary concern of successive governments towards the continent has been aptly summarized by James Mayall as one of damage limitation. During this period, Mayall (1986) argued, Britain's Africa policy revolved around the need to turn its imperial legacies 'from liabilities into assets'. This required the creation of 'a network of low key, but still special, relationships between Britain and her former colonies' (1986: 54). Successive British governments pursued this goal through three main mechanisms: the organization and management of the international economy; bilateral relations – primarily economic in character; and the political organization of international society.

Fundamentally, little has changed in Britain's relationship with Africa after the Cold War. More sympathetic interpretations of Britain's Africa policy have described it as 'reactive rather than proactive' and 'pragmatic in the extreme' (Spence in Styan 1996: 262), but it remains true to say that the Thatcher, Major and Blair governments have all been primarily concerned with damage limitation of one sort or another. In this sense, each government inherited the traditional post-colonial British mindset that saw Africa 'as a source of trouble rather than opportunity' (Clapham 1996: 88). It is also the case that each administration has used the familiar tools of economic, political and bilateral leverage to ensure their relations with African states run smoothly. But while the objectives and methods of Britain's Africa policy display a large degree of continuity, they are no longer so strictly confined to so-called anglophone or Commonwealth Africa, especially since the election of Tony Blair's New Labour Party in May 1997. Along with the scope, the discourse and language used to present and describe British foreign policy has also changed after the Cold War (see Williams 2002). This development is not unique to Britain but is representative of the language adopted by most Western states with a declared commitment to promoting liberal values abroad (Kahler 1997). After the disintegration of the Soviet Union and the concomitant increase in the power of neo-liberalism, British officials have presented their Africa policy as being fundamentally concerned with the promotion of peace, prosperity and democracy on the continent. More recently still, and particularly after 11 September 2001, the reasons for serious engagement with Africa have increasingly been wrapped up in the language of 'threats', 'risks' and 'security' (see Abrahamsen 2002). Britain's Africa policy is thus once again displaying a primary concern with damage limitation.

This chapter provides a critical evaluation of Britain's Africa policy after the Cold War with reference to the three themes of peace, prosperity and democracy. But first it is necessary to describe the evolving context within which these policy themes have been developed and their implementation attempted.

What is the political context for Britain's Africa policy?

In 1996, David Styan (1996: 261) noted how 'Africans and students of Africa will search in vain for sustained debates or literature on contemporary British policy in Africa'. Today, there are tentative signs that this situation is changing, but Styan's point is indicative of the fact that Africa has not been a priority for Britain's foreign policy elites for several decades. Their attention has consistently focused on other parts of the world, especially Europe, the former Soviet Union and East Asia. South Africa, Zimbabwe and (briefly) Sierra Leone are the only African states that have temporarily become major issues in Britain's post-Cold War foreign policy. But this lack of priority does not mean, as is sometimes suggested, that Britain has had no African policy, only that it has been of marginal concern to the major players in Westminster and Whitehall.

This lack of concern has been reflected in several trends in Britain's relationship with Africa. During the Conservative years (1989–97), while Britain increased its diplomatic engagement with eastern European and successor states of the Soviet Union, the number and size of diplomatic missions in Africa were reduced (five were closed in 1991 alone) against, it should be noted, the advice of those diplomats with significant expertise on the continent.[2] Little information was widely available on the topic; budgets were cut (including a reported 18 per cent cut on spending on Africa between 1994 and 1997); and policy became almost solely the concern of the Overseas Development Administration (ODA), which encouraged a tendency within Whitehall to see African policy as being synonymous with the British aid programme and for policy to be heavily influenced by the former *de facto* 'Minister of Africa', Lynda Chalker at the head of the ODA (Styan 1996: 262–3, 266). African issues have since climbed higher up Britain's foreign policy agenda under the New Labour government (1997–present), culminating in a series of speeches and policy documents that suggested the continent was 'a scar on the conscience of the world' and was urgently in need of international support (Blair 2001). In practice, however, African affairs have rarely been a priority for British politicians or makers of foreign policy. As one Kenyan parliamentary group visiting London in 1998 lamented, virtually no one in the British parliament had any knowledge about contemporary events in Kenya (Khadiagala 2000: 101). One suspects this holds true for the vast majority of African countries.

Not only has Africa been a marginal concern for British foreign policy, when it has attracted greater attention, policy has concentrated upon certain parts of the continent and neglected others. First, British policy has split the continent into two parts, with separate concerns and ministerial structures for dealing with North Africa and the Mahgreb, and Africa south of the Sahara. Within policy circles, Britain's Africa policy is usually taken as shorthand for policy towards sub-Saharan Africa. This chapter also follows this convention. Second, within sub-Saharan Africa, British aid, trade, investment and interests have been concentrated, at times almost exclusively, on Commonwealth Africa. The most startling example of this tendency was the almost total indifference displayed by John Major's government to the 1994 Rwandan genocide. Since Rwanda was deemed to lie outside its zone of interest, the signals from London to British diplomats in the region were that this was a 'country of which we knew little and cared less'.[3] At the time, the Foreign Secretary, Douglas Hurd, was apparently preoccupied coaxing the eastern Europeans 'into the same bed as the West'; selling the idea of a less interfering but benevolent EU to his party and public; and maintaining unity within the Conservative Party (*Economist* 12 March 1994: 34).

It is hardly surprising that on such a large and diverse continent policy should be concentrated upon a few key states. Until very recently, with the exception of Nigeria, British policy has focused upon southern and east Africa, particularly South Africa, Kenya, Zimbabwe and Uganda. Apart from a few minor initiatives in 1994, it was only after the Anglo-French summit at St Malo in December 1998 that a significant declaration was made to move beyond the mindset of post-imperial spheres of influence in Africa with regard to British and French policy towards the continent. This change in policy would, it was claimed, include greater cooperation and the sharing of information and diplomatic premises. Yet arguably even this symbolic step towards a more coordinated Anglo-French policy in Africa was a reaction to growing US influence in world politics in general and in their former African colonies in particular. Moreover, little practical evidence has emerged of moving beyond a 'spheres-of-influence' approach, with Britain and France subsequently disagreeing over policies on the wars in the Democratic Republic of Congo (DRC), Liberia and Sierra Leone (Ero 2001: 63–5) and how best to deal with Zimbabwe's President Robert Mugabe.

A third significant contextual factor is the way in which throughout the post-Cold War era the British state has worked in tandem with a variety of non-state actors including transnational corporations (TNCs), humanitarian and development NGOs and international organizations to pursue its policies. Under the Conservatives there was little evidence of close partnerships with humanitarian NGOs. Indeed, the Foreign and Commonwealth Office (FCO) was keen to retain as much control over foreign policy as possible.

This included letting as few 'outsiders' as possible become genuinely involved in the policy-making process. In contrast, New Labour has developed a much closer working relationship with numerous humanitarian and development NGOs, including a steady flow of staff exchanges with Amnesty International and Save the Children. On the economic dimensions of policy, especially trade and investment, both Conservative and Labour governments have actively promoted British TNCs and worked closely with the country's business elites through such organizations as the Commonwealth Development Corporation, the Confederation of British Industry, Trade Partners UK and the British Overseas Trade Board. The British state has also pursued its objectives through a variety of multilateral institutions. The most important of these in relation to the promotion of peace, prosperity and democracy in Africa have been the United Nations (UN), the International Monetary Fund (IMF) and World Bank, the Commonwealth, the European Union (EU) and the G-7/8.

The impact of the two main political parties, Conservative and Labour, on Britain's post-Cold War Africa policy also merits consideration. Although the attributes each party brings to Africa policy are difficult to quantify, the different concerns and traditions of the Conservative and Labour governments do appear relevant. At a general level, during the 1990s the Conservatives spent much of their period in office with a slim parliamentary majority. Consequently, the party's attention was focused on domestic issues, internal bickering over who should lead the party, and Britain's relationship with the European Community (see Wallace 1994). In contrast, New Labour swept to power with a massive majority and devoted far more attention to international issues, not least because of the efforts of the Foreign Secretary, Robin Cook, and because, in comparison with John Major, Tony Blair's political philosophy gave ideas of globalization and international interdependence central roles (see Blair 1997, 1998). Under New Labour, African affairs have received considerably more attention and funds than under the Major government, although in policy terms evidence of continuity is greater than of a fundamental change of direction (Abrahamsen and Williams 2001, 2002). Arguably the most important institutional difference between the two parties is New Labour's establishment of the Department for International Development (DFID), which has devoted considerable time and resources to African affairs. As noted above, under the Conservatives the ODA (DFID's predecessor) was run as an autonomous wing of the FCO.

The final contextual factor relates to the representation of Africa in the British media. Over the course of the 1990s trends in British media coverage of Africa have helped frame public discussion about Britain's relationship with the continent. Within Western media outlets, coverage of international affairs in general has significantly reduced after the Cold War. In relation to Africa, there are also far fewer expert Africa correspondents. The result has been a marked deterioration in both the quantity and quality of journalistic writing from and on Africa. In addition, the continent has been plagued by the editorial tendency to adopt a 'coups and catastrophes' approach to African affairs (Styan 1996: 276). On the rare occasions when the media spotlight has been turned on Africa it has been incredibly selective in its choice of issues worthy of reporting and has often bought into simplistic and stereotypical perspectives about the role of tribes, ethnicity, corruption and religion in Africa, especially in the descriptions of the continent's recent conflicts. This was particularly evident in the early journalistic descriptions of the 1994 Rwandan genocide (see McNulty 1999; Melvern 2001). As with other parts of the world, stable and flourishing political systems have not been considered newsworthy. But unlike other parts of the world, Africa has been consistently characterized as 'hopeless' (*Economist* 13 May 2000). Similarly, while some wars, coups and fraudulent elections have attracted the media's gaze, others have been neglected. And yet the issue that has attracted the greatest volume of media commentary in Britain – refugees seeking political asylum and immigration more generally – has been discussed with little reference to the terrible political circumstances which force many Africans to leave their homes in the first place (see Styan 1996: 278–82). This has meant that the minority of the British public interested in African affairs has been shown the continent through a very restricted and simplistic set of lenses. In relation to policy, combined with the reduction in diplomatic personnel based in Africa, media trends have meant that NGOs such as the International Crisis Group and Human Rights Watch have become far more important as sources of information about current events.

What are the objectives of Britain's Africa policy?

After the end of the Cold War and the collapse of the Soviet Union a renewed power and self-confidence came over Western states, Britain included. This proved the catalyst for a raft of announcements stating principles about aid conditionality, good government and human rights. In June 1990, for example, Foreign Secretary Douglas Hurd publicly declared the need for economic development and 'good governance' to go hand in hand. In his words, 'economic success depends extensively on the existence of an efficient and honest government, on political pluralism and, I would like to add, respect for the law and free and more open economies' (Hurd 1990). Hurd continued to explicitly link these ideas to the goals of British foreign policy. 'Countries which tend towards pluralism, public accountability, respect for human rights and market principles,' he argued, 'should be encouraged. Governments which persist with repressive policies, corrupt management and wasteful, discredited economic systems should not expect us to support their folly with scarce aid resources which could be used better elsewhere' (Hurd 1990).

In many respects, these sentiments set the ideological tone that continues to shape Britain's Africa policy today. In this sense, the principal objectives of Britain's Africa policy after the Cold War have been relatively consistent, at least at the theoretical level.

These same priorities were reiterated in 1995 by Lynda Chalker, who presented British policy as having five main objectives: the promotion of 'good governance', economic reform and the alleviation of poverty; support for the peaceful resolution of conflicts; international cooperation over criminal activities in Africa (notably drugs, terrorism and illegal immigration); support for the new democratic order in South Africa; and furthering British commercial interests (in Styan 1996: 264). As Styan (1996: 264) noted, the core themes were economic reform, growth and governance; the commercial interests of British trade and investment; and bilateral relations with South Africa. In comparison, conflict resolution and combating criminal activities were far less of a priority.

Over the course of New Labour's period in office the excessive focus on South Africa has diminished and the themes of conflict resolution and prevention have assumed greater prominence. But the concern with economic growth, reform and governance and other commercial interests remains central. In addition, New Labour ministers have placed a greater weight on the need to promote human rights than had been evident in the pronouncements of the previous Conservative government. However, it soon became evident that the Blair government's Africa policy would revolve around the promotion of the three interrelated concepts of peace, prosperity and democracy. These were said to be the three key challenges facing Africa in the twenty-first century (see Cook 1998; Hain 1999a).

Promoting peace?

Without peace there can be little hope of establishing durable democracy and sustainable development in Africa. Unfortunately, Britain's post-Cold War attempts to promote peace in Africa have been selective, inconsistent, under-resourced, narrowly focused and preoccupied with managing rather than preventing violent conflicts. However, there have been positive results, including attempts to regulate conflict trade goods such as diamonds and recent suggestions that more attention, and crucially more (human and financial) resources, will be devoted to conflict prevention.

During the Conservative years, Britain significantly disengaged from the continent as both its economic and geostrategic interests there dwindled. Within this context, John Major's government devoted only marginal attention and resources to promoting peace in Africa and at times pursued policies counterproductive to its stated aims. Ironically, Major was one of the few British prime ministers who had hands-on experience in Africa, having worked in Nigeria. On the positive side, some 650 British troops participated in the UNAVEM III operation in Angola and the government provided more than £36m of aid to help provide relief, food, shelter, de-mining and to demobilize soldiers (FCO 1995). The British government also contributed to a UN trust fund to help pay for ECOMOG's activities in Liberia; provided police training to over thirty African countries; and started deploying military advisory training teams (BMATTs) more heavily outside anglophone Africa, including to Angola and Mozambique. In November 1994, Major also endorsed French President François Mitterand's proposal made at the Franco-African summit that 1,000–1,500 African troops should be trained, equipped and financed for peacekeeping duties by France and other European powers, and eventually by the EU. Britain's initiative was aimed at establishing structures to prevent conflict and manage crises as they arose; help African states train their troops for peacekeeping; and support provision of equipment and logistics to enable rapid deployment (Rifkind 1996: 630).

But these positive developments were overshadowed by other less constructive policies. Despite calling for peace, Major's government continued to sell weapons to a variety of African states, including regimes that openly flouted democratic principles and human rights standards. For instance, although Britain provided military instructors to help train the post-apartheid South African armed forces, in early 1995 the British Defence Secretary, Malcolm Rifkind, visited South Africa as part of a two-week arms sales drive in the region. Rifkind pressed the case of British arms suppliers, including Yarrow shipbuilders, seeking a contract for four corvettes; British Aerospace, marketing its Hawk trainer as a replacement for South Africa's Impala; and Westland, offering its Lynx helicopters for the new corvettes (*Financial Times* 11 April 1995). Similarly, from 1991 Britain sold eighty Vickers battle tanks, CS gas and rubber bullets, and issued over thirty export licences for non-lethal military equipment, to Nigeria's military junta, many of which were in defiance of European Political Cooperation agreements to suspend military cooperation with Nigeria (*Economist* 8 July 1995: 60). And in Sierra Leone, Major's government was accused of offering a military advisor to the military junta government for six months from April 1995; a procurement expert to study defence purchase problems; and a short-term training team for senior officers in early 1995. Simultaneously, a contingent of ex-Gurkhas was helping to train the Sierra Leone army (*Economist* 8 July 1995: 60). Nor was Major's government fully committed to peacekeeping in Africa. In Somalia, for example, the British government declined to commit troops to either UNOSOM I or II, yet Douglas Hurd was quite happy to call for others to establish a UN 'trusteeship' over the country (Olsen 1997: 312). The government was also unable and apparently unwilling to prevent British mercenaries operating on the continent, such as those who provided security for certain mining complexes in Zaire as well as propping up the tottering regime of Mobutu Sese Seko (*Africa Confidential* 13 December 1996).

However, arguably the biggest stains on the Major government's attempts to promote peace emerged from its failure to respond effectively to two crises in Africa's Great Lakes region. First, Britain, along with the rest of international society, ignored what the US Committee for Refugees called a 'slow-motion coup' in Burundi that began in October 1993 and in which democratically elected president Melchior Ndadaye was killed. This sparked off a wave of violence, which according to Amnesty International left approximately 100,000 people dead by January 1994 and saw thousands of Hutu civilians ethnically cleansed from the country's capital city, Bujumbura. In response, the UN Security Council sent a small number of civilian observers but refused to offer military assistance to the stricken country. Apart from the allocation of some £4.5m of bilateral and emergency aid between 1993 and 1996, the British government has remained largely indifferent to the persistent violence in Burundi since 1993, preferring regional actors to find their own solutions. Since Nelson Mandela's retirement as president in 1999, South Africa has assumed the role of leading international mediator. Six months after Burundi's slow-motion coup began, British officials in Whitehall and the UN were making the extraordinary argument that responding to genocide in Rwanda was less important than ensuring the credibility of UN peacekeeping operations (Melvern 2000: 227–38). Not only did this line of reasoning assume that ignoring genocide would boost the UN's flagging credibility after the debacle in Somalia but it reinforced the signal that, in Africa at least, the British government was not prepared to put its own troops into harm's way for the cause of peace. Rwanda was considered an unimportant country that fell well outside Britain's zone of interest. As *The Economist* put it, Rwanda was apparently 'too difficult, too remote, maybe too black' and suffered because its 'agony was not played out on television' (7 May 1994: 15). The country also suffered from the political fallout of the interventions in Somalia, with politicians subsequently reluctant to become entangled in another African civil war. After the genocide was over, Britain deployed over 600 troops to the country for three months to provide technical and humanitarian assistance and established a diplomatic embassy. Before the genocide Britain had only a non-resident ambassador to both Burundi and Rwanda based in Uganda. This was indicative of the traditional view that Britain had very little to do with these countries.

In comparison with the Conservatives, the Blair government has engaged in far more initiatives intended to promote peace on the continent. These activities can be divided into those designed to respond to violent conflict and those designed to prevent it. Like the Conservatives, however, New Labour has pursued policies that have been selective and at times selfish and contradictory. Selectivity has been evident in the concentration of criticism on some fraudulent elections (as in Zimbabwe) while virtually ignoring others (as in Zambia and Madagascar). Selfishness was prominent in Kenya where, in the wake of the US-led 'war on terrorism' and the search for Islamic militants in Nairobi and Mombassa, New Labour decided to ignore then President Daniel arap Moi's poor human rights record in favour of renewing a military cooperation agreement that allowed British troops to use bases in the country (*Africa Confidential* 21 December 2001). And there have also been contradictions, as in the case of pushing for peace in the DRC but refusing to openly criticize friendly states such as Yoweri Museveni's Uganda and Paul Kagame's Rwanda for their involvement in the war.

New Labour has employed a variety of policies in response to war in Africa, including diplomacy and enforcement measures such as sanctions and military intervention. Politically, Blair's government has sought to manage conflicts by providing support for conflict resolution, and by consolidating peace through assisting in the disarmament, demobilization and reintegration of former combatants and boosting Africa's own peacekeeping capacity (Lloyd 1999). These activities have involved the Ministry of Defence (MoD) and DFID as well as the FCO. In relation to the military dimensions of its strategy, New Labour arrived in power keen to distance itself from the Major government's approach. To this end a Strategic Defence Review was quickly convened that reported in 1998. Among other things, this acknowledged the need to restructure Britain's armed forces to conduct small- or mid-scale power projection operations, such as the one deployed to Sierra Leone in 2000. This was also a theme of New Labour's attempts to develop a common European Security and Defence Policy with other EU member states, notably France and Germany. Declared hypothetically operational in December 2001, the Security and Defence Policy includes scope for a European Rapid Reaction Force (ERRF) of up to 60,000 troops deployable within sixty days' notice and sustainable for up to one year. Although the ERRF's exact remit, in terms of both function and geography, remains unclear, officials from Britain (and other EU states) have not ruled out the possibility of it operating in Africa.

Blair's government has also used so-called smart sanctions as a tool for promoting peace in Africa, especially to help reduce the trade in conflict goods such as oil, timber and diamonds in Angola, DRC, Liberia and Sierra Leone. In Angola, for example, Blair's government pledged to help isolate and defeat Jonas Savimbi's UNITA (Hain 1999b). Similarly, evidence presented by Robin Cook of Charles Taylor's support for the Revolutionary United Front of Sierra Leone and other insurgent groups in the region was instrumental in getting EU ministers to agree to freeze a two-year development aid programme for Liberia in 1998 and UN sanctions imposed in May 2001, which included a ban on the import of rough diamonds from the country. And in response to the ongoing crisis in Zimbabwe, Britain has also (with one or two problems) ceased its military cooperation with the country and, along with the EU and US, imposed smart sanctions upon certain members of Robert Mugabe's ZANU-PF regime (Taylor and Williams 2002).

On the negative side, one area where New Labour has received sustained criticism is over its continued arms sales to Africa, which the Campaign Against the Arms Trade estimates will exceed US$200m in 2003. In 1999, for instance, the government granted 970 single individual export licences in the small arms category, including exports to Eritrea, Kenya and Zimbabwe (CAAT 2001). Similarly, like its predecessors, Blair's government has continued to aggressively court South African arms contracts; BAE Systems and other British businessmen were alleged to have supplied spare parts for Zimbabwe's fleet of Hawk jets and other material while over 12,000 of Mugabe's troops waged war in the DRC (*Africa Confidential* 25 October 2002); and British-made weapons found their way into the hands of child soldiers fighting in Sierra Leone's war (*Daily Mail* 30 May 2000).

However, the incident that attracted the most media attention was the so-called 'Arms-to-Africa' affair in which the FCO was found to have colluded with the military consultancy firm Sandline International to bring 30 tonnes of arms and ammunition into Sierra Leone in contravention of the UN arms embargo (see FAC 1999). Although many Sierra Leonean civilians welcomed the results of this policy, it raised two dilemmas for Blair's government. First, if it is serious about promoting peace in Africa it has to make some tough decisions in relation to its domestic arms industry, which supports 45,000 jobs directly and another 45,000 indirectly (Goodie 2002). To date, there is little indication that the government intends to purposely reduce these numbers. Second, it raised the issue of what to do about British mercenaries and private military companies. Much to the embarrassment of the FCO, the point was reiterated when, during the war in the DRC, Avient, a company run by a British businessman, supplied military assistance to the DRC's air force against a variety of rebels (*Financial Times* 17 April 2001). In response, the government released a Green Paper in February 2002 discussing its plans for regulating the private military industry. However, British mercenaries have continued to operate in Africa, most recently in the Ivory Coast's ongoing conflict (*Guardian* 22 February 2003).

The biggest practical test of New Labour's ideas about promoting peace and security in Africa is its ongoing engagement with Sierra Leone. After years of neglecting the country's war under the Conservatives, New Labour became deeply involved in the diplomatic efforts to end the conflict and intervened militarily in May and again in October 2000. In retrospect, the British government's decision can be understood as deriving from a mixture of five imperatives: to protect British citizens; to avert a humanitarian crisis like that which had engulfed Freetown in January 1999; to defend the democratically elected government of President Kabbah; to live up to its stated foreign policy principles; and to support the UN operation, UNAMSIL, to carry out its mandate (Williams 2001). The presence of British troops helped to stabilize the UN force in and around Freetown, and as a semblance of order was restored to parts of the country the British scaled back their military contingent. Since then, the British have concentrated upon supporting President Kabbah politically, establishing a truth and reconciliation commission and a special court (despite significant criticism, see Penfold 2002), and undertaking security sector reform.

Soon after the intervention in Sierra Leone and as part of its Africa Conflict Prevention Initiative, Blair's government elaborated its position on the changing nature and extent of conflict in Africa during the 1990s and identified what it saw as the root, secondary and tertiary causes of conflict on the continent (UK Government 2001). The root causes of conflict were identified as inequality between groups, economic decline, state collapse and a history of resolving problems by violent means. Secondary causes included widespread unemployment, lack of education, population pressure, 'the abuse of ethnicity', and the availability of small arms. Tertiary causes that hinder conflict resolution efforts included the regional and interlocking nature of many conflicts, a lack of external guarantors to peace processes, inadequate and inappropriate mediation, and misplaced humanitarian assistance. The government sees its own role as being multidimensional and comprising of both short- and long-term commitments. The most pressing are considered to be enhancing small arms and light weapons controls; encouraging responsible investment practices in conflict zones; reducing the exploitation of mineral resources for the purposes of war; promoting inclusive forms of government; supporting security sector reform; and providing assistance to Africa's regional organizations, especially in relation to peacekeeping capacity (UK Government 2001: 22). However, this analysis has been criticized for containing little that is innovative; ignoring the globalized nature of war in Africa; analysing the continent as if it was somehow disconnected from the rest of the world and in a permanent state of crisis; and for generating inflated expectations about what Britain can 'deliver' (Ero 2001: 60–1).

More positively, New Labour's policy statements have consistently empha-sized that 'the most effective way to end human rights violations in conflict is by preventing conflict in the first place' (FCO 1998: 19). The British approach to conflict prevention concentrates on five areas for action: addressing the root causes of conflict by fighting poverty and promoting sustainable development; supporting forms of governance that have the consent of local people; curbing the flow of small arms and light weapons; preventing the trade of conflict goods, including diamonds; and countering the emerging 'culture of impunity' for those who break international humani-tarian law (Cook 1999). DFID has played a particularly important part in developing this approach and has also had significant input into the wider OECD strategies for preventing violent conflict. In 1998 DFID established a Conflict and Humanitarian Affairs Department as the administrative expres-sion of its move towards integrating conflict and development objectives (Kapila and Wermester 2002: 303). The focus on conflict prevention has also highlighted the need for a 'joined-up' foreign policy where different ministries and departments work with, not against, each other. It has also highlighted the need for British and other TNCs to behave responsibly in conflict situa-tions (Kapila and Wermester 2002: 306–7). One practical result of this line of thinking has been the establishment of the Africa Conflict Prevention Initiative led by DFID, which became formally active in spring 2001 and allo-cated approximately £50m per year between 2001 and 2004. The aim is 'to ensure that the government gets a maximum return on the resources it allo-cates to conflict-prevention activities' (Ero 2001: 59). It is also designed to fit into the British government's philosophy that offering combatants a brighter economic future is a necessary part of building peace in Africa.

Promoting prosperity?

As what Napoleon described as 'a nation of shopkeepers' it was not surprising that, during the Cold War, Britain's bilateral relations with African states were often preoccupied with the protection of trade and investment. It was also a position energetically pushed by the major British TNCs active in Africa, including Lonrho, Unilever, ICI, British Petroleum, Marconi and British banks such as Standard Chartered and Barclays, which currently have full retail and corporate banking facilities in twelve and ten African states respectively. After the Cold War, Britain's attempts to encourage economic growth in Africa have been through the promotion of free trade; encouraging profitable foreign direct investment (FDI); reducing the burden of debt; and providing development aid.

Both the Conservative and Labour governments have subscribed to liberal assumptions about the relationship between economics and politics, and the ostensibly mutually beneficial nature of international trade and FDI. This stance has frequently met with criticism from a variety of African states seeking fairer structures of international trade and left British governments with little space to criticize the negative social consequences of economic liberalism in states such as Zambia and South Africa (Abrahamsen and Williams 2001: 254–8).

In practical terms, there has been an 'overwhelming predominance of South Africa in Britain's commercial links with the continent', with the country consistently representing over 40 per cent of Britain's exports and imports to and from the continent throughout the post-Cold War period (Styan 1996: 271). Only South Africa has consistently been among Britain's top twenty countries for imports (between 2001 and 2004 its average growth rate in this regard was second only to China) while no African state has figured in the top twenty for exports. During the Conservative years, without South Africa, sub-Saharan Africa represented less than 2 per cent of all imports into Britain and less than 3 per cent of British exports (Styan 1996: 271). As with peace initiatives, Britain's other commercial relationships have remained predominantly within Commonwealth Africa, although recent signs indicate that British business is seeking to expand beyond this sphere.

British exporters have been given state support through a variety of mechanisms including the Commonwealth Development Corporation or by the Department of Trade and Industry (DTI) and the FCO through Trade Partners UK. The latter has some 2,000 staff worldwide dedicated to helping British business compete successfully across the globe. In addition, the government's trade promotion policy is guided by advice from 200 businesses that serve on the British Overseas Trade Board.

Between 1994 and 2001, compared to the world's other major regions, the annual average growth rate and total of British exports to sub-Saharan Africa were higher only than those of British exports to South America. In contrast, British imports from sub-Saharan Africa were larger than those from North Africa and the Middle East and South America, and grew by an annual average growth rate of 12.26 per cent, which was second only to eastern Europe (see Table 2.1). In other words, there are signs that Africa is becoming of increasing economic significance to Britain. By 2001 the five biggest African states exporting goods to Britain were (in descending order) South Africa, Nigeria, Kenya, Ghana and Angola (Britain's largest market outside Commonwealth Africa). For British imports the top five African states were (again in descending order) South Africa, Botswana, Mauritius, Namibia and Kenya.

British business is currently most active in seeking openings in the oil, gas and other natural resources sectors. Along with the larger markets, for instance, there has recently been heightened activity in Congo-Brazzaville's oil sector and the prospect of more to come with offshore discoveries all along the Gulf of Guinea. British Petroleum, for example, has also invested in prospecting for gas in Mozambique and seen its profits there increase fivefold over the last three years. The company now has operations in thirteen African states mainly in southern Africa, employs about 1,300 people in South Africa alone, and expects to invest approximately $7bn in Angola before 2010. Outside the natural resources sector, British TNCs, with the help of the British state, have looked to the so-called 'gateway economies'. The largest and most trusted gateway into southern Africa's market of 185 million people is South Africa. Here the UK–South Africa Partnership Programme has helped to build partnerships between South African and British companies. However, since the end of apartheid, South African companies have launched increasingly successful ventures throughout the continent, in many places, including Kenya and Uganda, at the expense of British companies. Partly as a result of this, British TNCs have started to look for gateways into francophone West Africa. Traditionally, Ghana has fulfilled this role, but more recently Cameroon, Senegal and the Ivory Coast have been actively courted. In the Ivory Coast, for example, the British government and private business worked in tandem to win the first major contract for a British company, TCI, in 2000. Similarly, in Cameroon a variety of companies including Guinness, Shell, Standard Chartered Bank and British American Tobacco have sought to use the country as a gateway into West Africa.

As the dominance of neo-liberal economic theories grew after the disintegration of the Soviet Union, many African states (especially Egypt, Mauritius, South Africa and Tunisia) initiated economic reforms aimed at increasing the role of the private sector and attracting FDI. These reforms included regulatory frameworks for FDI, trade liberalization, bilateral investment treaties and

Table 2.1 British trade relations with sub-Saharan Africa (in £ millions)

	1994	1995	1996	1997	1998	1999	2000	2001
Exports	3,137	3,664	3,840	3,574	3,312	2,961	3,170	3,466
Imports	2,248	2,552	2,885	2,840	2,865	3,242	4,201	5,669

Source: Adapted from UK Trade Statistics, http://www.hmce.gov.uk (accessed March 2003)

double taxation treaties (UNCTAD 1999). The recent FDI frontrunners in Africa have been Botswana, Equatorial Guinea, Ghana, Mozambique, Namibia, Tunisia and Uganda, with most analysts agreeing that 'natural resources have been among the main determinants for the attraction of FDI to almost all the frontrunners' (UNCTAD 1999: 25).

The need to promote private investment in Africa has been a persistent theme in both the Major and Blair governments. Although there was a significant period of disinvestments by British companies immediately after the Cold War, Britain remains among the largest investors in Africa, with cumulative flows between 1988 and 1997 totalling approximately $5,458m (UNCTAD 1999: 52). British FDI stock in Africa is no longer concentrated in the primary sector but instead embraces the manufacturing and services sectors. In 1989 the sectoral composition of British FDI stock in the continent was 37 per cent primary, 37 per cent secondary and 26 per cent tertiary. These figures had remained constant when New Labour took office in 1997 (UNCTAD 1999: 16). British investments have proved very profitable, with the net income accrued between 1989 and 1995 in sub-Saharan Africa (excluding Nigeria) increasing by 60 per cent (UNCTAD 1999: 17). To encourage more private investors, successive British governments have emphasized the need for African states to adopt 'good governance' and neo-liberal economic reforms. To this end, by January 1999 the British government had signed eighteen bilateral investment treaties[4] and twenty-nine double taxation treaties[5] with African states in an attempt to build environments conducive to FDI by British companies (UNCTAD 1999: 48–51). While the profits that have accrued to British firms as a result of these initiatives are obvious, the benefits to ordinary Africans are far from clear.

In relation to debt relief it was the Conservative government that in September 1990 first announced its intention to cancel two-thirds of the official debts of fifteen of its poor African debtors, so long as they kept to IMF rules (*Economist* 22 May 1993: 66). Since then, a complicated series of initiatives have been proposed. These culminated in the British government (led on this issue by the Chancellor, Gordon Brown, and International Development Secretary Clare Short) eventually settling on the terms of debt relief and/or cancellation provided the debtor states concerned continued to adopt neo-liberal economic reforms and abide by the World Bank's definition of 'good governance'. In practice, however, most heavily indebted African states are yet to see the supposed benefits of this relief under either the World Bank's reformed Heavily Indebted Poor Countries (HIPC) initiative or the G-7's Cologne Initiative (1999). Indeed, some African states have actually seen their levels of debt increase with the implementation of these schemes. Uganda, for instance, whose current debt stands at approximately $3,409m, saw its terms of relief persistently altered by its creditors until it was actually worse off than before (Dixon and Williams 2001: 167–8). Similarly, in 2003 Ethiopia, Malawi, Mozambique and Zambia had to pay approximately $325m to the IMF, World Bank and Paris Club states even as they were experiencing famines

(*Guardian* 6 January 2003). Upon reflection, the British government's actions on debt relief have remained largely symbolic. And with the closing down of the NGO coalition Jubilee 2000 in the new millennium, the intense levels of public protest surrounding the issue have subsided as international attention has become preoccupied with the US-led 'war on terrorism'.

On the issue of aid, it appears that after the Cold War the motives of the major donors in sub-Saharan Africa have been fivefold: to promote *development* in recipient states; *diplomatic* – as a tool of foreign policy (indeed, aid was a useful tool to ease Britain's withdrawal from active engagement in the region); *commercial*; *cultural* – including promoting language, religion and values; and *humanitarian* (Lancaster 2000: 213–16). However, aid to Africa has tended to be the least effective of any aid worldwide. Certainly, it has been the least sustainable, often with fewer than half of aid-funded projects surviving after aid was terminated. The least effective types of projects have been those involving 'complex interventions', requiring the management of multiple activities and organizational actors and/or social and political changes within African societies to be effective and sustained (Lancaster 2000: 225).

Under the Major government, aid programmes to Africa in the forms of cash grants and concessional loans were reduced from £636m in 1989 to £563m in 1995. This was in line with a reduction in Britain's overall aid budget from 0.31 per cent of Gross National Income (GNI) in 1989 to 0.26 per cent in 1997. The Blair government in contrast increased the size of the aid budget and bilateral programmes to Africa. The former rose to 0.3 per cent of GNI in 2001 and is apparently set to rise to 0.4 per cent by 2005–6 (DFID Press Release 3 April 2003). However, these levels are still only equivalent to 1989 levels and fall well short of the UN's recommended target of 0.7 per cent. Currently (2001–2), excluding humanitarian assistance, three of the top five recipients of DFID's expenditure were African,[6] and sub-Saharan Africa receives 43 per cent of all bilateral aid allocable by region compared with 36 per cent going to Asia (DFID Press Release 14 October 2002). (See Table 2.2.)

Table 2.2 British bilateral aid: top ten African recipients, 1999–2000 (£ millions)

Uganda	81
Tanzania	64
Ghana	48
Malawi	47
Mozambique	44
Sierra Leone	30
South Africa	30
Kenya	27
Nigeria	15
Rwanda	14.5

Source: Adapted from *The Economist* 23 February 2001: 35

Under the New Labour government there has also been an increased tendency to channel development expenditure through civil society organizations, with £191m disbursed in this manner in 2001–2 (DFID Press Release 14 October 2002). DFID has also been keen to work more closely with the private sector, one significant example being the Emerging Africa Infrastructure Fund. Established in 2002 and led by DFID and the Standard Bank Group, this earmarked $305m of public and private monies for projects including power generation, telecommunications, transportation and water facilities (DFID Press Release 30 January 2002).

Currently, Blair's government is trying to tie the themes of peace and prosperity together by supporting the New Partnership for Africa's Development (NEPAD) launched by African states in October 2001. Britain has endorsed NEPAD's liberal rationale and stressed two important strengths of the initiative. First, because it was designed by African states it is an example of Britain working in partnership with the continent rather than dictating the terms of the relationship. Second, it provides a framework for a variety of international actors, including the G-8, to cooperate across a broad range of areas such as peace and security, governance, investment, economic growth, development, agriculture, debt relief, health and information. Blair's brief tour of Nigeria, Senegal, Ghana and Sierra Leone in February 2002 was used partly to reiterate his government's support for the vision set out in NEPAD. The following month, however, the political storm surrounding Mugabe's 'victory' in Zimbabwe's presidential elections and the support he gained from many African states led British officials to question NEPAD's viability if its proponents failed to condemn Zimbabwe's plunge into crisis. Then, in June, Blair faced Japanese and US resistance to the plan at the G-8 summit in Kananaskis, Canada, despite the fact that NEPAD essentially endorses the G-8's version of the problems afflicting Africa and the necessary solutions (see Taylor and Nel 2002). Despite these problems NEPAD remains the current framework within which these issues will be addressed.

Promoting democracy?

After the World Bank's 1989 report *Sub-Saharan Africa: From Crisis to Sustainable Growth*, democracy or 'good governance' became the buzzwords of development discourse (Abrahamsen and Williams 2001: 258–60). Within a year most major state donors and international organizations made development assistance conditional on democratic reforms.

As noted above, Britain adopted such a stance in mid-1990 and practical evidence of the new policy was soon visible in the government's decision to cut its aid programmes to Sudan (1991), Kenya (1991) and Malawi (1992). A similar decision was taken through the EU to cut aid to The Gambia following the military coup that deposed President Dawda Jawara in July 1994. Again, however, Major's government applied this supposed principle selectively. Jerry Rawlings' Ghana and Yoweri Museveni's Uganda, for example, did not face such sanctions despite refusing to adopt liberal democratic reforms. Indeed, because it adhered to the prerequisites of World Bank structural adjustment, Ghana was even dubbed 'the darling of British aid overseers' and received more aid than any other African state except Zimbabwe (*Economist* 29 May 1993: 66). Similarly, little external criticism of Uganda's one-party movement for democracy has appeared because it too has followed the official adjustment rules.

More recently, the biggest tests of this position have been developments in Nigeria, Zimbabwe and, to a lesser extent, Rwanda. However, like the Conservatives, New Labour has also imposed sanctions on weak states while turning a blind eye to the vagaries of friends or stronger states. In Togo, for example, the EU (pushed by Britain and Germany) suspended aid following President Gnassingbé Eyadéma's fraudulent elections in June 1998 (*Africa Confidential* 2 April 1999).

In Nigeria, on the other hand, Britain's oil and other commercial interests were consistently considered paramount. Throughout the early 1990s, Nigeria was Britain's second largest export market in Africa, accounting for £457.9m of British exports in 1994 (*Hansard* 16 May 1995: col. 156). It was thus not especially surprising that when in 1995 General Sani Abacha announced the postponement of elections for more than three years, Britain's official reaction was to describe this as 'disappointing' (*Economist* 28 October 1995). Concerns about the military junta had not caused Britain to suspend its aid programme or stop selling weapons to Nigeria or supporting (politically and financially) its activities in both Liberia and Sierra Leone under the cover of ECOMOG. Following the execution of nine Ogoni activists in late 1995, Major's government did withdraw its ambassador from Nigeria, supported Nigeria's suspension from the Commonwealth and decided to terminate its arms sales to the country. However, although Britain supported an arms embargo against Abacha's regime, for commercial reasons it did not support the idea of oil sanctions proposed by Germany and the Nordic states. In Zimbabwe's case, Blair's government imposed a variety of sanctions bilaterally and through the EU after the country's parliamentary elections in 2000 in protest at Robert Mugabe's increasingly authoritarian rule (Taylor and Williams 2002).

For both the Major and Blair governments, democracy appears as an unproblematic concept with little attention paid to its inherently contested and controversial nature. In Africa, as elsewhere, democracy means very different things to different people and these competing definitions have been glossed over by successive British governments (Abrahamsen 2000). Both Conservative and Labour governments have advocated a particular form of multi-party liberal democracy that is said to be compatible with economic liberalization. Although this conception of democracy has appealed to many African elites, the continent's poorest people have usually defined democracy as including the provision of social and economic rights as well as civil and political ones.

Conclusion

This analysis suggests that Britain has a mixed record in terms of promoting peace, prosperity and democracy in Africa after the Cold War, with both Conservative and Labour governments pursuing selective and sometimes counterproductive policies. The brand of liberal internationalism exported by successive British governments has won favour with many African statesmen but has far fewer supporters among the continent's impoverished majority. This is at least partly because neither the Major nor the Blair governments have seriously addressed the tensions within their philosophical approach as it applies to Africa, particularly how neo-liberal economic policies have contributed to war, poverty and authoritarianism.

African affairs are undoubtedly higher up the British foreign policy agenda than they were immediately after the Cold War's end but it is inaccurate to suggest that, with the occasional exception, they occupy anything other than a marginal position in British politics more generally. Arguably, however, dramatic changes in Britain's policy towards Africa require substantial changes to be introduced at home. Not least, the British government must take some difficult decisions on issues like its domestic arms industry and invest the time and resources to explain to their electorates why Africa's predicament is an important political issue for Britons. These issues are important because, for all the talk of disengagement, Britain continues to play a significant part in African affairs through its bilateral relations, the activities of British TNCs and NGOs, and through its membership of the major multilateral institutions, most notably the UN, IMF, World Bank, World Trade Organization, G-8, Commonwealth and the EU. At present, however, the nature of Britain's relationship with Africa appears still to revolve around extracting profits and preventing 'their' problems ending up 'over here'. In this sense, Britain has still not moved beyond a damage limitation approach.

Notes

1   I would like to thank Rita Abrahamsen, Michael Kargbo and Ian Taylor for their comments on an earlier draft.
2   In 2002 Britain had thirty embassies and High Commissions in Africa with a total of over 1,750 staff, a total second only to the Asian Directorate within the FCO. There were thirty-one African diplomatic missions in London.
3   Author's interview with British official, February 2003.
4   Benin, Burundi, Cameroon, Congo, Egypt, Ghana, Ivory Coast, Lesotho, Mauritius, Morocco, Nigeria, Senegal, Sierra Leone, South Africa, Swaziland, Tunisia, Tanzania and Zimbabwe.
5   Algeria, Botswana, Cameroon, Congo, Egypt, Ethiopia, The Gambia, Ghana (x3), Ivory Coast, Kenya, Lesotho (x2), Malawi, Mauritius, Morocco, Namibia, Nigeria, Sierra Leone, South Africa (x2), Sudan, Swaziland, Tunisia, Uganda (x2), Zambia, Zimbabwe.
6   India (£180m), Uganda (£68m), Tanzania (£65m), Bangladesh (£61m) and Ghana (£55m).

References

Unless otherwise stated, all speeches by British government officials and government publications are available at www.fco.gov.uk

Abrahamsen, R. (2000) *Disciplining Democracy: Development Discourse and Good Governance in Africa*, London: Zed Books.

—— (2002) 'Blair's Africa: Securitisation after 11 September', paper presented to the African Studies Association of the UK biennial conference, University of Birmingham, 9–11 September.

Abrahamsen, R. and P. Williams (2001) 'Ethics and Foreign Policy: The Antinomies of New Labour's "Third Way" in Sub-Saharan Africa', *Political Studies*, 49: 249–64.

—— (2002) 'Britain and Southern Africa: A Third Way or Business as Usual?' in K. Adar and R. Ajulu (eds) *Globalization and Emerging Trends in African States Foreign Policy-Making Process*, Aldershot: Ashgate, pp. 307–28.

Blair, T. (1997) 'Principles of a Modern British Foreign Policy', speech at the Lord Mayor's banquet, London, 10 November.

—— (1998) *The Third Way: New Politics for a New Century*, London: Fabian Society Pamphlet 588.

—— (2001) Speech to Labour Party annual conference, Brighton, 2 October.

CAAT (2001) 'Labour's Hypocrisy over Small Arms', news release, 13 February. www.caat.org

Clapham, C. (1996) *Africa and the International System: The Politics of State Survival*, Cambridge: Cambridge University Press.

Cook, R. (1998) 'Promoting Peace and Prosperity in Africa', speech to the UN Security Council, 24 September.

—— (1999) 'Conflict Prevention in the Modern World', speech to the 54th session of the UN General Assembly, New York, 21 September.

Dixon, R. and P. Williams (2001) 'Tough on Debt, Tough on the Causes of Debt? New Labour's Third Way Foreign Policy', *British Journal of Politics and International Relations*, 3, 2: 150–72.

Ero, C. (2001) 'A Critical Assessment of Britain's Africa Policy', *Conflict, Security and Development*, 1, 2: 51–71.

FAC (Foreign Affairs Select Committee) (1999) *Second Report: Sierra Leone*, London: House of Commons, 9 February.

FCO (1995) *Angola: The Long Road to Recovery*, FCO Briefing Paper, October.

—— (1998) *Annual Report on Human Rights*, London: FCO and DFID.

Goodie, I. (2002) *The Employment Consequences of a Ban on Arms Exports*, London: CAAT Report, September. www.caat.org

Green Paper (2002) *Private Military Companies: Options for Regulation*, London: House of Commons.

Hain, P. (1999a) 'Africa: Backing Success', speech at the 'Challenges for Governance in Africa' conference, Wilton Park, 13 September.

—— (1999b) 'Angola Needs Our Help', speech to the Action for Southern Africa Annual Conference, London, 20 November.

Hurd, D. (1990) 'Prospects for Africa in the 1990s', speech to the Overseas Development Institute, London, 6 June.

Kahler, M. (ed.) (1997) *Liberalization and Foreign Policy*, New York: Columbia University Press.

Kapila, M. and K. Wermester (2002) 'Development and Conflict: New Approaches in the United Kingdom' in F. O. Hampson and D. M. Malone (eds) *From Reaction to Conflict Prevention: Opportunities for the UN System*, Boulder, CO: Lynne Rienner, pp. 297–320.

Khadiagala, G. M. (2000) 'Europe in Africa's Renewal: Beyond Postcolonialism' in J. W. Harbeson and D. Rothchild (eds) *Africa in World Politics: The African State System in Flux*, Oxford: Westview Press, 3rd edn, pp. 83–109.

Lancaster, C. (2000) 'Africa in World Affairs' in J. W. Harbeson and D. Rothchild (eds) *Africa in World Politics: The African State System in Flux*, Oxford: Westview Press, 3rd edn, pp. 208–34.

Lloyd, T. (1999) Speech to the Africa Day Conference, Lancaster House, London, 26 May.

McNulty, M. (1999) 'Media, Ethnicization and the International Response to War and Genocide in Rwanda' in T. Allen and J. Seaton (eds) *The Media of Conflict*, London: Zed Books, pp. 268–86.

Mayall, J. (1986) 'Britain and Anglophone Africa' in A. Sesay (ed.) *Africa and Europe: From Partition to Interdependence or Dependence?*, London: Croom Helm, pp. 52–74.

Melvern, L. (2000) *A People Betrayed: The Role of the West in Rwanda's Genocide*, London: Zed Books.

—— (2001) 'Missing the Story: The Media and the Rwandan Genocide', *Contemporary Security Policy*, 22, 3: 91–106.

Olsen, G. R. (1997) 'Western Europe's Relations with Africa since the End of the Cold War', *Journal of Modern African Studies*, 35: 299–319.

Penfold, P. (2002) 'Will Justice Help Peace?', *The World Today*, 58, 11: 21–3.

Rifkind, M. (1996) 'Africa – Time to Take Another Look', speech to the Royal Institute of International Affairs, 28 November, cited in RUSI, *Documents on British Foreign and Security Policy: Vol. I: 1995–1997*, London: TSO (1998), pp. 629–36.

Styan, D. (1996) 'Does Britain Have an African Policy?' in *L'Afrique Politique*, Paris: Karthala, pp. 261–86.

Taylor, I. and P. Nel (2002) '"Getting the Rhetoric Right", Getting the Strategy Wrong: "New Africa", Globalization and the Confines of Elite Reformism', *Third World Quarterly*, 23: 163–80.

Taylor, I. and P. Williams (2002) 'The Limits of Engagement: British Foreign Policy and the Crisis in Zimbabwe', *International Affairs*, 78: 547–65.

UK Government (2001) *The Causes of Conflict in Africa*, London: DFID, FCO, MoD Consultation Document.

UNCTAD (1999) *Foreign Direct Investment in Africa: Performance and Potential*, New York and Geneva: UNCTAD/ITE/IIT/Misc. 15.

Wallace, W. (1994) 'Foreign Policy' in D. Kavanagh and A. Seldon (eds) *The Major Effect*, London: Macmillan, pp. 283–300.

Williams, P. (2001) 'Fighting for Freetown: British Military Intervention in Sierra Leone', *Contemporary Security Policy*, 22, 3: 140–68.

—— (2002) 'The Rise and Fall of the "Ethical Dimension": Presentation and Practice in New Labour's Foreign Policy', *Cambridge Review of International Affairs*, 15, 1: 53–63.

3 France's policy towards Africa

Continuity or change?[1]

Daniela Kroslak

The end of the Cold War and the genocide in Rwanda in 1994 had a significant impact on French policy towards Africa. A continent of particular
importance to Paris, post-Cold War events and circumstances have
contributed to the revision of French involvement in Africa and triggered
several political, economic and military reforms. This chapter highlights the
changes that French African politics have undergone over the last decade
and argues that although a substantial revision has taken place, the effects of
which should not be underestimated, certain aspects of the special relationship between France and francophone Africa remain firmly in place. This is
even more so since a new government (led by Jean-Pierre Raffarin) was
elected in 2002.

The chapter analyses French African policy and its changes in four parts:
the systemic characteristics and institutional intricacies of French policy
towards Africa; the political and cultural features that mark the Franco-
African relationship; French economic activities and development aid; and
France's military involvement on the continent.

Systemic characteristics

Traditionally France's African policy rested on two main pillars: the exclusive power of the President and the continuity of a cross-party policy. This
has given a highly personalized character to Paris' policies towards Africa.
Due to the French President's prerogative in foreign policy, which is
enshrined in Articles 14 and 52 of the Constitution, French African policy
has been almost solely under the control of the Elysée (Presidency). Via the
Cellule Africaine (African Unit) of the Elysée (headed between 1986 and
1992 by Mitterrand's son Jean-Christophe), all important decisions
concerning Africa were made by the Presidency, and not as one would
expect by the Quai d'Orsay (Ministry of Foreign Affairs).

In addition to the President's power over foreign policy, he alone has 'the
power to dispatch regular ... troops overseas without reference to parliament or ministers' (McNulty 1997: 6). This is a result of the President being
the Chief of Staff of the Armed Forces (Article 15 of the Constitution).

During his term in office François Mitterrand made sure that his authority remained uncontested. As Mitterrand said in *Le Monde* in 1993, 'Not my ministers, but I am the one who determines French foreign policy ... Of course, my ministers are allowed to have their own opinion, but a policy which does not have my approval is unthinkable' (Brüne 1995: 135). African politics in particular has emerged over time as the French President's favourite fiefdom. As Smith and Glaser (1997a: xiii) have argued, 'if, under the Fifth Republic, French foreign policy is considered the *domaine réservé* of the head of state, Africa, even inside this exclusive notion, constitutes the *chasse gardée* (private hunting ground)' of the President.

Although the Presidency and its African Unit play the predominant role in French policy towards Africa, a great number of subordinate actors are involved in African politics: the Ministries of Foreign Affairs and of Defence, the former Ministry of Cooperation, and of Finance, the Caisse Française du Développement and the French Secret Service (DGSE), as well as a powerful network of directors of important public and private companies, the so-called *réseaux* (Chafer 2002: 347).

Jean-François Bayart (1995: 46), scholar and former advisor to the French Foreign Ministry, would add a few more agencies, namely 'the Prime Minister's Cabinet ... the treasury ... the high command of the armed forces ... [and] the Ministry of the Interior'. This coterie indicates not only the complexity of French African politics but also the effective lack of transparency, reinforced by an absence of democratic control and the influence of a small powerful elite. According to Marchal (1998: 357), this multiplicity of actors dilutes 'the political priorities that are officially proclaimed', promotes 'secret alliances' and has given 'remarkable leeway to African heads of state to pursue their own objectives'. Commenting cynically on this system, Verschave (1995: 29) remarked that 'the demoralisation of the actors of this system are such that one could compare them with the Chernobyl nuclear power plant: any accident becomes possible'. French African politics was thus dominated and managed by a small, tightly knit community of politicians, diplomats and businessmen surrounding the President. As mentioned, Mitterrand's son Jean-Christophe became presidential advisor in October 1986, ensuring that the President's and his own entourage's interest were preserved. Some experts have even insinuated that 'the majority of political leaders responsible for France's African politics are "masons"', alluding to the secretive and elitist character of Paris' activities on the continent (Smith and Glaser 1997a: 173).

In addition to the selected few involved in the decision-making of Franco-African affairs, the President has ensured that other governmental agencies, such as the Ministry of Cooperation and the DGSE, work within the parameters set by the Elysée's policies. Intelligence on client states in Africa has been invariably first class[2] and first hand since: 'Beside almost every president of France's African *pré carré* (backyard) is a colonel of the DGSE' (Smith and Glaser 1997a: 104). With the creation of the Ministry of Cooperation in 1961 (designed to manage French African policy with regards to decolonization), the Elysée found a way to side-step the Quai d'Orsay and 'continue its peculiar form of personalised diplomacy with African autocrats' (Adebajo 1997: 148). Politics towards Africa has thus traditionally been marked by a lack of control by and consultation with the National Assembly and various ministries which would normally have their say in foreign interventions, such as the Foreign Ministry or the Ministry of Defence.

Having said this, several factors have encouraged the reform of French African policy in general and the systemic intricacies that were so specific to Paris' policy. First, several setbacks on the African continent have contributed to change. The Rwanda debacle, the crisis in Zaire and the rebellions in the Central African Republic made a new generation of leaders, such as Alain Juppé and Lionel Jospin, realize that French African politics urgently needed an overhaul. Second, the election of such leaders impacted upon Paris' African policies as these new leaders were much less convinced of the benefits of such a closely knit relationship with Africa and did not enjoy any significant personal links with the continent. Third, a succession of scandals that involved parts of the *réseaux* deeply affected the political elite in Paris.

The structural consequence of the first and second factors was that the Ministry of Cooperation (the ministry often considered by African leaders as 'theirs') was integrated into the Ministry of Foreign Affairs. Although many attempted in vain to abolish the so-called 'Rue Monsieur', such as Foreign Minister Michel Jobert in March 1974 or Mitterrand's Minister of Cooperation, Jean-Pierre Cot, it took until 1998 for the integration to be finalized. The battle had started in June 1995 when Prime Minister Juppé decided to confront his Minister of Cooperation, Jacques Godfrain, with the incorporation into the Ministry of Foreign Affairs. Jacques Chirac, however, blocked the merger in 1996 on the advice of Jacques Foccart, the 'Monsieur Afrique' of several administrations (Bourmaud 1996: 438). It was on Jospin's initiative in 1998 that the Ministry of Cooperation came under the authority of the Ministry of Foreign Affairs. Yet compromise between modernizers (Jospin) and traditionalists (Chirac) prevailed and the ministry was not entirely absorbed into the Quai d'Orsay. It maintains a position in the Cabinet through its Minister for Cooperation and *Francophonie*. Furthermore, a government official affirmed that the collaboration between the 'Rue Monsieur' and the Quai d'Orsay remains sporadic.[3]

The election of a new generation of leaders was, as suggested, key to transforming French African policy in the 1990s. Until then, cross-party agreement had characterized policy. However, the second *cohabitation* with Edouard Balladur as Prime Minister (1993–5) significantly changed the direction and led to a 'radical transformation of the Franco-African complex' (Bourmaud 1996: 435). Alain Juppé, his Foreign Minister (who became Prime Minister 1995–7), also wanted to reform a discredited system. This was, as one commentator put it, managed by people responsible to the Elysée [who] were diplomats inclined to sacrifice their professional prerogative to certain ambiguous middlemen who, while ostensibly representing France's interests, in fact were doing little more than acting [for] private interests or financing their own political structures.

(Marchal 1998: 358–9)

It was, however, Prime Minister Lionel Jospin (1997–2002) and his Minister of Foreign Affairs Hubert Védrine, who, during another period of *cohabitation*, launched a multilateral approach to Africa, much to the dismay of many African leaders. It is important to underline two aspects: first, these modernizers come from both sides of the political spectrum and opposed adversaries from within their own political camps; second, since the 2002 elections the idiosyncratic African Unit of the Presidency has been sidelined by de Villepin, which added to a more transparent policy (in relative terms) towards Africa.[4]

However, old 'Africa hands' retain a presence in France's Africa policies. Jacques Chirac, for example, belongs to, as Bourmaud (1996: 435) put it, 'the galaxy of "Africans"'. A Gaullist to the core, Chirac has clearly absorbed the idea of the *'grandeur de la France'* that so marked French African politics of the Fifth Republic. Also a pragmatist, Chirac has tried to reconcile both reformers and traditionalists, reflected in his appointments to key posts where, 'for lack of an established personal doctrine', he aimed to strike a balance in order to counter radical reform attempts (Bourmaud 1996: 436). The case of the Ministry of Cooperation is an excellent example of this approach.

In addition to the above, a set of scandals has recently sent shockwaves through the French political system, the most famous being the Elf–Aquitaine sleaze scandal which involved not only the top managers of the previously state-owned oil giant but also high-ranking politicians, such as Roland Dumas and Charles Pasqua. Furthermore, President Chirac was accused of illegal party financing during his time as mayor of Paris. Although not directly to do with French African policy, it is interesting that Michel Roussin, Minister of Cooperation (1993–4) and a staunch advocate of a 'traditional' role for France in Africa, was accused of having organized a system of commissions to finance Chirac's *Rassemblement pour la République*. He is now vice-president of the group Bolloré, which has major interests in Africa. Notable accusations were also made against Mitterrand's son Jean-Christophe concerning his involvement in illegal arms dealing and money laundering (the so-called 'Angolagate'). These revelations, combined with the accusations against France in relation to the Rwandan genocide a few years earlier, triggered uproar in French society and bolstered the modernizers' case for reform.

Although it is true that the personal relationships between French and African elites have been considerably affected, one should not underestimate the power of the *réseaux*. Despite the fact that French African policy has been altered over the last decade, French interest and influence on the continent remains significant. Indeed, many traditionalists remain in positions of power and influence to defend the old way of France doing business in Africa.

Political and cultural features

The long overdue revision of French African policy has been in the making since the early 1990s. A number of political reforms have been undertaken to change or, as many officials insist, to 'normalize' the Franco-African relationship. This 'normalization' has its roots in several significant political developments, such as post-Cold War geopolitical circumstances and the domestic policy context as well as the arrival of a new generation of political leaders in Africa. The era of France's supposed 'neutral' position on the continent between the two superpowers has ended and the effects of globalization have meant that Africa is increasingly marginalized. Consequently, the political, economic and strategic benefits of France's engagement in Africa have turned out to be much less lucrative than before; reform thus became inevitable.

Traditionally, French African policy was marked by a cross-party consensus. Throughout the Fifth Republic all French presidents, from Georges Pompidou to François Mitterrand, continued General de Gaulle's 'activist Africa policy' (Adebajo 1997: 148). This tacit agreement between the parties was especially peculiar under a socialist leader, Mitterrand, who led a policy 'accompanied with a great discourse on democracy' (Franche 1997: 76). Even though Mitterrand initially set out to loosen the ties between the former colonies and the Métropole, he was soon convinced of French strategic, political and, especially, economic interests in Africa.

In order to maintain its influence, the French government pursued a policy of close relationships between the Elysée and African heads of states. Personal friendships and favouritism formed the basis of political and military decisions concerning francophone Africa. These 'friendships' were cultivated with regular meetings (mostly at the expense of the French taxpayer) and via the African Unit at the Elysée, headed by Jean-Christophe Mitterrand. The families of high African officials received special treatment in Paris, including higher education in France's best schools for the children and extravagant shopping trips for African 'first ladies'. These 'informal, intimate, and secretive politico-diplomatic relations, typified by the bi-annual Franco-African summit meetings', demonstrated cross-party complicity (Martin 1995: 1).

Paris fed these personal relationships to extract the most benefit from its former dependencies. Guy Martin (1995: 3) points out that 'although camouflaged under the mantle of cooperation, France's Africa policy is, in fact, primarily motivated by a narrow conception of its national interests, and blatantly disregards African concerns and interests'. Former President

Valéry Giscard d'Estaing underlined this point with his comment that 'I am dealing with African affairs, namely with France's interest in Africa' (Martin 1995: 6).

This interest was a reflection of the political importance that France attached to its links with Africa. As Gaston Monnerville commented back in 1945, 'without the empire, France would only be a liberated country today. Thanks to its empire France is a victorious country' (Ela Ela 2000: 87). This sort of thinking has dominated Paris' policies towards Africa. Here, three aspects are particularly relevant. First, the sentimental bonds linking Paris to francophone Africa (Ela Ela 2000: 90).[5] Second, the idea of France's *rayonnement* in the world: that is, the projection of French identity and values overseas (Chafer 2002: 345). Third, the desire to maintain France's status and influence in international politics. In addition, Louis de Guiringaud poignantly remarked that 'Africa is the only continent that remains within France's capacities and means. The only one where it can still change the course of history with 500 men' (Bayart 1998: 275).

The cultural side of France's *rayonnement* has always been of great importance and an integral part of French foreign policy. Paris cultivated its interest and influence via a cultural and linguistic crusade fought under the mantle of the *Francophonie*, a concept revolving around the organization of French-speaking countries whose people share French civilization and identity. The historian Fernand Braudel insisted that *'La France, c'est la langue française'*, a conviction shared amongst the highest echelons of the French ruling class. Hence, French influence was not only registered in the economic and military sphere, the cultural legacy of the former colonial mother country also represented an important dimension of Franco-African relations. In this sense Franco-African links appear mutually constitutive; France needs Africa for its own image just as much as Africa needs France. However, despite all the efforts to bolster France's cultural influence, only 15 per cent of the populations included in the *Francophonie* actually speak French (Adebajo 1997: 148). This implies that the francophone idea is very much an elite-driven agenda with little realization at the grass-roots level. While the 'big men' of francophone Africa identify strongly with a certain French heritage, it is doubtful whether the ordinary citizen shares this identity.

Closely related to this obsession with 'civilization' and the dissemination of French culture is the fear of anglophone encroachment. This has been nurtured by centuries of Anglo-French rivalry and, on the African continent, first and foremost by the humiliating incident at Fashoda in 1898 (where British troops forced the French to withdraw), resulting in the infamous 'Fashoda syndrome'. Today, French anglophobia does not so much lie with Britain any more but with what it sees as the undesirable spread of American influence on the African continent (Bayart 1995: 49). The stark contrast between the two powers lies between Paris' deep suspicion of other powers in Africa and its willingness to become militarily involved on the continent.

It is important to understand the intricacies of the post-colonial Franco-African relations in order to appreciate the reforms and changes in France's policy towards Africa in the 1990s. Several factors triggered its overhaul, but the end of the Cold War certainly had the most significant impact. A wave of democratization heralded a new era of political regimes on the continent and, similar to the former Eastern bloc, a spirit of *renouveau* marked the early 1990s. In January 1990, the Minister of Cooperation, Jacques Pelletier, realized that the changes underway in eastern Europe would affect Africa too and remarked, somewhat cryptically, '*Le vent de l'Est secoue les cocotiers* (The wind from the East shakes the coconut palms)' (Bayart 1998: 257).

The new geopolitical setting, the constraints and consequences of globalization and the rise of a new generation of political leaders in Paris and Africa have led to far-reaching reforms. However, it is important not to forget Africa's importance to France and the influence of certain circles on the political elite. These two factors still dominate French African politics and have been nurtured and cultivated since independence. Even though the reforms that have been undertaken by successive French governments in the 1990s represent a significant change, the French African lobby remains significant.

The change was also prompted by certain domestic developments: first, the economic weight of the Franc zone; second, a succession of prime ministers for whom Africa did not hold any great significance; third, the repercussions and media coverage of the Rwandan genocide drew attention to the chicanery of the French government in Africa. The political scandals mentioned above also made the French public aware of the corruption that seemed to permeate Franco-African ties.

Last, certain developments in Africa encouraged the reform of French policy. Chafer (2002: 354) outlines problems such as the debt crisis, economic failure, political instability, and conflict and humanitarian crises which made involvement increasingly costly. Again, the French role in Rwanda played an important part in the changing scenario. Jospin (1998: 11) alludes to the parliamentary investigation into the French role in the Rwandan genocide, insisting that 'the first of its kind, [it] allowed for the establishment of certain rules' previously virtually non-existent in relation to French policy in Africa leading, in relative terms, to more transparency. Furthermore, France's support for Mobutu in 1997 discredited and isolated Paris. François Léotard, Minister of Defence (1993–5), claims that

> events in Zaire have produced a triple failure for France: tactically because Mr Kabila was backed by the United States and anglophone African countries, morally because France had given the impression of supporting the discredited Mobutu to the end, and geo-politically because Zaire was an essential element in the French presence on the continent.
>
> (Gregory 2000: 441)

President Mitterrand launched the earliest initiative to reform French policy at the Franco-African summit in La Baule in 1990: 'French aid will be lukewarm towards authoritarian regimes and more enthusiastic for those initiating a democratic transition' (Martin 1995: 14). The so-called 'Paristroika' (Adebajo 1997: 148) envisaged a direct link between democratic reforms and continued aid. Considering France's involvement with authoritarian regimes on the continent, this seemed to constitute an enlightened step. French African policy, however, remained marked by 'a half-hearted support for democratic reforms guided by little principle' which resulted in the probability that 'France's African political traditions, its democratic demands and the attempt to preserve economic interests will also in future be in conflict' (Brüne 1995: 7). Equally, the French government maintained a paternalistic attitude towards the governments of the continent. Jacques Chirac, for example, considered democracy to be a 'luxury' for Africans and in February 1990 declared himself in favour of the one-party system in Africa (Adebajo 1997: 149; Brüne 1995: 144).

Despite the declaration at La Baule to help with democratization while continuing bilateral aid and military assistance, French African politics were nevertheless marked by financial support for non-democratic regimes and a willingness to rescue them whenever their internal security seemed in peril (France carried out ten military interventions on the continent from 1986 to 1994). This approach assumed that it was better to help crony governments to adopt pseudo-democratic measures and to remain influential rather than having to deal with new governments who would often be rather hostile towards the former colonial power. As Bernard Debré, Minister of Cooperation (November 1994 to May 1995) put it, 'democratisation in Africa leads to instability and institutional weakness. We must therefore encourage, assist, and help stabilise those regimes and leaders who are progressing on the path to democratisation at their own pace' (Martin 1995: 17–18).

Mitterrand himself commented on the substance of his proposal at the summit: 'My speech at La Baule? But it doesn't change anything! We already worked like that before!' (Bayart 1998: 264). Again, Rwanda serves as a good example. President Habyarimana made his discontent with the propositions known, although he quickly realized that paying lip service to the rhetoric of La Baule would be beneficial to him. Internal pressure and the civil war forced him to launch a half-hearted democratization process. Contrary to the apparent change in French policy, Paris did not support the newly established democratic parties but remained very close to the established authoritarian elite that committed the genocide in 1994 (Kroslak 2002: 229–34). In short, 'the results [were] not in keeping with the hopes born in La Baule' (Bourmaud 1996: 432).

Although President Chirac denounced 'sham democracies' and coups d'état, Paris retains its ambiguous relationship to democracy on the African continent (Wauthier 1997: 124–5). It remains willing to maintain contact with the continent's pariahs, such as Togo's Gnassingbe Eyadéma or

Zimbabwe's Mugabe. The latter was invited to the Franco-African summit in Paris against considerable resistance from the EU, especially Britain. The EU also condemned the 2003 election campaign in Togo and refused to send election observers because of irregularities. Several Assembly members in Paris decided, however, to override this decision and went to Togo to act as 'observers'.

This is relevant to another policy change that has been much heralded under the Jospin government: multilateralism. The idea was to integrate French policy towards Africa within a European framework. The bilateral involvement that used to be at the core of French African politics was loosened in favour of a multilateral approach. Since the St Malo agreement of December 1998, France and Britain also committed themselves to harmonizing their policies 'to promote the EU common position on human rights, democratic principles, the rule of law and good governance, and to contribute to the stability of the continent by tackling the debt problem and maintaining a significant level of development assistance' (Chafer 2002: 350). To date this Franco-British initiative is stuck on a diplomatic level. The political divergences between Paris and London over several conflicts on the continent such as Zimbabwe or the Great Lakes region seem to hamper a deeper cooperation on political issues, although the intervention in Ituri might signify a change.

Indeed, since the 2002 French election and the end of *cohabitation*, Chirac and his new Foreign Minister, Dominique de Villepin, have stepped back from this policy of multilateralism. Both Chirac and de Villepin are much more enthusiastic about Africa than Jospin and Védrine ever were, and Chirac is of the generation that holds strong personal ties with Africa. He is nevertheless aware that France–Africa links have been in urgent need of revision, though this has created a dilemma since it seems that Chirac seeks to reconcile traditional policy with the reforms of recent years. That is why there is a return to the bilateral relationship with African states (the so-called support of African initiatives) at the expense of policy coherence and multilateralism, as the Togo and Zimbabwe examples show. Yet the multilateral Ituri intervention defies a generalization in this respect. In general it seems that Africa has regained significance in the Elysée and the Quai d'Orsay (Kröncke 2003).

The Jospin government always underlined its wish to develop a new partnership with Africa. This is often interpreted as disengagement, notably by formerly close allies; officials insist, however, that 'France is not indifferent towards Africa's fate … it is still heavily committed for geopolitical, historic and almost moral reasons' (Combles 1998: 12). But Jospin's rhetoric and the significant changes in French policy did not stop his government becoming discreetly involved in Guinea-Bissau or Congo-Brazzaville. The recent interventions in the Ivory Coast and the Ituri region of the Democratic Republic of Congo (DRC) display a renewed confidence that France had lost during the 1990s and is reasserting under the new conservative government.

France's difficult and ambiguous role in the Ivory Coast since the beginning of the civil war in September 2002 reflects this rediscovery of French power in Africa. At first reluctant to get embroiled in the conflict, Paris decided, despite its little esteem for President Laurent Gbagbo, to intervene militarily and politically. This was partly due to the number of French citizens living in the country but also because Paris has rediscovered the use of long-established mechanisms, or what Smith (2002: 324) calls 'the extraordinary opportunism of French "policy" towards the Ivory Coast'.

During the 1990s, Paris launched a number of ground-breaking political reforms to adjust French policy to the new international setting. Although these reforms have significantly changed Franco-African relations, one should not over-exaggerate their impact. Several established mechanisms remain or have been rediscovered since the 2002 election. The *réseaux*, even if partly dismantled, still exert important influence on the 'normalization' of French policy. Chirac and de Villepin aim to find a compromise between the reforms introduced by Balladur, Juppé and Jospin and the more traditional bilateral approach that has marked French policy. At the same time, Chirac seems to want to reassert France's role in Africa after several years of crisis.

Development and economic aspects

In terms of France's economic involvement on the African continent one can distinguish between the economic activity of French business and the intricacies and changes of its involvement over the last decade, and French development policy.

As in the political sphere, Africa has always been an important economic partner for France in maintaining its grandiose ambition to be seen as a world player. France has relied on Africa as a source of strategic raw materials,[6] as a market for her manufactured goods and as an outlet for capital investment (Martin 1995: 9). Even though the economic aspects of French African politics were played down by President Valéry Giscard d'Estaing, who claimed that 'there is no relationship whatsoever between the Government's policy and economic interests' (*Le Monde* 29 January 1981), until the early 1990s Africa was important to the French economy.

Founded on a high degree of post-colonial dependency, trade relations between Paris and francophone Africa were very unbalanced. After independence Franco-African trade remained in the hands of renamed colonial trading companies (*La Compagnie française de l'Afrique occidentale* and *La Société commerciale de l'ouest africain*) that greatly benefited from the protective nature of the Franc zone (Martin 1985: 198). As Martin (1985: 198) pointed out in 1985:

A quarter of a century after independence, the foreign trade of African countries is still functioning according to the rules of the trade economy, according to which the African territories were restricted to the function of suppliers of raw materials and agricultural products, while the European metropoles reserved for themselves the exclusivity of industrial production and the export of manufactured goods.

To ensure that African economies worked in its favour Paris resorted to a monetary cooperation arrangement – the Franc zone and the CFA franc – aimed at controlling 'their issuance and circulation of currency, their monetary and financial regulations, their banking activities, their credit allocation and, ultimately, their budgetary and economic policies' (Martin 1985: 200). With the quasi-control of the African central bank resulting from these agreements, monetary and financial policy remained firmly in French hands.

The toppling of the Berlin Wall and subsequent developments heralded far-reaching economic changes. The La Baule summit was the first sign of major adjustments of French economic policy towards Africa, but it was the Abidjan doctrine presented by Prime Minister Edouard Balladur in 1993 that incorporated the new increasingly liberal economic approach. Two reforms impacted heavily on Franco-African trade relations. First, the devaluation of the CFA franc, and second, the opening up of French African policy to non-francophone states, such as Nigeria, Kenya, Zimbabwe and South Africa. The latter meant the reallocation of French investment in economies outside the Franc zone, which was in part due to the former, the devaluation of the CFA franc.

The 50 per cent devaluation of the CFA franc[7] in January 1994, which had been tied to the French franc at a fixed rate since 1948, was the result of several developments. The 'strong franc' policy, the devaluation of the dollar a decade earlier and the drop in raw material prices had devastating effects on the terms of trade between the Franc zone and the rest of the world, with African exports being issued in US dollars and African imports in strong EU currencies (Chafer 2002: 361; Bayart 1998: 257). The resulting economic crisis in Africa put significant pressure on the French treasury because of the rocketing cost of assisting bankrupt regimes in francophone Africa (see Bayart 1995; Hibou 1995).

This drastic measure implied a move away from the traditionally close post-colonial relationship between France and its former dependencies, and indicated the abolition of one of the pillars of the Franco-African system. The devaluation represented one of the major steps towards 'normalization' in French African politics, even if and because it signified the gradual loss of economic and perhaps even political power and influence in Africa. African leaders, however, were relatively unprepared for this change of policy, despite the changing rhetoric in Paris since the La Baule summit in 1990, and saw this decision as 'sudden, unilateral and therefore contemptuous' (Bourmaud 1996: 433). This perception was reinforced when the new policy was conveyed to fourteen African heads of state by a 'mere' minister, the Minister of Cooperation, Michel Roussin (Bourmaud 1996: 434).

After the disaster in Rwanda in 1994 and the debacle in Zaire in 1997, the political and military consequences for Paris were far-reaching. Economically, however, France has not suffered important losses in Africa (Sada 1997: 180), since over the years Africa has become less and less important to French business, which is more and more integrated into the EU economy. Marchal (1998: 360) insists that for Jospin 'Africa no longer represents a primary economic concern for France'. Yet Africa still accounts for about 5 per cent of France's external trade (Utely 2002: 130) and it is the one continent in the world where France is one of the most important actors. Therefore, Africa persists in its – at the very least symbolic – importance to French *rayonnement*.

The traditional post-independence relationship, the so-called *coopération*, was much less cooperative than its name would suggest. In fact, the cooperation agreements put in place after independence were, in Martin's (1985: 192) words, 'mere adjustments to previous agreements that in no way affected her [France's] hegemony'. These agreements were bilateral accords which enabled Paris to control the economies of its *pré carré*. Although France always preferred bilateral relationships with Africa prior to the reforms in the 1990s, Paris realized that it could not bear the burden of Africa's economic development alone. The Lomé Convention between the EEC and forty-six African, Caribbean and Pacific (ACP) countries in February 1975 enabled Paris to maintain its influence in 'her' part of Africa while sharing the cost with its European allies and rivals on the continent. As Sheth (1999: 82) points out, 'it was a classic case of neo-colonial control through multilateral cooperation'.

There were several reasons for changes in development policy towards Africa in the early 1990s. The collapse of the bipolar power structure diminished France's stronghold on its former colonies. Furthermore, certain legacies from the previous decade had become an increasing burden: the failure of structural adjustment programmes, the poor performance of the Franc zone and the recession in France. All these factors led to Mitterrand's speech at La Baule (discussed above). In economic terms the message was made clear: 'no development without democracy'. However, it became apparent that, as in the political domain, this policy was soon – if not dropped – toned down, arguing that African leaders needed to be given the time to reform at their own pace and on their own terms. In fact, 'French politicians began to link aid more with economic conditionality than with democratic political reforms ... [Consequently,] the countries which moved towards democratisation found their French aid more curtailed than that received by others' (Sheth 1999: 84).

In September 1993, Balladur set out to take La Baule a step further by announcing during his first official visit to the continent what was later labelled the Abidjan Doctrine (July 1994). This doctrine distinguishes clearly between aid linked to specific development projects involved in education, sanitation or equipment, and aid not related to specific projects, i.e.

budgetary aid, which would be conditional on a prior agreement with the Bretton Woods institutions (Bourmaud 1996: 434). Although this was very much in line with what was planned at La Baule, Balladur was much more serious about restructuring African economies according to the neo-liberal principles of the new world economy.

At the same time, inspired by the benefits of multilateralism, the EU became the preferred forum for development aid for French governments. For Paris this had two advantages. On the one hand, it redistributed the financial burden, since it was less expensive than maintaining constant bilateral flows. This was a measure that had already been practised since the Lomé Accords but was now reinforced. On the other hand, it was a symbolic gesture which depicted Paris in a favourable light as the 'caring mediator between the African states and the [European] community' (Bourmaud 1996: 440). The objective was clear: keeping the economic advantages without paying too high a price.

In terms of debt, France cancelled the arrears of the so-called 'least advanced countries' (*pays les moins avancés*, PMA) after the devaluation of the CFA franc. In July 1995 Chirac announced the conversion of the debt of four African countries into investments into development projects in exchange for an equivalent reduction in their external debt (Wauthier 1997: 123). In November 1995, however, Paris cancelled 60 per cent of its voluntary contributions to UN agencies, which heavily affected many development projects, notably those fighting HIV/AIDS (Wauthier 1997: 123).

These changes reduced French development assistance to Africa. As mentioned above, the era of Jospin and Védrine emphasized the opening of French African politics beyond the traditional *pré carré*, which meant that those countries that benefited from the special relationship rose to fifty-five at the end of the 1990s (Cumming 2001: 409). Due to the multilateral approach to Africa that Jospin favoured, bilateral aid steadily declined, and due to the enlargement of the traditional sphere of interest, aid to the former dependencies decreased drastically: in 1994 France's aid budget amounted to 0.64 per cent of GDP whereas in 2000 it was little more than half of that figure, namely 0.37 per cent. The proportion of the French aid budget earmarked for bilateral aid declined from 75.6 to 64.7 per cent in the same years (Chafer 2002: 352).

Since the elections in 2002, Chirac has aimed to return to a more bilateral structure of aid and to increase development aid spending. In fact, at the Franco-African summit in Paris in February 2003 the French President announced that he was against an increase in agricultural subsidies in developed countries and promised his African counterparts that he would try to persuade the G-8 countries in Evian to suspend this rise (Colette 2003: 79). Here, however, Chirac was being cynically opportunistic. After all, within the EU Chirac resists reform of the European agricultural policy, a measure that could be of enormous help to African agriculture. As Patrick Sabatier recently remarked in *Libération* (30 March 2003: 3):

[whether] Chirac be sincere or cynical, the government of [Prime Minister] Raffarin sets itself apart neither in the protection of the environment, nor in the generosity towards poor countries, nor in the calling into question of agricultural subsidies, nor in the opening up of the markets for products from the South. Anti-globalizationists [*altermondialistes*] have been able to realize that there is often quite a gap between Chirac's fine words and Raffarin's inaction.

Nevertheless, the rhetoric *has* changed on the aid front since the 2002 elections. Only recently de Villepin (2003) emphasized Paris' support for African initiatives, and notably for NEPAD. And in an interview the Director-General of the French development agency (AFD), Jean-Michel Séverino, implied that mistakes had been made over the last decade that needed to be adjusted without, however, dismissing the reforms in French African politics. He pointed out that 'France [had] undervalued poverty and its implications on the continent' over the last decade. However, while the

> personal links between French leaders and African heads of state were very close ... these links are slack today. This is not a bad thing: the reasoning is more pragmatic; *France-Afrique* and sleaze are not a phenomenon that structures the relations between Paris and the continent. But, simultaneously the investments have decreased. We have lost contact. The decade of the 1990s was one marked by an error of judgement.
>
> (Kappès-Grangé 2003: 80)

This being so, France's policies towards Africa retain a strong strategic element that aims to bolster Paris' standing as a global player. The next section analyses these strategic impulses.

Strategic elements

The political and economic control over its *pré carré* have gone hand in hand with extensive military engagement on the ground. According to Martin (1995: 14), France's military involvement and presence has been mainly determined by three factors: 'the size and degree of her economic interests and involvement; the number of French residents; and the nature of the links existing between France and the national ruling elites'. But as in the political and economic spheres, French military involvement has been considerably revised. Several measures have altered the Franco-African military relationship. First, the professionalization of France's armed forces, which resulted in a reduction of personnel and bases on the African continent. Second, France reviewed its defence agreements with African states in order to avoid becoming involved in internal conflicts. Last, with the integration of the Ministry of Cooperation into the Ministry of Foreign Affairs, military cooperation missions are now under the auspices of the Ministry of Defence (Marchal 1998: 362).

Prior to reform two types of military engagement were prevalent on the African continent. On the one hand, there was military cooperation, i.e. giving military assistance to African states (mostly resulting from bilateral agreement between a state and France, an *Accord de Coopération*). This cooperation could be extended to other aspects such as arms transfers, technological transfers or military–industrial cooperation (Dumoulin 1997: 9). On the other hand, when it came to the deployment of troops, such as the 1990 Operation Noroît in Rwanda, the mandate and command came from the Ministry of Defence rather than the Ministry of Cooperation, reflecting the official sharing of responsibilities. In the field, however, the distinctions between the two kinds of missions were not as clear-cut, and responsibilities and involvement often overlapped.

As with civilian cooperation accords, these defence and military cooperation agreements maintained French hegemony on the continent and became a tool to intervene at will in the name of regional 'stability'. Twenty-three countries in francophone Africa are tied to France through such accords; most benefit(ed) largely dictatorial regimes. As Richard (1997: 7) points out, 'the troops stationed in Africa are considered as a lightning conductor by the regimes in place'.

The multilateral drive of the Jospin administration obviously affected these accords. The aim to form a European rapid reaction force and 'closer co-operation with NATO have made it more difficult for France to play a distinctive, "exceptional" role in foreign policy' (Chafer 2002: 354). Furthermore, France realized that the internal conflicts that spread across national borders and involved several of its allies simultaneously could create serious problems if France was asked to stick to its defence/cooperation accords. Most significant for the review of these accords was, as Chafer (2002: 355) points out,

> the new international strategic environment in the 1990s ... [which] led France to redefine its security priorities and it was this that underpinned the wide-ranging defence reforms of 1994–1996, one consequence of which has been the restructuring of the French military role and presence in Africa.

One of the pillars of Franco-African military cooperation was the training of African troops. To this end France trained many Africans in French military schools and sent military advisors to restructure various African armed forces. Partly because of the criticism relating to the Rwandan genocide and the international isolation after Mobutu's defeat, but mainly because of the reform of the French armed forces, the training component of Franco-African military cooperation also obtained a multilateral spin.

Two measures were taken to this effect. First, the aim was to regionalize African security. In September 1998 Védrine stated that the 'regional contagion of crises justifies that regional organisations play a greater role in the prevention and resolution of conflicts' (Utely 2002: 138). In order to achieve this restructuring, Paris reallocated considerable sums to the OAU's conflict prevention programme and to the ECOWAS Moratorium on Small Arms. It also provided financial and logistic support for the ECOWAS peacekeeping mission in Guinea-Bissau, and continues to do so for Ecoforce in the Ivory Coast. Moreover, France decided to delocalize the training of African officers from France to Africa by creating regional training schools (*écoles nationales à vocation régionale*, ENVR) (Ela Ela 2000: 92–6).

Second, the aim was to link up with Western allies (who at the same time are perceived as France's rivals on the continent) to enhance regional peacekeeping in Africa (Chafer 2002: 349). As with civilian cooperation, the multilateral approach aspires to reduce the risks and cost, as well as share the responsibilities among partners (and competitors). Inspired by the summit in St Malo, a trilateral peacekeeping initiative was launched in May 1997 which united the efforts of three peacekeeping programmes, RECAMP (*Renforcement des capacités africaines de maintien de la paix*), ACRI (Africa Crisis Response Initiative) and BMATT (British Military Advisory and Training Teams) (Berman and Sams 2000: 267–332). Insisting on the new geopolitical and economic realities, Jospin maintained in 1997 that 'France cannot assure, alone, the security of its African partners' (Utely 2002: 138).

RECAMP aims 'to provide African states with the tools they need to conduct successful peacekeeping operations' (Berman and Sams 2000: 298) because, as Prime Minister Lionel Jospin (1997: 9) put it, 'France is particularly concerned with the stability and peacekeeping on this continent.' Following the policy of viewing Africa in its entirety (Jospin 1998: 16), this new initiative was not exclusively reserved for France's traditional sphere of influence. Although an effort was made to integrate anglophone and lusophone states, the bulk of the benefactors remain French-speaking, largely due to the fact that 'the French intention [is] to contribute to peacekeeping and international security ... through a reinforcement of our cooperation with the countries that are located in the zones where France has strategic interests' (Jospin 1997: 8). As in the civilian sector, the opening up of French Africa and the multilateralization of French policy towards Africa meant a redistribution of French funds and resulted in a significant reduction of bilateral military aid.

French justifications for its provision of military assistance have always hinged on the argument that it contributes to the stability and economic benefit of its former colonies. One need only look at the war-stricken ex-colonies of the British, the Portuguese or the Italians, so the argument goes, to understand why it was important to extend a 'guiding hand' to former dependants. Sierra Leone, Angola or Ethiopia is what happens when the colonial powers simply turn their backs, so the discourse goes. In fact, Paris insisted that through military cooperation it contributed to the development of 'its' part of the African continent. Giscard d'Estaing explained the official logic in 1981: 'Why do certain states ask us to take care of their security? It is because they just do not have the resources to build up modern armed forces. Africa must allocate her resources to development projects' (Martin 1985 : 205).

French military involvement on the African continent was unlike that of any other Western power. It was the only Western state to maintain military bases throughout Africa, with the most important ones in Bangui (Central African Republic), Franceville (Gabon) and Abéché (Chad). In addition to these bases, France had around 9,000 troops stationed on the continent. In 1997, Dumoulin (1997: 113) claimed there were 1,500 men in the Central African Republic, 840 in Chad, 3,425 in Djibouti, 600 in Gabon, 530 in the Ivory Coast and 1,500 in Senegal. Martin found similar figures in 1994. He confirmed French troops in the Central African Republic (1,200), Chad (750), Ivory Coast (500), Djibouti (4,000), Gabon (800) and Senegal (1,200), and highlights that 'a further 792 French military advisers are currently assigned to twenty African countries' (Martin 1995: 13). These troops could be deployed very rapidly in cases of internal turmoil or external aggression against any African client state.

However, the 1990s saw a gradual reduction in French troop numbers on the continent and a phasing out of its military bases. In August 1993 France set up a *Force d'action rapide* composed of five units totalling 44,500 men. This force was ostensibly 'capable of intervening at short notice almost anywhere in Africa from bases in France' (Martin 1995: 13).

In accordance with the policy changes outlined above, the number of military personnel stationed on the continent was equally affected. Two additional reasons were significant in this context. First, influenced by the new world order after 1989, the populations of several African countries grew increasingly resentful of French military presence on their soil (Ela Ela 2000: 89). Second, the armed forces were reorganized, gradually professionalized and reduced in strength by more than 23 per cent (Utely 2002: 134). This reform, which aimed to enhance the armed forces' efficiency, was issued in a European context (Jospin 1998: 8) and in view of a European rapid reaction force. As Utley (2002: 134) points out, 'both the 1994 defence white paper and the 1997–2002 military planning law emphasized clearly the European and Euro-Atlantic cooperative frameworks within which future French military actions were envisaged'.

The vision of these more efficient and professional French armed forces, appropriate for 'delicate and varied missions' (Jospin 1997: 5), would also be felt in Africa. The bases in Cameroon and the Central African Republic were closed because of this measure and for budgetary reasons, in order, in Defence Minister Alain Richard's words, to 'pursue its evolution towards an ever more balanced and more flexible relationship with friendly African forces' (Utely 2002: 137). Instead of the approximately 9,000 French troops previously stationed on the continent, around 6,500 French personnel remain in Africa: Djibouti (3,300), Senegal (1,300), Chad (850), Ivory Coast (530) and Gabon (600) (Ela Ela 2000: 94).

The most contested aspect of French African politics has always been the frequent military intervention on the continent since independence. The complex web of accords and agreements, and the political and economic involvement on the continent, 'has enabled the French army to intervene at least thirty times in Africa since 1963' (Martin 1995: 13). What was most disconcerting about these interventions is the fact that Paris remained in a position to control the political and military realities on the continent. Martin (1985: 194) notes that 'a number of *coups d'état* have occurred in various Francophone countries precisely when French economic, political, and strategic interests were being directly or indirectly threatened'. Or, in Giscard d'Estaing's revealing words, 'we have intervened in Africa whenever an unacceptable situation had to be remedied' (*Le Monde* 29 January 1981).

This 'traditional' approach to Africa reigned in Paris until its total failure in Rwanda. For the first time a rebel regime took power in a client state. This combined with the serious accusations against French support for the Rwandan regime prior to, and even to some extent during, the genocide (Kroslak 2002), represented a heavy blow to French prestige on the continent and impacted upon its willingness to intervene militarily.

A new phase of Franco-African relations, which started in the early 1990s, was pursued even more fervently by a number of actors in Paris after 1994. This was also felt in the military sphere. One can distinguish between the technical changes, such as the restructuring of the army, and the policy changes that altered (to some extent) French interventionism in Africa. The rhetoric towards interventionism has indeed changed. Prime Minister Jospin made clear that the era of clientelism was over by stating that 'the complementary principles "non-intervention" and "non-interference" allow for mutual respect, the development of a well-balanced partnership and the promotion of African interests within international institutions' (Jospin 1997: 16). Similarly, in November 1996, President Chirac declared 'the time of unilateral interventions is over' (Ela Ela 2000: 91).

Yet these reforms should be seen within the context of continuity within French policy. For example, as Chafer (2002: 358) has highlighted, French interventions in Comoros in 1995 and in the Congo in 1997 'allowed Chirac's friend and long-standing ally of *"la Françafrique"*, Denis Sassou Nguesso, to return to power in 1997'. This appears to indicate 'the continuation of France's long-standing policy of grandeur and the maintenance of stability in its *pré carré* through military intervention' (Chafer 2002: 358). French interventionism was not going to stop suddenly (Smith and Glaser 1997a: 65–93; 1997b).

However, the crisis in the Central African Republic in 1996–7 seemed to indicate a relative change and reflect a multilateralization of military interventionism. France was tied to a defence agreement with Bangui but decided not to be drawn into the conflict but rather support MISAB (*Mission*

Internationale de Surveillance des Accords de Bangui). This initiative was heralded by some as 'a major turning-point in the adaptation of France's African policy' (Utely 2002: 140). Considering the influence of the 'old boys' in French policy towards Africa, Chafer's (2002: 350) analysis that France's aim was rather to maintain 'influence (and lucrative arms markets) while reducing political risks and economic costs of unilateral military interventions' appears accurate. There is still a willingness to intervene on the continent but Paris is less prepared to take the financial and political risk of large-scale unilateral engagement. Paris has ceased to be the *Gendarme d'Afrique.*

After several years of disengagement and of confusing relationships between France and its African partners, 2003 seems to be the year of the normalization of 'normalization', combining old policies with the reforms and rhetoric of the last decade. Two developments signal this in military terms: the intervention in the Ivory Coast and the mission to Ituri under UN auspices.

The Ivory Coast sheds light on complex changes in French policy towards Africa. Paris was unwilling to intervene in the 1999 Christmas coup, arguably because 'Chirac was not ready to take the risk for the cohabitation. He knew that Bédié wasn't worth it' (Smith 2002: 312). Certain high-ranking figures pushed for intervention, arguing that the security of French citizens in Abidjan could be taken as a pretext to intervene (Smith 2002: 313). Paris later decided to abandon Bédié. After all, General Gueï, who had been trained in France, had good contacts with the French establishment and its military. At the time, the non-intervention in the Ivory Coast in 1999–2000 was justified along the lines of the new partnership with Africa. But upon closer inspection certain circles in Paris were not at all disconsolate about Bédié's departure – Gueï at the time seemed a safer bet for French interests.

In September 2002, however, the circumstances were slightly different. After the dispatch of a force to protect French citizens on 22 September, the French Minister of Defence, Michèle Alliot-Marie, declared that there would be no military intervention. After three months of an uncertain mandate (not unlike the one of Operation Noroît in Rwanda in 1990, where France sent in a force to evacuate and protect its citizens but stayed to support the government army), the French government decided to send additional troops. Through its political initiatives (most notably the Marcoussis agreement of January 2003) and its decision to intervene militarily Paris became more and more involved in the country. However, its role remains ambiguous. Paris is suspicious of President Gbagbo, who has criticized France's role on the continent, and its position as a mediator is delicate. Moreover, at the end of May 2003, *Liberation* reported that the Foreign Legion has been charged with securing the west of the country to act as a buffer force between the (former) warring parties and to create a 'zone of trust' (26 May 2003). By June 2003, France had 4,000 troops in the Ivory Coast (de Villepin 2003). Paris is thus significantly embroiled in the conflict.

Another major change of the new administration is the return of the French army into the Great Lakes region after six years of isolation. Under the aegis of the UN this French-led European force is seen as an opportunity for Paris to regain its credibility. The first French troops arrived in the town of Bunia on 6 June 2003 with the mission to contribute to the stabilization of Ituri. The warring faction linked to Rwanda (*Union des patriotes congolais*, UPC) made it clear that it would consider French troops as enemies (*Libération* 14 May 2003) despite Rwanda's approval of the intervention. This intervention is a significant step towards Chirac's vision of the future Franco-African relationship, combining the idea of reform in terms of multilateralism (UN mandate, EU framework) and traditional French interventionism in the name of 'stability' in Africa.

Conclusion

Maintaining status and prestige has always represented one of Paris' main goals in Africa. Reflecting the view that France needed its sphere of influence in Africa in order to play a role on the world stage, in 1953 Mitterrand wrote that 'the France of the 21st century will be African or nothing at all' (Bayart 1998: 260). This goal was to be achieved through economic, military–strategic and cultural means, and the French developed far-reaching influence in their former colonies and client states with the capacity and willingness to intervene militarily and diplomatically.

The Rwandan genocide and the political scandals of the 1990s, however, sent shockwaves through the political elite in Paris. These and several other events and personalities contributed to a long overdue revision of French African politics. The reduction of French military presence on the continent, the integration of the Ministry of Cooperation, the question of economic 'viability', the multilateralization of French aid policy and of French military interventionism, the support for African initiatives and the increasing even if relative transparency of French African politics are all major changes in the Franco-African relationship. However, the *réseaux* still constitute an important link between Paris and Africa. Despite the fact that French African policy has been altered over the last decade, French interest and influence on the continent remains significant. Many traditionalists remain to defend French interests. Chirac and de Villepin are searching for a compromise between the reforms introduced by Balladur, Juppé and Jospin and the more traditional bilateral approach that has marked French policy since independence. For his part, Chirac apparently wants to reassert France's role in Africa after several years of crisis. This is especially visible in the interventions in the Ivory Coast and Ituri. Thus, although the reforms and changes in French policy towards Africa are important, one should not lose sight of the continuity in the foundations of French African policy and the rather wide discrepancy between rhetoric and action in Paris' policies towards the continent.

Notes

1 I would like to thank the editors for their comments and express my gratitude to Priska Moser and Anne Baraquin.
2 Although some experts doubt the effectiveness of the DGSE, such as Gérard Prunier; interview, Paris, 28 September 1999.
3 Interview, Ministry of Foreign Affairs, Paris, 12 June 2003.
4 Interview, Ministry of Foreign Affairs, Paris, 12 June 2003.
5 Interviews, Ministry of Foreign Affairs and Ministry of Defence, Paris, 12 June 2003.
6 Strategic raw materials are minerals that are vital to the functioning of the European high-technology industries. France's dependency in 1985 was: 100 per cent for cobalt, 87–100 per cent for uranium, 83 per cent for phosphates, 68 per cent for bauxite, 35 per cent for manganese, and 32 per cent for copper (Martin 1985: 197).
7 At independence the former French colonies adopted a single currency, the franc CFA. Created in 1945 as the franc CFA of the Colonies Françaises d'Afrique (French African Colonies), it became the franc of the Communauté Financière Africaine (African Financial Community) after independence. Until 1994, this currency was attached to the French franc with a fixed exchange rate between the franc CFA and the French franc, which gave Paris control over African monetary policies.

References

Adebajo, A. (1997) 'Folie de Grandeur', *The World Today*, 53, 6: 148–9.

Barry, M. A. (1997) *La Prévention des conflits en Afrique de l'Ouest*, Paris: Karthala.

Bayart, J.-F. (1984) *La Politique africaine de François Mitterrand*, Paris: Karthala.

—— (1995) 'Réflexion sur la politique africaine de la France', *Politique Africaine*, 58: 41–51.

—— (1998) '"*Bis repetita*": la politique africaine de François Mitterrand' in S. Cohen (ed.) *Mitterrand et la sortie de la Guerre Froide*, Paris: Presses Universitaire de France, pp. 251–93.

Berman, E. G. and K. Sams (2000) *Peacekeeping in Africa: Capabilities and Culpabilities*, Geneva/Pretoria: UNIDIR/ISS.

Bourmaud, D. (1996) 'La Politique africaine de Jacques Chirac: les anciens contre les modernes', *Modern and Contemporary France*, NS4, 4: 431–42.

Brüne, S. (1995) *Die französische Afrikapolitik. Hegemonialinteressen und Entwicklungsanspruch*, Baden-Baden: Nomos.

Chafer, T. (2002) 'Franco-African Relations: No Longer So Exceptional?' *African Affairs*, 101, 404: 343–63.

Chipman, J. (1989) *French Power in Africa*, Oxford: Blackwell.

Colette, E. (2003) 'France-Bénin. Opération séduction', *Jeune Afrique/L'Intelligent*, 2200: 80.

Combles de Nayves, D. de (1998) 'La Nouvelle Politique militaire française en Afrique', *Défense Nationale*, 54, 8 and 9: 12–16.

Cumming, G. (2001) *Aid to Africa: French and British Aid from the Cold War to the New World Order*, Aldershot: Ashgate.

Dumoulin, A. (1997) *La France militaire et l'Afrique. Coopération et interventions: un état des lieux*, Brussels: Editions Complexe/GRIP.

Ela Ela, E. (2000) 'La Nouvelle Politique de coopération militaire de la France en Afrique', *Défense Nationale*, 56, 2: 86–100.

Franche, D. (1997) *Rwanda. Généalogie d'un génocide*, Paris: Editions Mille et Une Nuits.

Gaulme, P. (1995) 'La France et l'Afrique: De François Mitterrand à Jacques Chirac', *Marchés Tropicaux*, 50, 2585: 1112–14.

Golan, T. (1981) 'A Certain Mystery: How Can France Do Everything that It Does in Africa – and Get Away with It?' *African Affairs*, 80, 318: 3–11.

Gregory, S. (2000) 'The French Military in Africa: Past and Present', *African Affairs*, 99, 396: 435–448.

Guichaoua, A. (1997) 'Les "Nouvelles" Politiques africaines de la France et des Etats-Unis vis-à-vis de l'Afrique centrale et orientale', *Polis*, 4, 2: 68–82.

Hibou, B. (1995) 'Politique économique de la France en zone franc', *Politique Africaine*, 58: 25–40.

Jospin, L. (1997) 'La Politique de défense de la France', *Défense Nationale*, 53, 11: 3–20.

—— (1998) 'Évolution générale de la politique de défense de la France', *Défense Nationale*, 54, 11: 5–20.

Kappès-Grangé, A. (2003) 'Jean-Michel Sévérino: "Nous avons perdu le contact avec les Africains" ', *Jeune Afrique/L'Intelligent*, 2200: 80.

Kröncke, G. (2003) 'Vertrauen in Afrika', *Süddeutsche Zeitung*, 21 February.

Kroslak, D. (2002) 'The Responsibility of External Bystanders in Cases of Genocide: The French in Rwanda, 1990–1994', University of Wales, Aberystwyth, unpublished PhD thesis.

McNulty, M. (1997) 'France's Rwanda débâcle', *War Studies Journal*, 2, 2: 3–22.

Marchal, R. (1998) 'France and Africa: The Emergence of Essential Reforms?', *International Affairs*, 74, 2: 355–72.

Martin, G. (1985) 'The Historical, Economic, and Political Bases of France's African Policy', *Journal of Modern African Studies*, 23, 2: 189–208.

—— (1995) 'Continuity and Change in Franco-African Relations', *Journal of Modern African Studies*, 33, 1: 1–20.

Richard, P. (1997) 'Afrique: quelle politique de sécurité?' *Damoclès*, 72: 3–12.

Rigot, M. (1998) 'La Mission militaire française de coopération', *Défense Nationale*, 54, 8 and 9: 17–25.

Sada, H. (1997) 'Quels nouveaux équilibres en Afrique centrale et australe?' *Défense Nationale*, 53, 8: 178–80.

Sheth, V. S. (1999) 'French Policy in Africa: An Assessment' *Africa Quarterly*, 39, 2: 69–87.

Silberzahn, C. (1995) *Au Cœur du secret*, Paris: Fayard.

Smith, S. (2002) 'La France dans la crise ivoirienne: ni ingérence, ni indifférence, mais indolence post-coloniale' in M. Le Pape and C. Vidal (eds) *Côte d'Ivoire. L'année terrible 1999–2000*, Paris: Karthala, pp. 311–24.

Smith, S. and A. Glaser (1997a) *Ces Messieurs Afrique. Le Paris-Village du continent noir*, Paris: Calmann-Lévy.

—— (1997b) *Ces Messieurs Afrique 2. Des réseaux aux lobbies*, Paris: Calmann-Lévy.

Utely, R. (2002) ' "Not to Do Less but to Do Better ...": French Military Policy in Africa', *International Affairs*, 78, 1: 129–46.

Verschave, F.-X. (1995) 'Arrêtons le massacre!', *Golias*, 43: 28–9.

—— (1998) *La Françafrique. Le plus long scandale de la République*, Paris: Stock.

Villepin, D. de (2003) 'Discours d'ouverture du 4ème forum de l'Institut des Hautes Etudes de Défense Nationale sur le continent africain', 13 June, http://www.diplomatie.gouv.fr/actu/article.asp?art=35365

Wauthier, C. (1997) 'La Politique africaine de Jacques Chirac', *Relations Internationales et Stratégiques*, 25: 121–8.

4   The 'all-weather friend'?

Sino-African interaction in the twenty-first century[1]

Ian Taylor

The link between the People's Republic of China (PRC) and Africa in the contemporary period traces its essential roots to three things: the crisis in China's international relations after the Tiananmen Square incident in June 1989; the expansion of Chinese trade in the 1990s; and the desire to take advantage of numerical support in the United Nations (UN) granted by African states, in part to prevent hostile votes against China *vis-à-vis* its human rights record *and* to ensure that Taiwan remains an unrecognized international outcast (see Taylor 1998a). Prior to this period, Africa's importance in Beijing's foreign policy had declined during the 1980s as China's Socialist Modernization project called for massive foreign investment and technology deemed unavailable from Africa (Lin 1989).

In addition, Chinese tensions with both Washington and Moscow lessened throughout the decade, further marginalizing Africa's importance in China's view (Taylor 1997). However, post-Tiananmen Square China has 'rediscovered' Africa and this renewed interest has been further spurred by the huge growth in Chinese firms and corporations – as well as ordinary Chinese entrepreneurs – who have embarked upon a concerted drive to discover markets and commercial opportunities. The twin motivations of diplomacy and economics now firmly drive China's developing linkages with the African continent. Both of these impulses help further China's overall political ambition: to be taken seriously as a 'great power' and for China to be restored to its 'rightful place'. The developing world – Africa included – plays a role in this, even though such an actuality is generally neglected in the literature on China's contemporary foreign relations.

Beijing's broader foreign policy essentially stems from the perception held at the elite level that China is actually relatively weak and that it is vulnerable within the international system. This assessment, however, clashes with the tangible if yet unquantifiable 'Middle Kingdom' (*Zhongguo*) mentality, which sees China as central to the world and assumes to China an importance which, at best, is exaggerated.[2] Such a contradiction – between aspiration and ability – is ironically exacerbated by conservative elements in the United States who talk up and exaggerate China's power through the 'China threat' thesis (Bernstein and Munro 1997; Swaine and Tellis 2000). But as one

Chinese observer asserted, 'Chinese people believe that China, which has the world's largest population, a glorious history and distinguished civilisation, deserves an enhanced, respectable place in the community of nations' (Wang 1994: 28). Thus, 'the attainment of ... great-power aspirations ... draws upon strong emotions, linked to nationalist sentiments, traditional cultural ethno-centrism and a deeply rooted sense of injustice at the hands of foreign (especially) Western countries' (Swaine 1995: 84).

Inherited from pre-revolutionary China, this 'feeling of superiority and ... determination to become a great power' (Chao 1986: 21) has compelled the PRC leadership to attempt to project China's presence and reputation abroad as a means by which Beijing could attempt to make good the gap between the ambitions and aspirations of a reinvigorated China (note Mao's comments in 1949 that 'the Chinese people have stood up'), and the actual rather limited ability of the PRC. That Beijing is incredibly sensitive to the notion that China is actually not as important or as powerful as it might think it is in world affairs (Nathan and Ross 1997), one need only think of the hysterical reaction to Gerald Segal's 1999 article asking 'Does China Matter?' The personal abuse and exhibition of Chinese chauvinism – asserting that the late Segal (then one of the foremost scholars of China) was 'run through [with] his Western values, arrogance and prejudice specific to conservative slow-witted Western scholars like him' – demonstrated that questioning China's 'rightful place' as a supposed world leader is beyond the pale as far as Chinese nationalists are concerned (see Gu 1999).

In fact, the desire to possess centrality and autonomy of action in the inter-national system has been a particular feature of Beijing's foreign policy. As Pye (1992) observed, China's self-image *vis-à-vis* the rest of the world has influenced the PRC's conceptualization of its relations with the international system. Early on in the PRC's diplomatic history it was proclaimed that 'the Chinese people have elevated their nation to its rightful place as one of the leaders of the world', and this assertion has staked out China's overall foreign policy ambitions. The developing world has been a particular area where Beijing's foreign policy has pursued this stance, using 'the development of common interests with [the] Third World to raise China's global stature and increase Beijing's bargaining leverage with the United States' (Swaine 1995: 87). All this is aimed at realizing 'our great aim in building up a powerful pros-perous modernised China' (*People's Daily* (Beijing), 16 September 1999).

Post-Tiananmen Square relations with Africa

After 4 June 1989 such policy calculations received a major impetus. The events surrounding Tiananmen Square resulted in a severe crisis in China's relations with the West, and the depth of Western condemnation caught the Chinese leadership by surprise. Until then, China's human rights record had been basically ignored by the West. Suddenly, foreign – that is, Western – criticism of China's human rights abuses became a major issue in the foreign policy formulation of the PRC. In contrast, while Tiananmen Square ended China's 'honeymoon' relationship with the West, Africa's reaction was far more muted, if not supportive. As one commentator noted,

> the events of June 1989 ... did not affect the PRC's relations with the Third World as it did with the Western world ... What changed [was] the PRC's attitude towards the Third World countries, which ... turned from one of benign neglect to one of renewed emphasis.
>
> (Gu 1995: 125)

As a result, the developing world was re-elevated in Chinese thinking to become a 'cornerstone' of Beijing's foreign policy. The 1970s rhetoric of China and Africa being 'all-weather friends' was dusted off and deployed with vigour. According to a pro-Beijing newspaper in Hong Kong:

> In the past, China's relations with Western countries have been over-heated, giving a cold-shoulder to the Third World countries and old friends [meaning Africa]. Judging from the events in this turmoil, it seems that at a critical moment it was still those ... old friends who gave China the necessary sympathy and support. Therefore from now on China will put more efforts in ... developing relations with these old friends.
>
> (*Cheng Ming* (Hong Kong) (in Chinese), 10 October 1989 cited in *Foreign Broadcast Information Service–China* (hereafter *FBIS–CHI*), 3 October 1989: 3)

The ability to 'put more efforts in' to cultivating closer ties with Africa was eased by the response of African elites to 1989. Such reactions and their motives by African leaders might be summarized by three essential points. First, the self-interest of African elites under threat from democratization projects (linked surreptitiously in their eyes to the human rights crusade). Second, solidarity and resentment at perceived 'neo-imperialist' interference in the affairs of a fellow developing country. Third, a pragmatic understanding that overt criticism of Beijing could/would mean an end to Chinese developmental aid and assistance.

The first point is elemental: a large number of African heads of state assumed and maintain office with little reference to (or often, directly *against*) the popular will. Any mass mobilization of an important segment of the population against an entrenched elite threatened to set a precedent that Africans could well draw from. Combined with the ongoing collapse of the Leninist system in East Europe and the Soviet Union, Tiananmen gave a large number of African heads of state pause for thought. This fear of the 'domino effect' should not be played down and probably spurred such leaders as Blaise Compaore of Burkina Faso (who seized power via a coup, executed his predecessor and was himself widely criticized for human rights abuses) to be the first foreign leader to visit Beijing post-Tiananmen. Ironically, Burkina Faso now maintains official diplomatic relations with Taiwan, not China.

The belief in certain quarters that the developed world's critique of Beijing was a cloak by which the West aimed to retard a rapidly modernizing China was also shared by many African leaders and acted as a powerful spur in rallying them to China's cause. A victim of past and present intrigues by the capitalist West, much of Africa was highly suspicious of the newfound 'discovery' that China's record on human rights in Western eyes was suspect. As Snow (1995: 285) pointed out, both China and Africa believed themselves to have experienced and to continue to face common enemies, namely imperialism and neo-imperialism from the developed world. This translated into a deep suspicion by Chinese and many African leaders of criticism of their regimes on the grounds of the supposedly Western-centric norms of human rights and democracy. As a Chinese diplomat in Africa asserted in a claim shared by many African leaders, human rights such as 'economic rights' and 'rights of subsistence' are the main priority of developing nations and take precedence over personal, individual rights as conceptualized in the West.

Many African governments viewed the emphasis by the West on human rights as a pretext to undermine China's development and interfere in its own path to modernization. Zimbabwe's comments, when it attacked the 'concerted efforts from Western circles to destabilise China', are typical of such an attitude (*Xinhua*, 29 September 1989, cited in *FBIS–CHI* 29 September 1988: 8). Whether such a plot exists or not is immaterial: it is the perception both in Beijing and in many African capitals that there is some conspiracy to retard growth in developing countries. Deng Xiaoping's somewhat paranoid comment in September 1989 that 'there are many people in the world who hope we will develop, but there are also many who are out to get us' sums up this attitude (Deng 1994: 309).

Finally, the understanding that China was an important source of external aid and that developmental assistance should not be threatened by involvement in the West's criticism of China no doubt added a further variable to much of Africa's silence on the matter. It must be remembered that from 1956 up to and including 1987, China had provided Africa with nearly US$4,783 million of economic aid and assistance (Bartke 1992: 7). Though the level of aid had stagnated in the 1980s, this aid was a most welcome source of assistance and would not be risked lightly, particularly in the cause of democratization (to which, in any case, many African leaders did not share a commitment). One can say, therefore, that a number of factors meshed together to explain much of Africa's reluctance to join in with the opprobrium heaped on Beijing by the West following Tiananmen Square.

China's response

For its part (temporarily) isolated by the West, China became introspective for a period and saw all foreign criticism of its domestic policies as interference and a violation of its national sovereignty. As a self-perceived great power and with a national myth centred on China's 'century of humiliation' at the hands of the imperialists, Beijing deeply resented the West's critique of its human rights record. As a result, China embarked on a concerted campaign to widen its contacts in the developing world in an attempt to counter this criticism (Yu 1991: 34). Hence between June 1989 and June 1992, the Chinese Foreign Minister Qian Qichen toured fourteen African countries on what were to become annual visits to the continent, while numerous African dignitaries visited China at the invitation of the Beijing government. This has continued: since 1997, nearly thirty heads of state or heads of government from African countries have visited China, and when they do visit there is major press coverage in the Chinese media regaling the reader with the warmth of Sino-African ties.

Chinese aid in the post-Tiananmen era increased dramatically as Beijing scrambled to win over allies and sympathetic associates. Such a policy was a quick and comparatively cheap way by which Beijing could reward those countries that had stood by China during the 1989 crisis as well as cementing relations for the future. Indeed, if one looks at the increase in Chinese aid commitments in the immediate pre- and post-Tiananmen period, one may see a definite policy change: in 1988 China only disbursed US$60.4 million to thirteen countries, yet by 1990 (i.e. a year after Tiananmen) this had risen to US$374.6 million a year and forty-three countries were now recipients (Lin 1996: 38). Such evidence points to a determined effort to widen the scope and amount of aid provided by Beijing in the post-1989 period.

Always mindful of the fact that the West is in numerical minority in such international organizations as the UN, the courting of support from developing nations enabled China to successfully resist Western 'hegemonism' at a time when the old bi-polar world was crumbling. Prime Minister Li Peng's comments in 1990 are illuminating on this point and worthy of quoting:

> [The] new order of international politics means that all countries are equal, and must mutually respect each other ... regardless of their differences in political systems and ideology. No country is allowed to impose its will on other countries, seek hegemony in any regions, or pursue power politics to deal with other countries. They are not allowed to interfere in the internal affairs of the developing countries, or pursue power politics in the name of 'human rights, freedom and democracy'.
> (*Xinhua Domestic Service* 12 March 1990, cited in *FBIS–CHI*, 12 March 1990: 1)

Non-interference in state sovereignty and freedom from 'hegemony' were increasingly reasserted as a major theme of China's foreign policy, something which has continued today. This posture was a reaffirmation of the Five Principles of Peaceful Coexistence, which had been formulated in the

1950s as the basis of Beijing's foreign relations. These Five Principles are, namely: mutual respect for each other's territorial integrity; non-aggression; non-interference in each other's internal affairs; equality and mutual benefit; and peaceful coexistence. Thus post-Tiananmen Chinese policy-makers were essentially returning to their roots in reasserting what by then was an old theme in Beijing's foreign policy (Armstrong 1994: 473–4).

Ideologically, China increasingly conceptualized the world as being threatened by a new and potentially unchallenged hegemon: the United States of America. China's diplomatic policy in Africa has thus become centred on gaining support from African states *vis-à-vis* a predominant Washington. This has remained today and was graphically seen at the Sino-Africa Forum in 2000 (see following section). China has maintained the position that in the 'complicated' international system, with the danger of a by now unrivalled and ambitious Washington, it is imperative that China and the developing world support each other and work together to prevent the rise of this new hegemon. Asserting that respect for each other's affairs and non-interference should be the basis of the emerging new international order is fundamental to this stance, with the added proviso that only by China and Africa pursuing these goals 'hand in hand' can they succeed (*Xinhua*, 24 January 1992, cited in *FBIS–CHI*, 29 January 1992: 20). Today, Sino-African unity remains as a focal point: '[China and Africa] support each other in international affairs, especially on major issues such as human rights, safeguard the legitimate rights of developing countries and make efforts to promote the establishment of a new just and rational international political and economic order' (Embassy of the PRC 2003).

Much of this is tied to the long-held stance by Beijing that it is the leader of the developing world (formerly the 'Third World'). At the opening of the Sino-Africa Forum in late 2000, this posture was cast within the rubric that while 'Africa [is] the continent with the largest number of developing countries', China is 'the largest developing country in the world' (*People's Daily* (Beijing), 10 October 2000). China's audacious ranking of its own Five Principles of Peaceful Coexistence on an equal footing with the Charter of African Union – and even the Charter of the UN – is an example of the way in which Beijing seeks to court Africa within the broader framework of global politics, while at the same time asserting its leadership claims. Indeed, Chinese policy has been to claim that the world is currently multi-polar and that China is one of the world leaders – this despite Beijing's manifest refusal to play any meaningful role in the UN or use its position within the Security Council to assert itself. Indeed, China's foreign policy has been characterized 'by the strategy of enhancing its own status with little if any global responsibilities' (Kim 1994: 161).

Paradoxically, as China increasingly integrates itself into the global economy and starts to tentatively play by essentially Western rules (as exemplified by its membership of the World Trade Organization), China has sought to strengthen ties with African countries more as a defensive mechanism, invariably to be deployed against these very same impulses. This irony reflects the overall tension in Chinese diplomatic policy of pursuing both engagement and a certain distant coolness *vis-à-vis* the global order. This, and the notion that China seeks to 'restore' its 'rightful place' in world politics by being seen as some sort of leader of the developing world, cannot be overlooked. Such coalition-building helps explain the recent diplomatic developments in Chinese links to Africa, so graphically exemplified by the Sino-Africa Forum in October 2000.

Forum on China–Africa Co-operation ministerial conference

The Forum met in October 2000 and was attended by nearly eighty ministers from forty-four African countries. The meeting essentially had three main objectives. First, the Forum was part of Beijing's overall strategy to at least rhetorically declare its aim of overhauling the global order and advance China's traditional hostility to what it sees as 'hegemony', in this case the domination of the overweening power of the United States. This domination, dressed up as 'globalization', is seen as detrimental to the autonomy and sovereignty of China and, by extension, the developing world. As the then Chinese Premier, Zhu Rongji, said at the Forum, Sino-African ties help 'build up our capacity against possible risks, which will put us in a better position to participate in economic globalisation and safeguard our economic interests and economic security'. They also 'improve the standing of the developing countries in North–South dialogue so as to facilitate the establishment of a fair and rational new international political and economic order' (Zhu 2000).

Such a position is based on the belief that 'when the new international economic order has not been established and countries differ considerably in economic development, the benefits of economic globalisation are not enjoyed in a balanced way'. Consequently, 'developed countries are benefiting most from economic globalisation; but the large number of developing countries are facing more risks and challenges, and some countries are even endangered by marginalisation'. As a result, the global community should 'give more considerations to the will and demands of developing countries [including, no doubt, China] so as to promote the establishment of a fair and rational new international economic order'. This can be advanced by developing countries building 'a sense of self-protection' (speech by Minister Shi Guangsheng at the Sino-Africa Forum, quoted in *People's Daily* (Beijing), 11 October 2000).

As mentioned previously, China is intensely suspicious of the West's promotion of human rights and regards such calls as a Trojan horse through which the West might undermine Beijing. Chinese policy in this regard has then been to consistently cast talk of democracy and human rights (and, occasionally, the environment) as a tool of neo-imperialism. This falls on many receptive ears in Africa at the elite level, and China is not unaware of this. Indeed, this has been fairly long-standing and China has long 'managed to piggyback on the Third World's power of numbers to escape international censure' (Kim 1994: 137). As part of this, the Forum was a means by which China could advance a position of moral relativism regarding human rights to a mostly sympathetic audience and thus consolidate its standing within Africa and the developing world as a device to resist American domination and hegemony, understood as Washington's ascendancy in the post-Cold War era. The assertion at the Forum that China and Africa 'should ... enhance their co-operation and consultation in multilateral ... organisations in order to safeguard the interests of both' is a reflection of this concern (*People's Daily* (Beijing), 12 October 2000). Hence the Beijing Declaration of the Forum on China–Africa Co-operation, released at the end of the meeting, asserted that 'countries, that vary from one another in social system, stages of development, historical and cultural background and values, have the right to choose their own approaches and models in promoting and protecting human rights in their own countries'.

Going further, the Declaration made the astounding claim that 'the politicisation of human rights and the imposition of human rights conditionalities' themselves 'constitute a violation of human rights' and that conditionalities for development assistance which are based on good governance and respect for human rights 'should be vigorously opposed' (ibid.) – all music to the ears of many of the African dictators sat in the hall in Beijing, no doubt, and all crafted as a means to promote an 'alternative' global order, based on the stance that 'each country has the right to choose different ways and modes of promoting and protecting human rights domestically' (Embassy of the PRC 2000). Of course, such a position would grant the elites of each country the role of being the arbiters of what are or what are not 'human rights', and also how such rights should be protected (or not, as the case may be). This stance is advanced by China even if such sentiments run counter to the prevailing belief today that state elites cannot and should not be allowed to hide behind 'state sovereignty' to abuse their own citizens. They nevertheless help bolster Beijing's claim to be the 'leader' of the developing world, at least in the eyes of dictatorial elites, if not the people.

The second objective of the Forum was to exhibit Chinese accomplishments from their Socialist Modernization programme (thus demonstrating the 'superiority' of China's economic policies), but also to try and encourage African countries to reform (using the Chinese model) as a way of lightening the burden of China's foreign aid. At the Forum, Beijing, as usual, emphasized that 'China never attaches any political string to its assistance to Africa or seeks any political privilege in doing so'.[3] However, then Premier Zhu also talked of the 'earthshaking changes' China has achieved since the launching of the 'reform and opening-up programme'. It was of no surprise that a special aeroplane transported more than two hundred senior officials and business representatives from Africa, all of whom had attended the Forum in Beijing, to Guangdong for discussions on economic ties and to visit China's economic showcase of reform and modernization (*People's Daily* (Beijing), 16 October 2000).

Finally, the Forum was certainly part of China's ongoing strategy to contain and limit Taiwan (on Sino-Taiwanese competition see Taylor 1998b; 2002). China has a number of motives for indulging in this. First, the PRC's state constitution asserts that it is the legitimate government of *all* of China, including the island of Taiwan. To allow Taiwan to gain political legitimacy and status as an independent republic or as an 'alternative' government of part of China would be an unbearable loss of face for the Beijing leadership and raise questions as to the hold the Communist Party has over the Chinese people. Taiwan is seen as the third unfinished project in the Chinese reunification agenda of the Communist Party that began with Hong Kong's transfer to Chinese sovereignty in 1997 and was augmented by Macau's transfer in 1999. Not to remain committed to the eventual assumption of sovereignty over Taiwan is, at present, unthinkable. This explains why Beijing invited eight African countries that maintain diplomatic ties with Taiwan to attend the Forum as 'observers'. However, of the eight (Senegal, Gambia, Burkina Faso, Liberia, Malawi, Chad, Swaziland and Sao Tome and Principe) only Liberia and Malawi accepted the invitations.

Also, as mentioned above, China postures an image of itself as being of the developing world, if not its effective leader through the possession of a permanent seat on the UN Security Council. This position is aimed at enabling Beijing to project China on to the global stage as a major player in its own right. But, if this image is to be sustained, Beijing feels compelled to maintain an active and visible interest in areas such as Africa, which at times act as a constituency to add political and numerical support to China's claims. With Taiwan sniping at its heels, China feels propelled to involve itself in the diplomatic tug of war on the continent.

The outcome of the Forum reflected the increased priority China was placing on Africa. As a goodwill gesture, Beijing announced that it would exempt Africa from repaying its $1.2 billion back to China. A cynic might point out that these debts would not have been repaid anyway, but such actions certainly put Beijing on the moral high ground when calling on the West to do the same with much larger quantities of debt owed to them by Africa. At the Forum, the Chinese also put forward a proposal on furthering Sino-African economic ties, calling for the removal of tariff and non-tariff barriers and the creation of better market access to each other. China also promised to establish special funds and incentives to encourage Chinese enterprises to invest in Africa, reflecting the growing economic imperative underpinning Sino-African linkages (*People's Daily* (Beijing), 12 October 2000).

Sino-African economic interaction

As China has become more and more active in the global economy, Chinese companies and corporations have increasingly begun to move offshore and seek markets elsewhere, beyond either the local Chinese market or the immediate Asia-Pacific region. Africa has emerged as one destination of choice. By the end of 2000, Chinese companies had established 499 companies in Africa with a total contractual investment of $990 million, of which $680 million was Chinese capital. As part of Beijing's encouragement to further develop Sino-African trade since 1995, China has established eleven Investment Development and Trade Promotion Centres in Africa. It can be said that Chinese trade links with Africa have indeed been blooming of late. However, Chinese trade figures need to be treated with caution. The part played by Hong Kong as a transit point for Chinese imports and exports makes bilateral figures very dubious when estimating the significance of other states for Chinese trade: it has been calculated that between 1988 and 1998, over half of all Chinese exports were routed through Hong Kong (Hanson and Feenstra 2001: 2). Besides, foreign-invested firms account for just over half of all Chinese trade: i.e. much of Chinese trade is not actually 'Chinese' at all; and if domestic Chinese producers who produce under contract for export using foreign components are included, the figure is nearer to 60 per cent (Breslin 2003). In actual fact, the majority of Chinese exports are produced by foreign-funded enterprises, often joint ventures but increasingly wholly foreign-owned. Of the actual 'Chinese' firms, a number are state-owned, but act as if they are independent corporations, while an increasing number are under local (provincial, towns, counties, etc.) control. Only the really large corporations might be said to be 'agents' of Chinese foreign policy, narrowly understood.

It thus remains true that Beijing's economic interest in Africa is based on three assumptions. First, Beijing seems to believe that the macroeconomic situation in Africa is taking a favourable turn. This analysis is based on the belief that (as the Chinese would no doubt assert), copying China, African countries have 'adopted a set of active measures to push forward the pace of privatization, open up international trade and reform based on bilateral and multi-lateral trade agreements'. As a result, 'most of the countries have improved macroeconomic situation greatly [sic]' (Embassy of the PRC 2002).

Second, Chinese manufacturers (and shopkeepers) believe that the types of goods (household appliances, garments and other domestic products) they produce and sell have immense potential in Africa, where the economy is not yet as developed as in Western nations and where the consumers are perceived to be more receptive to the type of inexpensive products that China typically produces.

Third, Africa is perceived by both the Chinese government *and* by Chinese companies to be rich in natural resources, particularly in crude oil, non-ferrous metals and fisheries. Indeed, China's rapidly developing oil requirements have helped propel Sino-African trade in recent years. In 1993, China became a net importer of oil, and oil will be the only feasible primary fuel for the foreseeable future that will be in a position to fulfil China's growing needs regarding both transportation and industry (Troush 1999).

China is projected to rely on imports for 45 per cent of its oil use by 2010. As a result, China has been faithfully developing linkages with oil-rich countries in Africa such as Angola, Nigeria and the Sudan. Analysing this situation, China has since around 1995 begun an 'outward-looking oil economy'. This is for primarily economic reasons: the average production cost of Middle Eastern oil is still under $2 per barrel, while the average production cost of Chinese onshore oil is between $9 and $23 per barrel, depending on the oilfield.

As a result, the China National Petroleum Corporation (CNPC), the China National Offshore Oil Corporation (CNOOC) and the China Petroleum and Chemical Corporation (Sinopec) were elevated to the status of ministries and located with the State Economic and Trade Commission. The corporations were also granted the task of buying operating rights overseas and of establishing overseas oil exploration. Chinese expansion into oil operations overseas has become obvious. Chinese oil companies now have a presence in places as diverse as Canada, Peru and Sudan. One way by which this policy has been cemented is to use what China refers to as 'special relationships'. Arms sales are one part of this policy and also help offset costs. Sudan is a particular example. That this has been problematic for the African continent will be detailed below.

Economic interest in Africa has been manifested through increased numbers of joint ventures, Chinese investment and economic interaction. An emphasis on trade and economic affairs now dominates Sino-African interaction. Between 1989 and 1997 Sino-African trade increased by 431 per cent.[4] This has taken a massive boost in recent years and is growing rapidly. Total trade between China and Africa increased by 63 per cent in 2000 and now exceeds US$10 billion. Traditionally, Sino-African trade has been vastly unbalanced in China's favour, but recently Africa's exports have begun to pick up (due to oil imports from Africa). Exports to China increased by 134 per cent in 2000 from 1999 figures, and Africa exported US$5.5 billion to China (*Business in Africa* (Johannesburg), February 2003: 19).

In contrast to the past heady days of Maoist 'solidarity', China's economic dealings with most African countries are today based on a cool evaluation of their perceived economic potential, and it is for that reason that Africa can expect a growth in Chinese economic activity in the future. Li Peng's statement in Ghana that Africa is a 'continent with great development potential and hope' underscores the perception that China has an eye on the future economic progress of the continent (*Agence France Presse* (Beijing), 14 September 1997). Beijing also sees Africa as playing a greater role in future world politics: a Chinese commentary recently asserted that 'as more African countries improve political stability and make headway in economic growth, the continent's nations will have more say in international affairs' (*China Daily* (Beijing), 9 January 1998), and China seems interested to raise the profile of Africa at forums such as the UN Security Council. Such actions are based on the assertion that China and Africa share 'identical or similar

opinions on many major international affairs as well as common interests'
(speech by Minister Shi Guangsheng at the Sino-Africa Forum, quoted in
People's Daily (Beijing), 11 October 2000).

At the same time, China has been keen to promote the idea that China
should be given privileged access to African markets on the basis of
South–South 'solidarity' and as a concrete manifestation of a broader
counter-hegemonic strategy which China is keen to encourage within
Africa. The self-serving nature of this stance is obvious. When Chinese officials claim that 'it could not be possible to continuously deepen and
develop South–South development without the policy support of governments of developing countries [and] without ... preferential treatment'
(ibid.), one must remember that, with the exception of oil exports to China,
Sino-African trade is lopsided in favour of Chinese exporters, who are
flooding African markets with cheap household products of limited quality.
Such imports into Africa most certainly help China's trade development
but do little to encourage indigenous African manufacturing. Any 'preferential treatment' for such imports from China would do little to change this
milieu. Indeed, the assertion at the Sino-Africa Forum that the Chinese
government would 'encourage' Chinese enterprises to 'give preference to
African goods in their imports *when all other conditions are the same* so as
to improve the trade balance between China and African countries'
(emphasis added) is a caveat of dubious standing and one that commits
Beijing to very little indeed (*People's Daily* (Beijing), 12 October 2000). Yet
this sort of benign non-commitment pales into insignificance when one
turns to one of China's big growth industries *vis-à-vis* its links with Africa:
arms sales.

Chinese arms sales to Africa

China's 'non-interference in domestic affairs' stance has not prevented
Beijing from involving itself closely in African politics, notably in the
support of various highly undemocratic regimes. As part of this, China has
been a long-standing exporter of weapons to the developing world
(Bitzinger 1992). At the same time, it has long been noted that 'China has no
principles, only interests, driving its arms sales to the Third World' (Kim
1994: 146). Although China stands far behind the leading arms exporters
such as the US, the UK, Russia and France, exports of Chinese weaponry –
either directly or through middlemen – are not inconsequential. In the
contemporary period this has taken on not only the guise of providing military supplies and weaponry to Africa, but also an active involvement in
actual conflict. Such involvement has passed by with relatively little international attention, yet needs examination.

China is currently the world's fifth-largest arms exporter behind the United
States, Britain, France and Russia, and exported an estimated US$500 million
worth of arms in 2001 (*Straits Times* (Singapore), 24 January 2003).

It has been apparent for some time that the Chinese government hopes to turn the country's arms industry into a top global player by 2020. China reformed its defence industry in mid-1999, dividing its top five defence corporations (space, aviation, shipbuilding, conventional arms and nuclear) into ten enterprises. This is consistent with the aims of the defence aspect of Socialist Modernization which was, in part, to convert military to civilian production. As part of this transformation of the operational mechanism of military–industrial enterprises, all military–industrial ministries were converted into industrial corporations as economic bodies and industrial groupings. However, concern that the People's Liberation Army (PLA) was becoming too involved in the economy meant that in 1998 Premier Jiang Zemin declared that businesses were being officially de-linked from the PLA. Like other state enterprises, China's military industrial enterprises carried out a 'contract responsibility system', i.e. such enterprises paid the state both taxes and a segment of their profits. Profits that remained from the production of civilian goods were either deployed to develop production and/or went to the military management. However, now that the PLA has been forced to withdraw from openly operating civilian businesses the search for profits is largely concentrated in increased arms sales. While it is true that most major Chinese weapons manufacturers are not owned or handled by the PLA but by one of the civilian ministries, the remuneration from arms sales returns to the Chinese state. Either way, there are compelling motives for actors within China to increase arms exports.

The classic contemporary example of Beijing's weapons-exporting policy in Africa is China's involvement in Sudan's long-running civil war, a war which has claimed nearly two million lives so far. Chinese actors have pursued a policy that is entirely based on narrow economic interests and have been keen to supply the Sudanese government with fighter aircraft and an assortment of weaponry. Apart from the profits accrued from these arms sales, the policy helps consolidate and protect Chinese shares in the exploitation of Sudan's oil reserves. Reliable reports say that Sudan has obtained thirty-four new fighter jets from China, and that the Sudan air force is equipped with $100 million worth of Shenyang fighter planes, including a dozen supersonic F-7 jets (13 July 2000, www.Worldnetdaily.com).

The motivation for such supplies is simple. The state-owned China National Petroleum Corporation (CNPC) owns the largest share (i.e. 40 per cent) in Sudan's largest oil venture. The Sino-Sudanese oilfield project covers 50,000 square miles in the southern non-Muslim region of the country and is expected to produce 15 million tonnes of crude oil annually. With proven reserves of 220 million tonnes, the project is amongst the largest China has undertaken overseas. At the same time, Sudanese government forces, armed with Chinese weapons, have used CNPC facilities as a base from which to attack and dislodge southerners in the vicinity of the new oilfields. The Center for Religious Freedom of Freedom House, America's oldest human rights group, has asserted that Khartoum is using hard currency generated by Chinese investment in oilfields there to finance its ethnic cleansing of non-Muslim insurgents and civilians in the southern part of the country. China, for its part, has cynically deployed its 'alternative' reading of human rights to block UN action in the country. For instance, the Chinese ambassador to Sudan, Deng Shao Zin, said in August 1999 that Beijing was 'opposed to any intervention by the United Nations in the internal affairs of Sudan under the pretext of human rights violations'.[5]

Chinese involvement in an ongoing civil war is not conducive to peace and development. However, one might proffer the defence that Beijing was invited to supply arms and equipment to support a beleaguered government and protect Chinese assets. This is not the case in Equatorial Guinea, where China has provided military training for equipment that the host country does not even have. It is reported that Chinese specialists in heavy military equipment have been sent to the country, presumably in order to sell such weapons to Equatorial Guinea in exchange for oil. Over a three-month period ending in November 2000, Chinese trainers worked with the local army – yet Equatorial Guinea has no heavy weaponry. The only guess that one may make is that Chinese arms exporters want to introduce such weaponry to Equatorial Guinea in exchange for either oil concessions or hard currency. This fits with China's broad economic ambitions in Africa, i.e. profits and oil supplies. Equatorial Guinea appears the perfect customer: climbing oil prices have provided the country with extra finances and, possibly concerned to defend their oil wells from Nigeria and Cameroon, China has stepped in to offer Equatorial Guinea military weapons and training. That this will no doubt fuel some sort of arms race in the Gulf of Guinea is clearly of no concern to China ('Seizing an Opportunity' 2001: 92).

In other parts of Africa, China plays a leading role in the provision of weaponry, often during times of conflict. China can thus be held responsible – alongside others – for the death and destruction that Africa's various wars have visited upon the continent's peoples. This behaviour has been cynical in the extreme. For instance, while Ethiopia and Eritrea were edging towards war, Chinese corporations transferred a substantial share of US$1 billion in weapons dispatched to both countries between 1998 and 2000. In 1995 a Chinese ship carrying 152 tonnes of ammunition and light weapons was refused permission to unload in Tanzania: the cargo was destined for the Tutsi-dominated army of Burundi, and Tanzania was concerned that ethnic conflict there would be exacerbated by the arms shipment (*Agence France-Presse International News* (Paris), 3 May 1995). This was not an isolated shipment, however. Human Rights Watch released a recent report that showed that at least thirteen covert shipments of weapons (three of which were in violation of regional or international arms embargoes) were delivered by China to Dar-es-Salaam, with the final destinations mislabelled and the weapons disguised as agricultural equipment (Overseas Development Institute 1998).

In the Democratic Republic of the Congo (DRC), Chinese exporters furnished Laurent Kabila with arms in 1997 and have been supplying Kinshasa with weapons, frequently through Zimbabwean middlemen. Sierra Leone's brutal civil war was fuelled by extensive shipments of Chinese arms: China was Sierra Leone's main arms supplier and stepped up shipments once the civil war began. In short, Chinese arms deals have repeatedly broken UN sanctions and have substantially helped damage the continent's aspirations for peace and development.

Concluding remarks

Chinese policy towards Africa in recent times, certainly post-1989, has been both consistent and changing. On the one hand, Beijing remains determined to reinforce its position *vis-à-vis* the West. China has felt increasingly vulnerable to the perceived threat of a unipolar world, even while it makes claims about a multi-polar globe with China as one of the supposed poles. Though Beijing's primary focus is naturally on East Asia and maintaining at least cordial links with the United States by vehemently advancing the theme of non-interference in domestic affairs and promoting a culturally relativist notion of human rights, China has been able to secure its own position and, at the same time, appeal to numerous African leaders.

On the other hand, the Chinese state has been increasingly encouraging Chinese corporations to play a role in broad Sino-African ties. This emphasis on economic linkages with Africa not only enables Chinese corporations to develop their export capabilities and reach, but also empowers the Chinese state to further project itself on the continent. As a result, the state encourages corporate activity as a means to maintain its commercial and political links with Africa. An important by-product of this is to carve out a reserve pool of friends and sympathizers from which it can draw moral and political support within the international system, as well as economic clients, naturally. A Chinese magazine article made this quite categorical when it revealingly stated that 'the vast number of Third World countries [will] surely unite with and stand behind China like numerous "ants" keeping the "elephant" from harm's way' (*Chinafrica* (Beijing), April 1990: 12–13). In this conceptualization, the 'elephant' of China – a dominant and central figure – is protected by the little countries against outside threat and coercion.

In an attempt to offset Washington's position in the international system, Beijing has sought and will continue to seek improved relations with non-Western powers. Africa has not been an exception to this policy, and this is likely to continue. Indeed, China's policies are essentially a bid for the leadership of the developing world. 'China wants to play a new international role as champion of Third World interests in international trade negotiations, and its partnership with Africa is fast emerging as its testing ground' (*Al-Ahram Weekly* (Cairo), 19–25 October 2000). As part of this strategy, China has over the last decade or so reformed its aid policies, moving away from bilateral economic co-operation schemes and the furnishing of outright aid or low-interest loans to a more focused policy that aims to build up trade, investment and joint ventures in Africa. Whether this linking of aid to the construction of joint ventures with Chinese firms amounts to conditionalities is a moot point. In addition, while it is true that China has stated that it will continue to supply aid to Africa, this is couched very much within the confines and limitations of what Beijing terms China's 'capacity' (Chinese Foreign Minister Tang Jiaxuan quoted in *People's Daily* (Beijing), 13 January 2003).

The stress these days is on improving the overall economic environment in Africa for Chinese trade, hence Beijing has been very keen to show off its reform and modernization policies as a possible model for Africa. At the same time, the development of Africa's mineral resources – particularly oil – has risen to major prominence, frequently lubricated by Chinese arms sales and the construction of 'special relationships'. In return, China has frequently promised that it will open the Chinese market to African producers.

However, what benefits might Africa expect from Chinese expansion on the continent? First, as one commentary noted, 'it is doubtful whether a more accommodating Chinese trade policy could ... help African countries ... For most African countries the greatest barrier to trade is the fact that they just don't have much to sell [to China]' (*Sunday Independent* (Johannesburg), 15 October 2000). It is a fact that China's trade figures with Africa have been wildly unbalanced for years (in China's favour). For instance, in 2002 Uganda earned US$5.6 million from its exports to China while China earned US$28.3 million from its exports to Uganda. This is not an isolated case but is typical. In fact, it is only Chinese oil purchases from selected African countries that generally moderate the overall Sino-African trade imbalance, otherwise the asymmetric trade relationship between China and Africa would be extreme (*New Vision* (Kampala), 3 April 2003). Between 2000 and August 2002, South Africa, Egypt, Angola, Nigeria, Sudan and Benin were China's six largest African trading partners: Angola, Nigeria and Sudan, of course, are oil-exporting nations. Indeed, from January to August in 2002, petroleum and petroleum products imported from Angola and Sudan were 94.2 per cent and 76.7 per cent of bilateral total trade volumes respectively (*Business in Africa* (Johannesburg), February 2003: 19).

Of equal concern is China's casual stance towards arms sales and proliferation. Its happy involvement in Sudan's civil war has already been detailed. There is a very real danger that Beijing's supposed 'non-political' stance merely masks its bottom line: the chase for profits and oil. This has been carried on with a nonchalance towards Africa's political stability and peace, never mind the rights of the ordinary African, that is most distasteful. As one report noted, 'unmoved by ideological concerns and without fear of political consequences, the Chinese government [seems] willing to fuel a small-arms race in sub-Saharan Africa to generate additional revenues for the PLA' ('Seizing an Opportunity' 2001: 92). Indeed, unlike virtually every other power involved in Africa (except perhaps Russia), China has no civil society worth talking about that might protest against various Chinese initiatives in the continent, whether it is arms sales to war zones or support for corrupt autocrats such as Zimbabwe's Mugabe. Indeed, a report has noted that US$1 million worth of Chinese small arms were exchanged for 8 tonnes of Zimbabwean ivory in May 2000 in an attempt by Mugabe to secure his precarious position (ibid.). Such amoral and opportunistic behaviour by Beijing critically undermines China's objectives to be seen as a leader of a developing world coalition or one that is qualitatively different from the 'traditional exploiters' of Africa, i.e. the West. Beijing does not seem to realize as yet that political instability sabotages the long-term possibilities of sustained Sino-African economic links and also helps maintain the situation where Africa remains at the bottom of the global hierarchy, plagued by dictators and human rights abusers. However, such elites are heartened and appreciative of China's frequent utterances on national sovereignty, non-interference in domestic affairs and the intriguing notion that every different country has the right to choose its own version of human rights. Whose interests such relativism serves can be readily surmised.

Chinese activity in Africa is, like all other countries' foreign polices, self-serving and based on economic and strategic considerations. On this it is no different, and it is on this that its success or otherwise must be judged. What is different in comparison to other countries' foreign policies is that Beijing is an actor in Africa providing a discourse that effectively legitimizes human rights abuses and undemocratic practices under the guise of state sovereignty and combating 'hegemony'. While one might argue that other actors' policies in Africa support the same ends, Beijing's spirited defence of elite sovereignty (or is it impunity?) is somewhat different and certainly jars against the growing international consensus that political leaders cannot escape justice for violations against an emerging – if fragile – global norm. This stance is then coupled with an opportunistic policy regarding arms sales to all and sundry in Africa, even if it is to widely reviled elites or those actively involved in genocidal practices. For such reasons, China's expansion into the African continent almost certainly does not contribute to the promotion of peace, prosperity and democracy on the continent. Thus Beijing's reassertion in Africa may prove to be a most negative development for the continent's peoples, although welcomed by many of its political masters.

Notes

1   I would like to thank Shaun Breslin and Jürgen Haacke for their helpful comments on an earlier draft.
2   An indicative example of this attitude was the announcement by the Chinese newspaper *Jiefang Ribao* (Shanghai) that 'the whole world is waiting to follow China as soon as it achieves its goal of founding a spiritual civilisation', *Hong Kong Standard* (Hong Kong), 26 September 1996.

3 'Strengthen Solidarity, Enhance Co-operation and Pursue Common Development by Zhu Rongji'. This, of course, is untrue as China refuses to provide aid to any country – African or otherwise – which recognizes Taiwan.
4 In 1989 total economic trade between Africa and China stood at $1,166,591,000 – *China's Customs Statistics Yearbook*, Hong Kong, Economic Information and Agency, 1990.
5 'Chinese Investment Spurs Civil War in Sudan', *CNSNews.com*, 3 September 1999. One report asserts that conflict diamonds were used to purchase arms and ammunition from China through Burkina Faso to Sierra Leone. See Conciliation Resources Occasional Paper, 'Resources, Primary Industry and Conflict in Sierra Leone', September/October 1997.

References

Armstrong, D. (1994) 'Chinese Perspectives on the New World Order', *Journal of East Asian Affairs*, 8: 454–81.

Bartke, W. (1992) *The Agreements of the People's Republic of China with Foreign Countries, 1949–1990*, Munich: Saur.

Bernstein, R. and R. Munro (1997) *The Coming Conflict with China*, New York: Alfred Knopf.

Bitzinger, R. A. (1992) 'Arms to Go: Chinese Arms Sales to the Third World', *International Security*, 17, 2: 84–111.

Breslin, S. (2003) 'Foreign Direct Investment in China: What the Figures Don't Tell Us', unpublished paper.

Chao, C. (1986) 'Communist China's Independent Foreign Policy: The Link With Domestic Affairs', *Issues and Studies*, 22, 10: 13–32.

Deng, X. (1994) *Selected Works Volume III (1982–1992)*, Beijing: Foreign Languages Press.

Embassy of the PRC (2000) 'Actively Carrying Out International Exchanges and Co-operation in the Realm of Human Rights', Embassy of the People's Republic of China in the Republic of Zimbabwe.

—— (2002) 'A Survey of the African Economy', Embassy of the People's Republic of China in the Republic of Botswana.

—— (2003) 'Sino-African Relations', Embassy of the People's Republic of China in the Republic of Zimbabwe.

Gu, P. (1999) 'What is Segal up to by Belittling China?', *People's Daily* (Beijing), 16 September.

Gu, W. (1995) *Politics of Divided Nations: The Case of China and Korea*, Westport: Praeger.

Hanson, G. and R. Feenstra (2001) 'Intermediaries in Entrepôt Trade: Hong Kong Re-exports of Chinese Goods', *NBER Working Paper 8088*, Cambridge: NBER.

Kim, S. (1994) *China and the World: Chinese Foreign Relations in the Post-Cold War Era*, 3rd edn, Boulder: Westview Press.

Lin, T. (1996) 'Beijing's Foreign Aid Policy in the 1990s: Continuity and Change', *Issues and Studies*, 32, 1: 32–56.

Lin, Y.-L. (1989) 'Peking's African Policy in the 1980s', *Issues and Studies*, 25, 4: 1–21.

Nathan, A. and R. Ross (1997) *The Great Wall and the Empty Fortress: China's Search for Security*, New York: Norton.

Overseas Development Institute (1998) 'Stoking Fires with Arms in Burundi', May. Available at http://www.odihpn.org

Pye, L. (1992) *Spirit of Chinese Politics*, Cambridge: Harvard University Press.

Segal, G. (1999) 'Does China Matter?', *Foreign Affairs*, 78, 5: 24–36.

'Seizing an Opportunity: The Changing Character of Chinese Arms Sales to Africa' (2001) *Armed Forces Journal International*, 139: 92–5.

Snow, P. (1995) 'China and Africa: Consensus and Camouflage', in T. Robinson and D. Shambaugh (eds) *Chinese Foreign Policy: Theory and Practice*, Oxford: Oxford University Press, pp. 29–70.

Swaine, M. (1995) *China: Domestic Change and Foreign Policy*, Santa Monica: RAND.

Swaine, M. and A. Tellis (2000) *Interpreting China's Grand Strategy: Past, Present and Future*, Santa Monica: RAND.

Taylor, I. (1997) 'The People's Republic of China's Foreign Policy towards Southern Africa in the post-Cultural Revolution Era', unpublished MPhil thesis, Department of Politics and Public Administration, University of Hong Kong.

—— (1998a) 'China's Foreign Policy towards Africa in the 1990s', *Journal of Modern African Studies*, 36, 3: 443–60.

—— (1998b) 'Africa's Place in the Diplomatic Competition between Beijing and Taipei', *Issues and Studies*, 34, 3: 126–43.

—— (2002) 'Taiwan's Foreign Policy and Africa: The Limitations of Dollar Diplomacy', *Journal of Contemporary China*, 11, 30: 125–40.

Troush, S. (1999) *China's Changing Oil Strategy and its Foreign Policy Implications*, Center for Northeast Asian Policy Studies Working Paper, Washington DC: Center for Northeast Asian Policy Studies.

Wang, J. (1994) 'Pragmatic Nationalism: China Seeks a New Role in World Affairs', *Oxford International Review*, 6, 1: 29–33.

Yu, G. T. (1991) 'Chinese Foreign Policy since Tiananmen: The Search for Friends and Influence', in T. Lee (ed.) *China and World Political Development and International Issues*, Taipei: Cheng, pp. 134–45.

Zhu, R. (2000) 'Strengthen Solidarity, Enhance Co-operation and Pursue Common Development by Zhu Rongji', Embassy of the People's Republic of China in the Republic of Zimbabwe.

5 Russia and Africa

Moving in the right direction?

Vladimir Shubin

Although Russia never had African colonies, it has had a long history of interaction with the continent going back to the Middle Ages, when Russian Orthodox pilgrims met fellow Christians from Africa (primarily Egyptians and Ethiopians) in the Holy Land. At the same time, Muslims from Russia met Africans in the holy sites of Islam. Later, Russian sailors and explorers visited many countries of Africa. At the end of the eighteenth century Russian consulates were opened in Cairo and Alexandria. Over a hundred years ago, pre-revolutionary Russia established diplomatic relations with Ethiopia and the South African Republic (Transvaal) in 1898. In the same year the Russian Consulate-General was established in Tangiers (Morocco).

Russia's contact with Africa continued after the 1917 revolution, albeit initially in a limited form, mostly through the Comintern machinery and the political training of Africans in the USSR. Much more active ties were developed from the late 1950s onwards, however, when African countries were gaining independence and when the Kremlin turned to the Afro-Asian world with offers of support for anti-colonial movements.

By the mid-1980s the Soviet Union had signed hundreds of agreements with African countries. About 53,000 Africans were trained in the Soviet/Russian universities and technikons in various fields, as well as thousands of graduates of military and political schools. Among such alumni are the current presidents of Angola, Cape Verde, Mali, Mozambique and South Africa. Besides, at least 200,000 specialists were trained by the Soviets on African soil.

No doubt, the so-called 'superpower rivalry' played its role in shaping Moscow's relations with Africa in the 1960s–1980s. However it would be wrong to reduce the essence of Soviet involvement to the search for geo-strategic positioning and public support in the international arena. One should not forget that in the Soviet Union its African friends were officially regarded not as 'proxies' or 'junior partners' in waging the Cold War but rather as one of the 'detachments' of the world struggle against imperialism. This explains the ideological component of Soviet policy, especially towards those countries whose leaders professed to adopt one or another kind of socialism. However, one point should be emphasized: even the most dogmatic political scholars could not name more than a dozen African countries as 'socialist-oriented'.

Another wrong assumption should also be clarified. It is commonly held that from the beginning of the 1990s onwards, the former socialist countries of Eastern Europe and former Soviet republics became rivals with Africa in competition for aid and investment. The reality is quite different, at least as far as Russia is concerned. Instead of benefiting from aid and credits, for over a decade Russia has been providing direct financial assistance to the West, at the level of approximately US$20–25 billion annually, due to capital flight. So, for each dollar received from the West (usually as credit to be paid back at a high rate of interest) Russia has sent five if not ten dollars back for good.

This does not mean, however, that the collapse or dissolution of the Soviet Union did not affect Russia's relations with African states. One should emphasize that the dismembering of the country was accompanied by radical systemic changes, i.e. the restoration of capitalism. One of the main reasons why Russia's new ruling class was eager to establish close relations primarily with major Western powers was because they regarded Washington and its allies as role-models and as guarantors against a 'social revanche' from the Left. In these circumstances, Russia's neglect of Africa was almost inevitable. Indeed, Africa became somewhat of a scapegoat for Russia's ills. Early on in his struggle for power Boris Yeltsin claimed that Soviet assistance to Africa and other developing countries was a major cause of the economic problems that the Soviet/Russian people faced in the late 1980s/early 1990s. The so-called 'democratic' (read: pro-Western) mass media followed suit and did its best to shape an extremely negative image of Africa and its relations with Moscow. Africa was portrayed as a 'black hole' which swallowed Soviet resources, and the myth that 'Africa ate us out of house and home' was disseminated.

Against such a background, Africa and the South in general were sacrificed as an important vector of Russian foreign policy in favour of the West in a vain hope for technology transfer and soft credits. The West applauded such changes. Meanwhile, as Russian Foreign Minister Igor Ivanov (2002) asserted later, Western states encouraged his country to adopt a more subdued global role, one that supposedly 'fitted' with the new situation. This new and more 'modest' role was particularly manifested in the closing down of a dozen Russian embassies and consulates in Africa: from Togo to Lesotho and from Burkina Faso to Sao Tome and Principe, plus a number of trade missions. Most of the aid projects initiated in the Soviet era have been terminated, including a multi-million dollar steel plant in Ajaokuta (Nigeria), which had been about 98 per cent completed (Deich 2003: 52).

Even positive steps in maintaining and advancing relations with Africa during Russia's transition period were often an attempt to somehow copy the West. For example, the meeting of the then Prime Minister Victor

Chernomyrdin with Russian ambassadors in Africa in 1994 reportedly followed a similar meeting of Vice-President Al Gore with heads of the American missions on the continent. Speaking at an academic conference on the 'Possibilities and Limits of Co-operation between Russia and the South' in 1999, Professor Alexey Vassiliev, Director of the Institute for African Studies in Moscow, noted that:

> Russia is a split society. There exist various social groups, or, if you wish, class interests, which are reflected in its foreign policy. Quite real interests of certain social groups, which became a part of the Russian economic and political elites, caused a chimerical orientation to integration with the West. These are exporters of raw materials, big financial speculators, who export a considerable part of their capitals to the West.
>
> (Vassiliev 2003: 169)

Nowadays in Russia, the 1990s (i.e. the Yeltsin era) are often regarded as a lost decade, and a new attitude in Russian foreign policy both towards the West and towards the developing world has emerged. This turn to realism in Russian foreign policy began even before Yeltsin's demise, symbolized by the replacement in January 1996 of Yeltsin's first foreign minister, Andrey Kozyrev, with Yevgeny Primakov, an outstanding expert on the Third World in general and on the Arab countries in particular. This occurred because after four or five years of Yeltsin's rule it became clear that a one-sided reliance on the West had not borne fruit. At the same time, the regime in the Kremlin had been stabilized and no longer needed the same degree of support from the West as it had sought during Yeltsin's confrontation with the Russian Supreme Soviet (i.e. the parliament) and especially during his 'presidential coup' in September–October 1993. Moreover, at the end of his rule, especially after NATO's aggression in Yugoslavia, even Yeltsin himself – visibly offended by Washington's disregard of Russia's opinion and interests – openly spoke against American global domination and diktats. If one ignores the reception held by Yeltsin for outgoing South African President F. W. de Klerk in the Kremlin in June 1992, it was not until 1997 that an African president, Hosni Mubarak of Egypt, visited Moscow after the collapse of the USSR. Eduardo dos Santos of Angola, Sam Nujoma of Namibia, Thabo Mbeki and Nelson Mandela of South Africa subsequently followed him. The intensity of summit meetings in Moscow grew after the changes in the Kremlin. Thus in 2001 Yeltsin's successor Vladimir Putin met in Moscow Abdelaziz Bouteflika of Algeria, Omar Bongo of Gabon, Lansana Conte of Guinea, Hosni Mubarak, Olusegun Obasanjo of Nigeria, and Meles Zenawi of Ethiopia.

Such a renewed interest in Africa sprang from a comprehensive review of Russian foreign policy, which took place immediately after Yeltsin's resignation in December 1999. Even before the presidential elections, Vladimir Putin, as Acting President, approved in January 2000 amendments to the

Concept of the National Security of the Russian Federation, which signified a departure from previous periods. The aims of Russian foreign policy stated in this document were further elaborated in another document, *Concept of the Foreign Policy of the Russian Federation*, signed by Putin on 28 June 2000.

The latter document spells out Russia's policy towards various regions and major international problems. It is clear from the *Concept* that Africa is not a priority for Russia. In fact, as a region it is mentioned second to last, just before Latin America. Nevertheless, the document envisages the expansion of interaction with African states and expresses Russia's readiness to assist the earliest possible settlement of regional military conflicts in Africa. Another positive aspect is classifying regional and sub-regional associations as a significant factor in regional and sub-regional security and peace-making. The need 'to develop a political dialogue with the Organization of African Unity (OAU) and with sub-regional organizations' is underlined. However, this provision is connected with the use of 'their capabilities for enabling Russia to join multilateral economic projects in the continent' (*Rossiyskaya gazeta*, 2000). In practice, this mostly means that Russian business hopes to become involved in projects financed from sources outside both Russia and Africa. Yet the *Concept* unfortunately does not elaborate on the prospects for bilateral economic relations.

Contemporary dimensions of Russo-African relations

Let us now consider the actual state of current Russian–African relations in various fields. Russia has established diplomatic relations with each and every African country (the last of them was Swaziland in 1999). Thirty-eight embassies of the Russian Federation operate in Africa, whereas thirty-six African countries maintain embassies in Moscow, and three more, Mauritius, Uganda and Senegal, are going to open (or reopen in the case of the latter two states) offices in Moscow shortly.

Moscow's intention to develop ties with Africa was confirmed during Igor Ivanov's visit to South Africa and three other countries in December 2001 (earlier, in July, Ivanov had also visited Libya, and then in November Egypt, both traditional partners of Moscow). This was followed in September 2002 by Prime Minister Mikhail Kasyanov's trip to attend the Earth Summit in Johannesburg. On the way there and back, he discussed matters of both political and economic co-operation with the prime ministers of Ethiopia and Tanzania. At his meeting with Meles Zenawi, Kasyanov expressed Russia's readiness to take part in the exploration for and production of gas and minerals, in the construction of power stations, and also in the modernization of various enterprises built in Ethiopia during the earlier period of co-operation with the USSR (Ministerstvo 2002). Yet the visit of the Russian president to Africa remains long overdue. Even during the Soviet era, when Moscow's profile on the continent was very high, Moscow's top leaders largely ignored the continent in the physical sense of actually visiting Africa. The only exception was Nikita Khrushchev's visit to Egypt in 1964. During his visit to South Africa the late Vassily Sredin, then Deputy Foreign Minister, publicly announced that Vladimir Putin would visit that country (and some others in Africa) in the first half of 2001. Later, other dates were mentioned as the proposed visit slipped from view. During Ivanov's 2001 visit to Pretoria and Cape Town, the Treaty of Friendship and Partnership between Russia and South Africa was initialled, and it was again announced publicly that the Treaty would be signed during the forthcoming visit of the Russian president. Alas, at the time of writing no date for this visit has been confirmed.

In the present world of insecurity and instability, relations between countries and the regions are largely determined by concerns about existing or latent threats. Perhaps following the example of Russia's Western partners, Vassily Sredin wrote in 2001 about 'transnational threats' such as 'streams of refugees, terrorism, and illegal arms trade and drug trafficking' which 'emanate from the African continent to other countries, including Russia' (Sredin 2001: 12). Sredin used this argument to justify Russia's assistance in the settlement of conflicts in Africa, which according to him was 'not altruism' but was 'dictated by our objective interests' (2001: 12). Indeed, there have been cases when Africans have come to Russia as narco-couriers or have been engaged in drug dealing in Russia. A small number of individuals from Africa, mostly Arabs, have also taken part in the terrorist actions of the Chechen separatists. A substantially greater number of Africans have tried to use the territory of Russia as a springboard for illegal migration into Western European countries.

However, in general it looks as though these threats from Africa have been exaggerated. According to a recent interview of the incumbent Director of the MFA Africa Department, Ambassador Alexander Makarenko, 'perhaps it is not very well-founded to speak about [Russian] security interests concerning Africa. There is no direct threat to our security in this case' (*Puls Planety*, 31 March 2003). Nevertheless, this has not precluded Russia from actively participating in efforts to prevent or resolve conflicts in Africa. This involvement has taken place under the auspices of the UN, primarily in observer-type missions in countries such as Egypt, Congo, Sierra Leone and Western Sahara (Yermolaev 2000). In the case of Sierra Leone, Russia dispatched a military contingent of 115 persons with four MI-24 attack helicopters (Vassiliev 2003: 130). Taking such steps, the Russian leadership takes into account a 'special responsibility' of the country as a permanent member of the UN Security Council. Indeed, it was the only permanent member of the Security Council to deploy combat units as part of the UNAMSIL mission in Sierra Leone. At the same time, Moscow proceeds from the assumption that transforming Africa into a 'continent of peace, tranquillity and stability' would contribute to the development of Moscow's bilateral relations with African countries (*Puls Planety*, 31 March 2003). According to Makarenko, 'in [Russia's] relations with Africa now there is no ideological context, no military strategic interests'; they are based 'first of all on our understanding of our trade and economic aspirations ... The approach is practical, I would even say, pragmatic' (*Puls Planety*, 31 March 2003).

In the field of trade and economy Russia and African countries are bound by many bilateral agreements, both inherited by the Russian Federation from the Soviet Union, which had agreements with thirty-seven African states on technical and economic assistance, and with forty-two countries on trade (Deich 2003: 52), and new ones. However, not much has been achieved in practice and the trade turnover of about US$1,000 million (*Puls Planety*, 31 March 2003), the bulk of it with North African states, is disappointing. One of the reasons for this state of affairs is the abolition of state management of foreign economic activity in Russia and numerous restructurings of government organizations in this field. There is a consensus that even in conditions of the so-called 'market economy' the development of broad economic ties with Africa is largely impossible without strong support from the state, and there have been calls for packages to support Russian businesses working in Africa, including tax reductions and credit guarantees. If earlier state credits played a major role in advancing national industrial goods to African markets, now, when the government has vacated the sphere of foreign economic relations, only the most efficient Russian companies and businessmen have managed to find niches for export to Africa. Several of them can be singled out – RUSAL (Russian Aluminium) in Guinea and ALROSA (Diamonds of Russia–Sakha) in Angola – but actions of individual companies or persons, even successful ones, cannot reverse the major decline in Russo-African economic relations.

Meanwhile, with the splitting up of the former Soviet Union, Russia has found itself deprived of many of the supplies of minerals vital for its economy and which came from sites within the USSR but now outside its borders. This has stimulated the search for sources from other locations, and there has been a rise in the importance of imports from Africa of manganese, chrome, nickel, zinc, lead, etc. In this regard, one might have thought that a considerable contribution to the Russian state in facilitating and encouraging economic co-operation with African countries would have been made through the bilateral commissions formed with a number of African countries. Unfortunately most of these are not active enough, and some are actually defunct. For example, although the agreement to create a relevant commission with South Africa was reached long ago, in the mid-1990s, its first inaugural meeting took place only in April 1999, during Nelson Mandela's visit to Moscow, and the first working session (in Pretoria) occurred three and half years later. Under the chairmanship of Valentina Matveenko, then Russian Vice-Premier, and Nkosazana Dlamini-Zuma, South African Foreign Minister, the Commission has had useful discussions. For instance, Pretoria has promised to grant Russia the status of a country with a market economy and Moscow granted South Africa the status of a developing country, steps which it is hoped will facilitate trade between the two countries. This status ensures that Russian importers of South African goods pay 75 per cent of the basic tariff import duty, and the export of South African fruits, for example, is expected to increase by 25–30 per cent.

Russian scholars and businessmen have proposed the creation of a financial–industrial group under the auspices of the Russian government specifically to facilitate the development of trade and economic relations with Africa (Deich 2003: 95). At the same time, Russian businessmen interested in Africa have taken some steps in self-organization by recently establishing the Russian–African Business Council, a kind of co-ordinating and lobbying body. To date, however, the Council remains in its embryonic stages and beset by internal conflicts.

A peculiar sphere of Russia's economic relations with Africa is the arms trade. The Soviet involvement in equipping and often advising the armed forces of various African countries is well known. In some of them, for example in Algeria, Angola and Ethiopia, up to 90 per cent of equipment was Soviet-made. However, the situation changed drastically in the early 1990s for several reasons. First, with the deterioration of the economic situation in the USSR arms export was moved from a credit to a cash basis. Then, after the dissolution of the Soviet Union, large quantities of arms were 'inherited' by the Ukraine and Belarus where Soviet troops were concentrated. These countries began actively selling their stocks, often in competition with Russia. At the same time, the 'democratic' mass media launched a campaign against arms sales, portraying them as immoral. This has resulted in a number of traditional markets for Soviet/Russian arms, such as Zambia and Tanzania, being captured by Western, primarily American and British, suppliers.

In the field of education the growing concern for problems of the South and of Africa in particular was demonstrated when in 1996 the Russian government resumed the granting of scholarships at Russian universities to citizens of developing countries (Deich 2003: 112). For example, in the People's Friendship University of Russia (formerly the Patrice Lumumba University) almost half of the 950 African students enjoy Russian government scholarships; the others study on a commercial basis. However, the scholarships are rather modest, covering only tuition and accommodation; airfares and other expenses have to be paid by the relevant governments or the students themselves. The graduates of Soviet/Russian universities can act as a channel of communication between Russia and Africa and act at a sub-state level to promote Russo-African links. Although previous African students often studied beyond the borders of Russia proper, i.e. in other Soviet republics such as the Ukraine, their teaching media were Russian and many activities, especially extra-mural, were co-ordinated in Moscow. They therefore often feel a certain affinity not only to their *alma mater* but to Russia as well. One of the Russian ambassadors in Africa said recently: 'Whatever party comes to power in the country, there will be two or three Soviet graduates in the cabinet.'

Domestic sources of Russia's Africa policy

After Yeltsin's 'victory' over parliament in 1993, he advanced a new constitution and Russia became a presidential republic, with very strong powers concentrated in the hands of the head of state. In particular, according to Article 86,

> The President of the Russian Federation shall: a) supervise the conduct of the foreign policy of the Russian Federation; b) conduct negotiations and sign international treaties of the Russian Federation; c) sign instruments of ratification; d) accept credentials and instruments of recall of diplomatic representatives accredited with him.
>
> (Constitution of the Russian Federation 1993)

Thus the Minister of Foreign Affairs is directly subordinate to the President, though he attends the cabinet meetings. In his ministry two departments are concerned with African affairs: the Department of (Sub-Saharan) Africa and the Department of Middle East and North Africa. Relevant divisions also exist in other foreign-policy making bodies, such as the Ministry of Defence and the External Intelligence Service (both of these organizations are also directly subordinate to the President and their heads, just as the Foreign Minister is a member of the Security Council chaired by Putin).

The Ministry of Economic Development and Trade, which includes the Department of Asia, Africa and Latin America, facilitates trade with African countries, or at least is supposed to do so. Some other ministries are also involved in Russia's African policy: for example, in 1996 the Ministry of Emergency Situations and Civil Protection signed an agreement with the OAU on humanitarian assistance in conflict zones (Vassiliev 2003: 180). The power of the Russian parliament – the Federal Assembly – is rather limited in the ongoing presidential republic, though both chambers (the State Duma and the Council of Federation) have Committees on Foreign Affairs and have to ratify international treaties. They also have to be consulted on the appointment of ambassadors and maintain bilateral contacts with African parliaments, for example in April 2003 hosting a South African National Assembly delegation.

Special attention should be paid to the role of civil society organizations in Russo-African relations. Although the process of 'democratization' should have enhanced civil society, the reality looks somewhat different. Among hundreds of political parties existing at least on paper (though only thirty-seven of them have so far registered for the next parliamentary elections), just one or two have some contacts with Africa. In particular, the Communist Party of the Russian Federation maintains contacts with the African National Congress and South African Communist Party, and Vladimir Zhirinovsky's Liberal Democratic Party of Russia used to have contacts with the White right wing in South Africa. The major Russian trade unions (as a rule, pro-governmental) hardly have any contacts with their African counterparts.

During the struggle for national independence many African organizations enjoyed political and practical support from the Soviet Afro-Asian Solidarity Committee, which had been funded by the Soviet Peace Fund and worked under the tight control of the CPSU International Department. This Committee survived the political storms surrounding the breakdown of the Soviet Union and was reorganized in 1992 as the Society of Afro-Asian Peoples' Solidarity and Co-operation. However, until recently this organization hardly dealt with Africa at all, concentrating on the problems in the Middle East and Asia. In April 2003 the Society elected a new president, Mikhail Margelov, who is young (by Russian standards) and energetic. Margelov is also Chair of the International Affairs Committee of the Council of Federation and an Arabic scholar by education.

Although not strictly 'civil society' but involved in much the same activity, an important role in expanding cultural ties with Africa was played earlier by the Soviet Association of Friendship with African Peoples (SADNA), a member of the government-funded Union of the Soviet Friendship Societies. Having undergone a number of transformations this Union is now operating as the Russian Centre of Scientific and Cultural Co-operation with Foreign Countries (*Roszarubezhtsentr*) under the MFA. Closely associated with it is the non-governmental Russian Association of International Co-operation (in fact, Valentina Tereshkova, the first woman cosmonaut, is currently chairing both of them). Unfortunately, in the 1990s approximately half of the Russian cultural centres in Africa were closed due to lack of funding, but the *Roszarubezhtsentr* still maintains centres in Congo-Brazzaville, Egypt (in Cairo and Alexandria), Ethiopia, Morocco, Tanzania, Tunisia and Zambia. As for the SADNA, it had been initially transformed into the Association for Business and Cultural Cooperation with Countries of Africa (ADEKS). But this organization has subsequently expanded its activities into Asia as well and has become known as the International ADEKS Foundation, engaged mostly in attempts to facilitate business between Russia and the South. On the other hand, societies of friendship with individual African countries such as Cape Verde, Egypt, Ethiopia and South Africa have been created (or, in most cases, resurrected). These organizations are trying (albeit with different degrees of success) to make the Russian public better acquainted with the situation in Africa. It should be noted, however, that such activities are conducted against the background of an often hostile anti-African milieu created by a good part of the Russian mass media.

According to a study conducted by Veronica Usacheva of the electronic media, newspapers and magazines, in the major news programmes of the NTV Channel in the space of nine months there were fifty-two stories on Africa, in which twenty-two African countries were mentioned. Out of these stories only six were positive, twenty were neutral and twenty-six were negative (Usacheva 2003: 2). Only two of the six positive stories had a socio-political content: about the relationship between the higher social status of women and the development of a national economy in Africa, and about the agreement on establishing the African Union. Another two of these stories told of two Africans, a Nigerian 'prince' and a former African prisoner in Russia, accused of drug dealing, who had devoted their lives to the service of the Russian Orthodox Church. In addition, there were stories about the best football player in Africa and about the possibility of selling Russian cross-country vehicles to North Africa (Usacheva 2003: 2–3).

Such findings fit a pattern in Russia. The Russian mass media often uses Africa as the 'zero baseline' for comparing countries. For example, in a story about the dire condition of the Yugoslavian economy, that country was compared to such African countries as Zambia or Sudan (Usacheva 2003: 4–5). In such circumstances, when an economy is destroyed, as in Yugoslavia, it is described as resembling African economies, an obviously negative and pejorative perception. Newspapers and magazines have tended to pay most attention to southern Africa, particularly to Zimbabwe and South Africa, and in such articles the situation is usually presented as a dispute between Whites and Blacks. The Zimbabwe conflict was actually personified as being between Ian Smith and Robert Mugabe, and in articles mentioning Ian Smith he is portrayed as a strong leader who confronted the British and the Blacks: a living legend of African politics, in fact, with a sincere though also unique form of African patriotism, and a person of high personal decency (in Usacheva 2003: 6). In fact, in an article entitled 'The Time of a White Person', telling the story of Ian Smith, the writer claimed that 'Whites put all in order and were responsible for all. They taught "careless Negroes" how to work and live' (in Usacheva 2003: 7). The situation in Zimbabwe is simply characterized as 'Black racism'. As a journalist for *Izvestia* newspaper put it,

> what will happen when after Zimbabwe and Kenya the [anti-White] pogrom makers will reach the Republic of South Africa, where [the] White population is more? ... The White minority in the Republic lives on [a] powder keg. It can blow up at any moment and then the world will run into [a] new humanitarian catastrophe.
>
> (Usacheva 2003: 6–7)

Usacheva suggests that although the image of Africa is not the main image of the 'alien' or 'other' for Russia, it is important for the Russian mass media. She believes that when Russian policy, proceeding from the premise of a multi-polar world, began to take up a position of Russia as 'the other' in relation to Western culture, Africa in the Russian mass media assumed the role of 'the other' culture in relation to Russia itself. The image of Russia thus became a median link in the chain made up of the West–Russia–Africa, emphasizing the 'civilized character' and 'developed nature' of Russia in contrast to 'wild Africa' (2003: 11).

As to the opposition ('left-patriotic forces' in the Russian political vocabulary) or progressive viewpoints within Russian civil society, their newspapers have a rather limited circulation and they are practically deprived of access to television. On the other hand, internet sites presenting favourable descriptions of Africa have been created in recent years, one on the whole continent and another specifically on South Africa (e.g. www.africana.ru and www.southafrica.narod.ru). In summary, it might be asserted that one of the obstacles to developing Russo-African relations is a lack of objective information on the African continent available within Russia (as well as on Russia in Africa) and the weak role of civil society in promoting such ties. The African mass media has a very limited number of correspondents in Moscow and the number of Russian media offices in Africa has been drastically reduced in comparison with the Soviet period. Such a situation facilitates the activities of xenophobic and even overtly racist elements. The reasons for this are multiple. First, one has to mention the negative influence of so-called 'Western standards' uncritically adopted by a part of Russian society in the 1990s. To give one example, practically all the racist graffiti in Russia is written in English – after all, 'skinhead' is not a Russian word! There are other reasons as well. A general degradation of social and economic conditions often provokes people (not only Russians) to view foreigners as 'scapegoats', supposedly controlling markets and rising prices and/or taking advantage of Russia's 'goodwill' to come and get education at the state's expense. The destruction of the Soviet-era system of youth organizations and facilities has left many Russian youngsters unattended and uneducated, and a drift to extremism and racism has proven an attractive destination for some.

To support this, the news on the www.africana.ru web-site sometimes resembles a report from the criminal world: unprovoked racist attacks, beatings and even murders of Africans and others are common. The situation has been aggravated by the fact that until recently Russian higher authorities preferred to consider these crimes as generalized 'hooliganism' and not as actual racist acts. Thus at the parliamentary hearings in the Duma in 2001, one of the Vice-Speakers did his best to prove the absence of racism in Russia by urging his audience not 'to look for a black cat in a dark room when it is not there'. Fortunately, albeit rather late, the authorities have had to recognize the reality and promise to try and change it.

Such developments directly affect thousands of Russian citizens of mixed race, whose fathers returned to Africa but whose mothers stayed in Russia or returned home. They include a popular actor, successful businessmen and juvenile delinquents. In recent years, several organizations have been founded to assist children of mixed origin; the most active of them is probably the Metis Children's Fund. Besides such organizations of 'half-Africans', apart from students' unions, those Africans who have settled in Russia permanently have begun to organize their own associations. Thus, the African Unity organization headed by Aliou Tunkara from Benin, who has been living in Russia for eighteen years, has been officially registered in St Petersburg. Its activists were positively surprised when the local training centre of the Ministry of Home Affairs invited them to deliver lectures 'in order to inculcate in young officials of the militia [police] the culture of communication with citizens belonging to various ethnic groups' (*Nezavisimaya gazeta* 2003). However, by and large the influence of such organizations is still rather limited.

Current developments

Not everybody in Russia necessarily welcomes the turn to a multi-vector foreign policy and the proclaimed intention of Russia's leadership to shape the multi-polar world. Certain pro-Western political elements such as the Union of the Rightist Forces (URF) openly criticize this course. For instance, soon after Putin's appearance in the Kremlin one of the URF leaders, Irina Hakamada, proposed that Russia should 'close the ring' around the globe by joining the US, Japan and Western Europe, thus distancing itself from the South. Such views received prominence after 11 September 2001, and in this regard many in Africa, who welcomed the idea of a multi-polar world, were somewhat worried by any rapprochement between Moscow and the US. Moreover, at that time Western propaganda did its best to present Russia as a passive collaborator, dependent on Washington if not actually following its orders.

Nevertheless, Vladimir Putin (2002a) soon reconfirmed Russia's commit-ment to the multi-polar concept and Foreign Minister Ivanov reiterated that Moscow's foreign policy has a multi-vector nature. Moscow's adherence to these principles became evident during the so-called Iraq crisis in late 2002 and early 2003 and the Iraq war; Russian public opinion highly appreciated the attitude of African countries towards these developments, which was seen as sharing Moscow's views on the matter. These developments proved once again that, far from being marginalized, Africa can play an important role in world affairs: although the war went ahead, the US, Britain and Australia failed to gain Security Council authorization, and of fifty-three African Union members just four or five offered political and moral support to the aggressors.

Russia's participation in the privileged club of the G-8 has to a degree allowed Moscow to advance its policies towards Africa. At the 2001 G-8 summit, Putin supported the so-called Genoa Plan for Africa, which involved, among other things, the appointment by each G-8 country of a personal representative for Africa who was to co-ordinate with the leaders of the African continent in working out a plan of action. Professor Nodari Simonia, Director of the Moscow Institute of International Relations and World Economy in Moscow, represented President Putin in this group. The group's activities met with approval at the next G-8 summit on the Africa Action Plan. In particular, at Kananaskis the G-8 expressed their support for the New Partnership for Africa's Development (NEPAD). Speaking at the press conference after the summit on 27 June 2002, Putin (2002b) said,

> As to Russia, traditionally with the African continent we've got very good relations. We subtly feel all the problems of the African continent ... I must say Russia's contribution is very noticeable in dealing with the problems of Africa. Suffice it to say that in the initiative adopted here [the Africa Action Plan], it is multilateral ... Among other things related to the writing off of a part of the debts of African countries, Russia makes a very great contribution: of all the debts of African countries to be written off, 20 per cent falls on the Russian Federation. It is 26 billion dollars ... We are ready to take part in humanitarian programmes, and in particular in the programmes fighting AIDS ... We grant African countries a considerable amount of scholarships for study in higher and secondary educational institutions of Russia, and intend to carry on this programme in the future as well. On the whole Russia's assistance to African countries is multi-pronged, and we are convinced that this activity ultimately meets the national interests of the Russian Federation itself and intend to continue this work jointly with the other G8 countries.

Conclusion

In an interview, Ambassador Makarenko disagreed with those who believe that big strategic mistakes in Russia's African policy were made after the disappearance of the Soviet Union. 'What we lost,' he said, 'was not worth keeping' (*Puls Planety*, 31 March 2003). Yet this statement resembles an attempt to put on a brave face. Indeed, the losses in Russo-African relations have been substantial, some of them irrevocable. Moreover, Russia in some aspects continues to lose its position in Africa. For example, the number of African capitals served by Russian airlines is decreasing and the offices of the state-owned Russian Information Agency (Novosti) in South Africa and Nigeria, as well as the African division of the agency, have just been closed. Yet all in all the tide seems to be turning back. Makarenko's final conclusion, in this sense, seems to be correct:

> Things are moving in the right direction, though they will move very hard and very slowly. We have to take into account the complexity of our own problems and the even bigger volume of the problems facing Africa. But the main point is that there is a positive movement and there has been already a practical return.
>
> (*Puls Planety*, 31 March 2003)

References

Constitution of the Russian Federation (1993) http://www.constitution.ru/en/10003000–01.htm

Deich T. (ed.) (2003) *Afrika vo vneshnepoliticheskih prioritetah Rossii* [Africa in the Foreign Policy Priorities of Russia], Moscow: Institute for African Studies.

Ivanov, I. (2002) 'Russian Foreign Policy Guidelines', *Kommersant–Vlast Magazine*, Moscow, 10 June 2002. English translation http:// www.ln.mid.ru/bl.nsf

Ministerstvo inostrannykh del Rossiiskoi Federatsii (2002) *Informatsionnyi byulleten* [Ministry of Foreign Affairs of the Russian Federation, Information Bulletin], Moscow, 3 September, http:// www.ln.mid.ru/ns-rafr.nsf

Nezavisimaya gazeta (2003) [*Independent Gazette*], Moscow, 10 February.

Putin, V. (2002a) 'Interview of President of Russia V. V. Putin with the Chinese newspaper *Renmin Ribao,* 4 June', http://www.ln.mid.ru/bl.nsf

—— (2002b) 'President of the Russian Federation Vladimir Putin Remarks at Press Conference following Big Eight Summit, Kananaskis, Canada, 27 June', http://www.ln.mid.ru/bl.nsf

Rossiya–Afrika Realii i perspektivy. Otchet o deyatelnosti deputatskoi gruppy po svyazyam s parlamentami stran Afriki. 2000–2003 (2003) [Russia–Africa: Realities and Prospects. Report on the Activities of the Group on Ties with Parliaments of African Countries, 2000–2003], Moscow.

Rossiyskaya gazeta (2000) [*Russian Gazette*], Moscow, 11 July.

Sredin, V. (2001) 'Russia and Africa', *Mezhdunarodnaya Zhizn* [International Affairs], 7: 8–14.

Usacheva, V. (2003) 'Africa in the Mirror of Russian Mass-Media', paper delivered at the Symposium 'Africa and the Challenges of Globalization in the 21st century', Africa Institute of South Africa, Pretoria, 27 February.

Vassiliev, A. (2003) *Afrika – padcheritsa globalizatsii* [Africa: A Stepchild of Globalization], Moscow: Vostochnaya Literatura.

Vremya novostei (2000) [*Time of News*], Moscow, 30 April.

Yermolaev, M. (2000) 'Russia's International Peacekeeping and Conflict Management in the Post-Soviet Environment' in Mark Malan (ed.) *Boundaries of Peace Support Operations*, Pretoria: Institute for Security Studies Monograph, No. 44.

6   Japan–Africa relations

Patterns and prospects

Scarlett Cornelissen

> I chose to visit Africa at the dawn of the new century because I definitely wanted to stand on the soil of the African continent and express directly to the African people the firm determination of the Japanese people to open our hearts along with you, to sweat and to expend all our might to aid in the process of Africa overcoming its difficulties and building a bright future. I believe this is an appropriate new beginning for Japan's global diplomacy.
>
> (Japanese Prime Minister Yoshiro Mori, South Africa;
> *Independent on Sunday*, 14 January 2001)

The relationship between Africa and Japan has historically been tenuous, characterized by limited economic and – for much of the earlier part of the twentieth century – political contact. Unlike other large powers, Japan had no imperial connection with the African continent, nor any obvious similarities or convergence points. Africa was thus often perceived as the 'dark continent' that offered little economic attraction (Morikawa 1997).

At the end of the twentieth century this situation changed dramatically, when ties between Africa and Japan became more concrete and in some respects significantly deepened. Beginning in the 1970s, Japan pursued a more robust approach in Africa, the apex of which was Prime Minister Mori's visit to the three regional powerhouses of Kenya, Nigeria and South Africa at the start of 2001. These visits were highly significant in that they represented the first diplomatic call to Africa by an incumbent Japanese leader. The visit also ushered in a new era in Japan's relations with Africa, one where the continent would move to the centre of a reinvigorated foreign policy, and through which Japan was seeking to graft a renewed role for itself as the self-styled custodian of Africa's development. This stance towards Africa is encapsulated in Mori's proclamation that there 'will be no stability and prosperity in the twenty-first century unless the problems of Africa are resolved' (*Independent on Sunday*, 14 January 2001).

The intensification of ties between Africa and Japan is conventionally attributed to modifications in the latter's foreign policy objectives, the reshaping of its external aims, and a broadening of its interest beyond the East Asian region and North America. From this perspective, Africa is generally viewed as the passive partner in an asymmetric relationship (e.g. Adem 2001). It can, however, be argued that much of the shifting relationship between Japan and Africa, while partly the result of changing Japanese interests and fortunes, can also be read as the outcome of political developments within Africa over the past two decades. In other words, Japan–Africa relations are affected by both African and Japanese agency.

Key themes characterize Japan's ties with Africa. First, aid constitutes a core element of this relationship, and in many respects forms the superscript to other aspects of Japan–Africa connections.[1] Second, much of Japan's professed Africa drive centres on its interaction with South Africa, with whom the country has had a relatively long-established strategic relationship. Japan's economic and political linkages with South Africa are of a very particular nature, and while it provides a certain context within which to read Japan's overall African policy, it also carries implications for the Asian country's involvement in the rest of the continent. Third, a significant element of Japan's activities in Africa is built on a notion of a common destiny and identity (see Cornelissen and Taylor 2000). This chapter reviews Japan's involvement in the African continent under these broad themes.

Aid: the foundation for ties between Japan and Africa

Between the 1960s and late 1990s, aid constituted the fulcrum of Japan–Africa relations. Aid remains a vital component of the relationship between the two, but following global economic and political events during the late 1990s, the nature, direction and purpose of Japan's aid to Africa is now qualitatively different. Japan's early relationship with Africa was shaped, first, by its larger economic goals, central to which was the need to secure access to, and the supply of, strategic energy resources and raw materials (Ampiah 1997). More broadly, this was also linked to the desire to assist in the development of a stable global economic order that would favour Japan's own growth.[2] Overall, these concerns and its political ambitions in the international arena played a key role in its involvement and interests in Africa.

Aid ties between Japan and Africa were inaugurated in the 1960s with aid disbursements to five African states: Ghana, Kenya, Nigeria, Tanzania and Uganda. These disbursements were modest, and mainly in reciprocation for these countries' lowering their import restrictions on Japanese goods (Morikawa 1997). It was only after the oil shocks of 1973 that Japan started to seek new sources of energy. Africa thus became significant for Japanese foreign economic interests and attracted more Japanese aid. This was one element of the larger resource diplomacy that Japan was starting to engage in. In 1974 the Japanese foreign minister visited Ghana, Nigeria, Tanzania and former Zaire, and declared a doubling in Japan's aid to African countries. Consequently, whereas at the beginning of the 1970s Africa received less than 2 per cent of Japan's total aid disbursements, by the end of that decade Japan's Africa aid payments had significantly increased, and were comparable to the volume of its aid to South America and the Middle East (roughly 10 per cent of its total aid payouts).

During the 1980s Japan's overall aid programme benefited from the country's rising current account surpluses and the appreciation of the yen against the dollar, and by 1989 the country became the biggest aid donor in the world, a position it retained throughout the 1990s. This expansion of Japan's aid programme is commonly understood as the consequence of two factors. First, Japan's rising international economic stature was accompanied by increased pressure from the US for international burden-sharing (Inukai 1993; Islam 1991). The extension of aid programmes provided the means for Japan to offset such pressure. Second, aid was one component of the international 'middle power' position Japan was progressively adopting, another element of which was increased activism in multilateral organizations (Yasumoto 1995).[3]

Africa, particularly those states south of the Sahara,[4] gained significantly from this (see Orr 1990; Rix 1993). By 1995, Japan was disbursing aid to all forty-seven sub-Saharan African (SSA) states, and it was the top donor for seven of these countries (Kenya, Ghana, Gambia, Malawi, Sierra Leone, Tanzania and Zambia). Altogether, in 1995 Japan's ODA to SSA stood at $1.33 billion, a tenth of the total aid contributions by the twenty-two members of the OECD's Development Assistance Committee (DAC) to SSA, and just over one-eighth (12.6 per cent) of Japan's total bilateral disbursements (MOFA 1996b: 87).

By the end of the 1990s, however, as Japan entered a prolonged phase of economic downturn, the rapid growth of its bilateral aid programme was severely curbed. In 1996 its net aid disbursements plunged some 35 per cent, from US$14.7bn in 1995 to US$9.6bn. There has been a strong decline in aid spending since then. Most recently, in 2001 the country's total net disbursements decreased by 27 per cent over the previous year, amounting in 2001 to US$9.8bn (DAC 2003). Its 2002 general account budget for aid (i.e. that share of the government's budget before borrowing for aid), furthermore, has been reduced by 10 per cent (MOFA 2003a). The expansive approach to its aid that the country has adopted since the 1980s has now clearly come to an end, and, in the face of mounting domestic opposition to a broad aid programme, the focus is on increasing the effectiveness and efficient implementation of aid (MOFA 2003a).

Japan's aid to Africa has concomitantly been affected. Between 1996 and 1997, for instance, aid disbursements declined by 24 per cent. While Africa has continued to account for approximately 10 per cent of Japan's total aid, disbursements to the continent have, in real terms, substantially declined from its apex in the mid-1990s.

Japan's emergence as an aid power has attracted a great deal of attention and criticism. This is due to the fact that, on qualitative measures, Japanese aid has consistently fallen below the criteria set by the Development Assistance Committee. Japan has been widely criticized for aid disbursals which are said to be low in concessionality, concentrated towards loan rather than grant assistance, with a focus, moreover, on financing economic infrastructure programmes in recipient countries (e.g. Nester 1992; Söderberg 1996; Yasutomo 1995). Critics take this as evidence of an overly mercantilist aid programme, the conjecture being that such infrastructure projects are aimed at smoothing the path for the advancement of Japanese trade and investment in these recipient countries, all to the benefit of the Japanese export industry (Cornelissen and Taylor 2000). Similarly, Japan's aid relationship with Africa has often been described as the outcome of 'carefully calculated self-interest' (Carim and Solomon 1994), a 'neomercantilist strategy [and] creating a classic dependency relationship' (Nester 1992), while Ampiah (1996) has questioned the proclaimed humanitarian motive of Japanese development assistance.

As will be discussed, the nature of the Japanese aid programme is largely the result of a particular development philosophy, one that also underlies the country's economic relationship with Africa. Nonetheless, the patterns of Japanese aid disbursements in Africa do attest to a high level of selectivity regarding the main recipients and a considerable degree of utility maximization. Japan has consistently extended the bulk of its African aid to a few key states (notably Ghana, Kenya, Tanzania and, of late, South Africa), i.e. those who either are resource-rich and for whom aid was provided on a *quid pro quo* basis, or those who are of strategic significance for Japan.

As regards the latter, many commentators have noted how Japanese aid to some African states has been designed around its larger United Nations (UN) ambitions (e.g. Ampiah 1997; Osada 1997). For example, Japanese assistance to Kenya and Tanzania in East Africa and to Ghana in the West African region has for a long time been based on the political influence these countries had in the continent and, importantly, the weight they carried in the UN (Inukai 1993; Moss and Ravenhill 1985). Ueki (1993) notes that UN-centred diplomacy has been a long-standing pronouncement of the Japanese government as a means to attain its international political objectives. Japanese officials believe that actively participating in the UN and supporting its goals and principles can enhance Japan's global stature (Yasutomo 1995). In the 1960s this UN-centrism played out multilaterally in Japan's support for the Afro-Asian bloc[5] within the UN General Assembly, of which Japan regarded itself a member. By 1991 Japan had been elected as a non-permanent member of the Security Council seven times (Osada 1997), largely on the votes of the Afro-Asian bloc.[6]

More recently much closer ties have been forged between Japan and South Africa, both of whom have keen Security Council ambitions, and whose relationship partly centres on the mutual buttressing of each other's international goals. Furthermore, the Japanese government has also extended its promotion of an Afro-Asian linkage, which worked so well for Japan in the 1960s, through several programmes and actions it has undertaken more recently

(Cornelissen and Taylor 2000). There are two key pillars to Japan's present ties with Africa: the Tokyo International Conference on African Development (TICAD), a multilateral initiative aimed at drawing funds for Africa's development; and a concentration of a significant degree of Japan's aid, economic and other resources on the Southern African region, particularly South Africa. Overall, South Africa has become the pivot of Japan's Africa interests and endeavours.

The TICAD process

Inaugurated in 1993, the TICAD has become the flagship of Japan's involvement in Africa. Under Japan's patronage it brings together representatives of the World Bank, the UNDP, the Global Coalition for Africa, DAC and EU donor countries, and representatives from several Asian – and all fifty-three African – countries. Its main objective, encapsulated in the Tokyo Declaration on African Development, released after the first TICAD in 1993, is to accelerate African development through political and economic reforms in African countries, the encouragement of private sector investments to promote economic development and employment creation, and enhanced African regional economic and trade cooperation and integration (MOFA 1993). In 1998 a second conference was held that sought to further develop cooperation among African countries, multilateral and bilateral donors, and other developing countries. Its conclusion saw the adoption of a number of quantitative targets on education and poverty reduction in Africa.[7] A third conference was scheduled for the end of 2003.

The role of Japan as instigator and sponsor of the TICAD process is significant. The Japanese government suggests the TICAD is a response to the aid fatigue that has characterized the North's relationship with the African continent over the past two decades and maintains that the process as a whole constitutes an effective counter to rising Afro-pessimism over this time (e.g. JICA 2000). Japan's involvement in the TICAD can, however, be read as an element of its specific international posturing, or 'middlepowermanship'. In this way, its patronage of the TICAD is aimed at drawing political dividends from raising the state's international profile as a benevolent collaborator in Africa's development. This is also evident in how Japan publicizes its role in championing Africa's cause in a number of other multilateral forums, such as the G-8.[8]

But the TICAD is also significant for its underpinnings, and the implications of the rhetorical foundations of the initiative. TICAD is aimed at fostering partnerships between African countries and donors towards the development of the continent, along with promoting South–South cooperation. The central philosophy of the TICAD is that African countries help themselves to develop (MOFA 1998). 'Ownership' (based on African initiative and self-help) and 'partnership' are hence the prime bases of the TICAD process. These are supposed to be operationalized through a commitment towards democratization and good governance on the part of African countries and an undertaking by Northern governments to aid Africa's efforts by creating favourable economic and trade environments.

It was only during the preparations for the second TICAD that there was a shift towards an overtly *political* aim for the Conference. The adoption of the Tokyo Agenda for Action at the conclusion of TICAD II entailed commitments towards political liberalization and suitable fiscal management. While on the one hand this was reflective of the larger discourse on the twin requisites of democratization and good governance espoused by all donor institutions (the so-called Washington Consensus), its inclusion in TICAD also represented a further means through which the Washington Consensus and its aims are propagated. As far as Japan is concerned, it is only relatively recently that it started attaching more explicit fiscal and political conditionalities to its aid programme, most concretely demonstrated with the adoption of its Official Development Assistance Charter in 1992.[9]

Importantly, the principles of African 'ownership' and 'self-help' that underlie TICAD echo Japanese developmental philosophy, which is based on the notion that 'developing countries should manage or regulate their economies with the objective of achieving self-reliance as soon as possible' (Hanabusa 1991: 89).[10] Their initial inclusion in the TICAD process was largely due to Japanese engagement. Since then, however, these have found resonance in the ostensible turn towards democracy and good governance by African leaders, most substantially with the establishment of the New Partnership for Africa's Development (NEPAD) in 2001. Recently, the Japanese government has placed much more emphasis on complementing the TICAD process with the NEPAD initiative.

Another crucial aspect of the TICAD is its emphasis on promoting South–South, and in particular African–Asian, cooperation. Since the first TICAD several initiatives have been taken to foster closer trade, investment and cooperation linkages between Southeast Asian and African countries. Most important of these were the establishment of the Africa–Asia Business Forum and the Asia–Africa Investment and Technology Promotion Centre in Malaysia at the beginning of the new millennium.

Japan has played an instrumental role in articulating and incorporating African–Asian cooperation into the TICAD process, and sponsors many of the collaboration initiatives. Underlying its efforts, however, is a belief in the relevance and importance of Asian countries' development trajectories for Africa and a focus on the lessons African countries can draw from Asia's development experience (Cornelissen and Taylor 2000). This is part of a larger thrust in Japan's development and aid policies, which seeks to extend to other regions the particular form of economic and aid programme that it has adopted in East Asia. Japan's promotion of an 'East Asian Development Approach' has been concretized in its Initiative for Development in East Asia (IDEA) (MOFA 2002).[11] Although this is primarily a multilateral project that in the aftermath of the Asian financial

crises of the late 1990s seeks to design new forms of development cooperation in the East Asian region, it is also aimed at advancing economic
development strategies derived from East Asian experiences to other parts
of the world.[12]

The notion of an Asian model of development can be criticized as ahistor-
ical, reductionist and ignoring the heterogeneity of development paths in
East Asia produced by local histories, domestic economies and politics, and
diverse experiences of the international economy (Bernard and Ravenhill
1995; Hatch and Yamamura 1996). Yet the nature of Japan's development
activities in the East Asian region – based on a comprehensive involvement of
the Japanese public and private sectors – and its claims to be employing a
similar strategy beyond East Asia are important. They also carry with them
implications for the character of Japan's broader economic links with Africa.

East Asia has traditionally been the focus of Japan's development efforts.
Its development programmes in the region functioned on the provision of
concessional and non-concessional resource (aid) flows and the conjunctive
channelling of Japanese investments. This triad of aid, trade and investments has been the foundation of Japan's system of economic
cooperation,[13] which in turn is based on a comprehensive approach to
'development'. Japan's format of aid provision, which in the East Asian
region was closely tied to the country's industrial policy (Hatch and
Yamamura 1996), was criticized as neo-mercantilist. From the Japanese
perspective, however, the propitious export-led economic advance that East
and Southeast Asia has seen between the 1970s and the early parts of the
1990s was due, in large part, to the type of assistance provided by the
Japanese government. The Japanese stance is encapsulated in official claims
that a 'review of the role played by [Japan's] development assistance in the
past economic development in the East Asian region ... demonstrates the
effectiveness of an East Asian Development Approach which addresses
poverty reduction through economic growth' (MOFA 2002). With regard to
Africa, Japan claims to be trying to 'adapt Asian models to the African
setting' (MOFA 1997). However, the low levels of Japanese investment in
and trade with the continent belie this.[14] The exception is Japan's relations
with South Africa and the Southern African region.

Japan's relationship with South Africa

Historically, Japan's relationship with South Africa has been more intimate
than with other African countries, but also more uneasy. The two countries
had long-standing trade ties, which intensified during the 1960s and 1970s.
Trade between the two countries was based on the strategic advantage that
South Africa possessed, as both source and supplier, of scarce minerals
such as platinum. This coincided with Japan's increasing dependence on
such minerals. In the 1980s, for example, South Africa held 80 per cent of
the world's reserves of platinum and was the single largest producer of the

metal. Japan in turn obtained 36 per cent of its platinum imports from South Africa (Ampiah 2002a). In addition, the relatively high level of economic growth that South Africa experienced also made it an important importer of Japanese industrial material and equipment. Yet it was exactly the persistence of these relations that was to become Japan's Achilles' heel in the rest of Africa, particularly as international censure of South Africa's regime mounted in the 1970s and 1980s, culminating in the imposition of sanctions. Morikawa (1997) designated this as Japan's *dual policy* towards Africa – its use of economic carrots to black African states which provided it with much-needed strategic resources or with political succour, and the provision of economic appeasements to objections raised against Japan's expanding trade with apartheid South Africa. Under increasing pressure from other African countries, and for fear of jeopardizing its alliance with the Afro-Asian bloc (and hence their support for its UN aspirations), Japan did finally levy sanctions against South Africa, and trade between the two substantially declined by the end of the 1980s.

The end of apartheid has seen a reinvigoration of economic and political ties with new linkages between the two countries aimed at founding ties of economic cooperation through enhanced two-way trade, and investment in South Africa. This is reflected in both the distinctive aid relationship the Japanese government has established with South Africa and the commercial and strategic stakes already vested in the country.

Aid

In 1994 the Japanese government announced measures to aid South Africa with an assistance package amounting to US$1.3 billion. It was a significant move for two reasons. First, the Japanese government diverted from its usual protocol of committing aid only upon the request of a recipient government. Second, the aid package considerably retracted from Japan's characteristic disbursements to other SSA states. It constituted substantially less concessional ODA (US$300m) than non-concessional, market-rate loan financing from the Japan Export–Import Bank (JEXIM), and a credit line for trade and overseas investment insurance, both of which amounted to US$500m. Moreover, the ODA package had a low grant element – much less of the ODA was destined for grants and technical assistance than for yen loans extended for the construction of infrastructure projects.

Closer scrutiny of the implementation of the JEXIM portion of Japan's aid reveals a further emphasis on infrastructure development. By February 1998 JEXIM loans had been taken up by three South African parastatals: to improve the transition and distribution line grid (extended to ESKOM, the national electricity supplier); to improve and construct railways and ports (extended to Transnet, which provides, maintains and monitors national transportation networks); and to foster small, medium and micro enterprises and agricultural modernization, and improve economic infrastructure (extended to the Development Bank of Southern Africa, a wholesale lender to the Southern African region). A fourth loan was disbursed to another parastatal, the Industrial Development Corporation (IDC) for 'export financing for South African companies to purchase machinery and services from Japan'.[15]

In 1999 the Japanese government indicated that, given South Africa's relative economic advance, it would not qualify for further grant aid disbursals from Japan, although the country would continue to provide technical assistance and concessional loans (*Independent on Sunday*, 21 March 1999). This was reflected in Japan's second aid disbursal to South Africa that year, which amounted to US$1.5bn. Two-thirds (US$1bn) of this package was destined for trade and investment insurance, while the remainder was in the form of yen loans (US$400m) and grants (US$100m) (Alden 2002). However, the aid relationship between the two countries has been somewhat strained because of a wariness on the part of South African officials about the motivations behind the Japanese disbursals (Osada 2001). Indeed, there have been suspicions that the disbursals were primarily aimed at serving Japanese commercial interests (Alden 2002). Criticism was also aimed at the costs that the non-grant portion of the package presented to South Africa. Thus by the end of the 1990s the bulk of Japan's initial 1994 aid package had not been taken up by South Africa, mainly because all of the loan financing that the Japanese government makes available is yen-dominated. To South Africa, drawing upon the yen loans poses an exchange risk, and hence was relatively expensive.[16] This has proved a point of contention between South African and Japanese officials (Alden 2002).

Nonetheless, the volume of aid disbursals (twice that provided to Kenya and Tanzania, the next-largest African recipients of Japanese aid) and the fact that these disbursals were made at a time of economic downsizing in Japan were a clear indication that it considered South Africa its central focus in Africa. This was borne out by the country's subsequent economic and political engagements with South Africa. In 2001, for instance, following Prime Minister Mori's visit, the Japanese ambassador to South Africa stated that, while 'Japan manifests her strong commitment in Africa as a whole, Japan considers South Africa as the main partner in pursuing her African policy' (in Enoki 2001).

Japan's emphasis on South Africa relates to the latter's economic prowess in the African continent, but crucially also to the political and moral stature the country has attained internationally. Political ties in many regards constitute the weightier aspect of the relationship between the two countries. Yet there is an important element of Japan's economic policy towards Africa that revolves around the fostering of (purportedly mutually beneficial) trade and investment opportunities. Japan's entire involvement in the TICAD process professes a desire to support economic expansion for the African continent. Its economic ties with South Africa in this regard, again, are central.

Trade and investment

Total trade between Japan and South Africa has risen substantially over the past decade, from a level of R9.7bn in 1992[17] to R36.5bn in 2001 (Embassy of Japan 1998; *Financial Mail*, 25 October 2002). Overall this makes Japan South Africa's fourth-largest trade partner after Germany, the US and Britain. In the East Asian region, however, Japan is South Africa's top trade partner, accounting for 38.7 per cent of all the trade with this region in 1997.

The trade balance is weighted in South Africa's favour. In 2001 the total value of the goods exported to Japan from South Africa was R22bn, while imports to South Africa were valued at R14.7bn (*Financial Mail*, 25 October 2002). The nature of the trade between the two countries has not altered considerably since the 1980s, however. The bulk of South Africa's exports to Japan are raw materials, ore and mineral fuels, iron and steel, and agricultural goods, while Japan's exports to South Africa mainly comprise machinery and equipment. Importantly, the largest component of South Africa's present exports to Japan is platinum; in 2001 the value of platinum exports to Japan was R11bn, half of the total exports from South Africa (*Financial Mail*, 25 October 2002).

Investments from Japan have also increased, from a zero level of growth in 1992 (mainly due to the sanctions of the 1980s) to a cumulative value of approximately R4bn (*Pretoria News*, 27 September 2001). The pattern of Japanese investments in South Africa is of a very particular nature. First, investments have primarily been made in sectors where Japan has a trade interest. The bulk of Japanese investments over the past decade have, for instance, been in the ferrochrome, lower-value coal, manganese, ferro-alloy and manganese metal sectors – that is, products utilized in the manufacturing industry – while some have been made in telecommunication products. Second, investments are mainly in the form of joint ventures with South African companies.[18] This is largely due to an attempt on the part of Japanese companies to offset economic risks, yet it has meant that Japanese investments have occurred at a much slower pace than initially anticipated by the South African government (Alden 2002).

Since the mid-1990s an interesting trend in one element of the investment ties between the two countries has emerged, one that is also starting to find reflection in their trade relationship. This centres around South Africa's automotive industry, a sector where, due to the long-established presence of several of the global motor corporations, South Africa has developed a reasonable competitive advantage, particularly in automotive assembly and the manufacturing of motor car components. In the post-apartheid era, Japanese investment in the South African motor industry started to intensify in 1996 when large-scale investments were undertaken by three companies: Toyota Motor Corporation, Nissan Motor Corporation and Bridgestone. Together these companies spent R1.2bn in the South African economy that year (*The Star*, 16 May 1997). At present investments in the automotive sector constitute more than half of total Japanese investments in South Africa (*The Star*, 7 August 2000).

Such investments have had important effects in enabling South Africa to increase its value-added exports to Japan, at least in the automotive sector. Between 1998 and 2001 auto exports from South Africa to Japan have increased thirty-fold year on year (*Financial Mail*, 25 October 2002). In 2001 the value of South African exports to Japan was nearly R2bn, still well-exceeded by Japan's automotive exports to South Africa for that year, which were valued at R7.5bn. But this represents a clear strengthening of South Africa's auto trade position *vis-à-vis* Japan. Moreover, automotive exports now make up a very significant portion of exports to Japan, second only to platinum. This is indicative of a significant shift in the strategic dynamics of the trade relationship between the two countries. Given the central location of the automotive sector in the industrial fabric of South Africa, and its ties with the Southern African region, this shift also portends the systematic penetration of Japanese automotive companies into the regional market, with South Africa as a base. Concomitantly, it draws the South African industry into the global Japanese automotive production system.

Early indications of this are found in the investment behaviour of Toyota Motor Corporation (TMC) which, since its initial large-scale venture in 1996, when it acquired a bigger share in Toyota South Africa,[19] has taken several other steps to implant itself more fully in the South African industry. In 2000 it entered into a joint venture with Toyota South Africa and another Japanese company to produce catalytic converters in South Africa. The joint venture was aimed at feeding Toyota's global network of catalytic production (*Business Day*, 12 July 2000). In 2002 TMC acquired a controlling stake in the South African company when it increased its ownership to 75 per cent. This step, intended to expand Toyota's export scope within and beyond Africa (*Business Day*, 18 July 2002), was augmented with a further investment early in 2003 to establish a programme for the export of vehicles from South Africa to Europe, Africa, Australia and the Caribbean (*Business Day*, 16 March 2003).

Other large Japanese companies have also used South Africa as an entry point into the rest of Africa, particularly Southern Africa.[20] For example, Keidanren, the Federation of Economic Organizations, one of the most influential bodies in Japan, has identified South Africa as a foremost destination for future Japanese investments, primarily for its richness in minerals and the access it provides to the resource base in the Southern Africa region (*Sunday Independent*, 20 February 2000). To some commentators (e.g. Ampiah 2002a; Draper 1998) patterns of Japanese investments in South Africa significantly resonate with Japan's post-war investment activities in East Asia, which were closely tied with a programme of industrialization that Japan followed in the East Asian region. Hatch and Yamamura (1996) argue that the development of the countries of the

Asian region has come about through the incorporation of these countries into a Japanese-dominated production complex. The authors maintain that the particular nature of the Japanese state – an intra-penetrated alliance of government and business elite – has been regionalized as they forged links with government officials and business elites in other countries in the region. Thus a network has evolved through the simultaneous process of Japanese foreign direct investment in these countries, as Japanese industries and firms shifted production off-shore, and the contriving of political ties with host regimes through the extension of aid. This is commonly termed the 'flying geese' pattern of development. According to this view, development in East Asia was the outcome of a regionally interlinked process of industrialization with its origin in Japan, which through Japanese investments spread concentrically outwards. Similarly, Japanese investment in South Africa, it is contended, is aimed at developing an industrial base from which Japanese goods can be exported to other parts of the world.

The large infrastructural and loans element of Japan's aid packages to South Africa suggests that the Japanese government also views South Africa as the major launching base for its development projects in Southern Africa. Indeed, official aid documents proclaim South Africa as constituting a viable foundation for propelling a programme of economic cooperation based on aid to, trade with and investment in Southern Africa, similar to Japan's involvement in East Asia's development (e.g. JICA 2000). Ampiah (2002b), however, notes that to date there has been an incongruity between the activities of the Japanese government and those of Japanese companies in Southern Africa. While corporations have shown an interest in investing in the region, they have not received adequate financial and logistical support from the Japanese government. This means that even though the government directs a considerable portion of its ODA for infrastructural developments in Southern Africa, it will not induce the broad-based investment by Japanese companies that is sought by the government.

Furthermore, despite the recent attention to the South African automotive industry, Japanese investment in South Africa is still heavily weighted towards projects of mineral extraction and processing, and while there is some move to further develop a market for Japanese consumer goods there is no indication that Japanese companies have any intention to divert their investment stakes in South Africa away from raw materials (including food products) and minerals in the foreseeable future.[21] This means that Japan's economic participation in South Africa, and more broadly the Southern African region, is still largely geared towards serving Japan's strategic interests.[22]

In many respects, Japan's political involvement in the region, and its ties with South Africa, can also be read in this way. There is a close interplay in the external objectives of the two countries. This, and the implications it carries for the remainder of the African continent, is discussed more fully below.

Nurturing political ties

After the systematic political withdrawal of Japan from South Africa during the 1980s, diplomatic ties were re-established in 1992. This set into momentum a series of actions by both sides to strengthen political bonds – what one Japanese official has termed 'the normalization of relations'. In 1994 Japan lifted its restrictions on travel to or from South Africa, and since then several high-ranking officials from South Africa have visited Japan. Although this included a state visit by President Nelson Mandela in 1995, the real cementing of ties occurred with then Deputy-President Thabo Mbeki's two visits to Japan in 1998. This is encapsulated in the statement of a Japanese official, according to whom Nelson Mandela's 1995 visit was 'only ceremonial', while that of Mbeki was 'very substantive,' with a 'success rating of nearly 100 per cent'.[23] Japanese policy elites warmed to Mbeki's depiction of the 'new mood in Africa', the rise of African leaders with renewed commitments to democracy and good governance, and proposals to reform regional organizations in Africa.[24]

Japan's present bilateral political relations with South Africa are driven through the Japan–South Africa Partnership Forum, a regular gathering of senior government officials through which the two countries collaborate in areas of international relations, trade and investment, economic cooperation, science and technology, and cultural exchanges. The initial founding of this Forum in 1998 was highly significant, since Japan usually conducts its bilateral relations by establishing a 'working dialogue' between its own bureaucracies and that of other states. Two fundamental purposes underlie the Forum. The first is to foster cooperation on multilateral issues. As a spin-off of Japan's own multilateral activism and South Africa's increased use of multilateral institutions to attain foreign policy goals,[25] the Forum seeks to synthesize the two countries' policies on issues such as nuclear disarmament, the banning of anti-personnel mines, democratization and human rights. A key element of this cooperation is the mutual support of each other's bids for a permanent seat on the UN Security Council.[26]

The second main objective of the Forum, and one where the full import of Japan–South Africa relations shines through, is the so-called 'Common Agenda' for Africa, an effort to coalesce mutual objectives regarding Africa's development into a joint programme. Over a number of years this Common Agenda has found expression in Japan's sponsorship of the TICAD process and South Africa's role in the NEPAD initiative. The vision of NEPAD's promoters (among whom Thabo Mbeki is a primary figure) of a 'new Africa' and 'African solutions to African problems' (see Taylor and Nel 2002) seems to mirror Japan's own self-help agenda for Africa. South Africa has played an effective part in steering Japan's policy towards Africa through initial espousals of the 'African Renaissance' and later the establishment of the NEPAD. South African elites have also capitalized on the willingness of the Japanese government to provide money and expertise for Africa's development.

Japan's approach to partnership with South Africa rests on an assessment of the cognate economic position both occupy in their respective regions, and hence the shared obligations to advance prosperity throughout these regions. But it also extends deeper, encompassing sentiments about both countries' unique location in the international system, analogous experiences of that system, and a shared necessity to balance a non-Western identity with efforts to insert itself into a Western milieu. This is encapsulated in the following statement by the Japanese ambassador to South Africa, Yasukuni Enoki (2001), who contended,

> both of us have been challenged by the need to harmonize Westernization with the preservation of traditional culture ... [As] a consequence of the above, both of us have an identity problem. If we succeed in creating our own respective identities, while putting one foot in one world and the other foot in another, we will be in a very important position to bridge the two worlds; Africa and the Western world in your case, Asia and the Western world in our case, or more broadly for both of us between the North and the South.

The ambassador's statement is an entreaty for the establishment of a global partnership between South Africa and Japan, based on shared non-Western identity and, stemming from this, mutual objectives, roles and responsibilities in the international system. Japan also invokes a professed African–Asian nexus in its broader dealings with the continent. Ostensibly, however, Japan gains more from such an appeal than African countries, particularly given that the present-day application of a purported African–Asian identity still largely echoes Japan's use of the Afro-Asian bloc in earlier times in an attempt to secure itself a seat on the UN Security Council. A clear illustration of this was found in 1996 when Foreign Minister Ikeda pledged financial assistance to the SADC in return for supporting Japan's bid to obtain permanent membership of the Security Council (*Kyodo*, 1 May 1996). This contradicted Japan's claims that philanthropy underlies its recent initiatives in Africa and also raises questions about whether some of the more substantive goals of the TICAD (i.e. assisting democratization, governance and the entrenchment of norms and institutions) are attainable.

Conclusion: Japan and Africa into the new millennium

The waxing of relations between Japan and Africa over the past three decades is largely due to changes in the external aims of the former. Nonetheless, particularly in recent years, African agency has been an important factor in the contriving of Japan–Africa relations. The role of South Africa in this has been especially important. On the political front South Africa and Japan have found a synergy in their foreign policy ambitions:

South Africa in its attempts to establish itself as a world paragon, and Japan in trying to attain international political prowess. The common ground is provided in the emergence of both as significant voices in multilateral forums.

The South African government's adoption of policies that echo the ethos of the 'Washington Consensus' (see Taylor 2001) has afforded it the assenting attention of influential industrialized countries. In this context, South Africa constitutes a key developing 'partner' for Japan. However, paradoxically, Japan's closer ties with South Africa are in stark contrast to its claims that Africa inhabits a central position in its foreign policy. Indeed, Japan's emphasis on South Africa is a perpetuation of its earlier 'dual policy' towards Africa, where South Africa is accorded a favoured position because of its economic and political importance. It is questionable if this situation, beyond fulfilling South Africa's goals, benefits the rest of Africa. Indeed, Japan's economic presence in the rest of the continent is still limited and primarily dictated by its strategic and resource interests.

The legacy of Japan's recent policy rhetoric concerning Africa will, however, persist: the continent still provides Japan with a serviceable ally in its search for international stature. Given that Japan has always applied, with relative success, a 'key country approach' to Africa, its recent focus on South Africa is not likely to imperil the political gain Japan can draw from the remainder of the continent. Indeed, Japan, like China (see Chapter 4) has effectively utilized its multilateral development policy through initiatives such as the TICAD as a lobbying instrument for African (and other) votes. Nevertheless, shrouding political goals within development policy rhetoric is likely to be a continued policy instrument of the Japanese government. Moreover, given that many of Japan's political relationships with African states are founded upon a supposedly common 'non-Western' identity, however contradictory and opportunistic this may be in practice, Japan's stance towards Africa will continue to be encapsulated within a rhetorical Afro-Asian nexus.

Notes

1 Although it will be used interchangeably in this chapter, a distinction needs to be drawn between Official Development Assistance (ODA) and aid. The former involves the transfer of resources from the government of one country to that of another, on concessional terms, and with the explicit objective of promoting welfare and economic development. Aid has the same basic purpose, but is extended at less concessionary terms and also comprises financial transactions between the public and private sectors of countries.

2 The Japanese government has traditionally justified its provision of development assistance on two grounds: that the problems of the developing countries constitute a serious threat to the world, and that the economic development of poor countries would contribute to global economic development, and therefore that of Japan (MOFA 1996a).

3 The concept of 'middle power' has traditionally been closely tied with the hegemonic equilibrium of the Cold War era. In this context, middle powers, states with medium political and economic capacities, generally fulfil a diplomatic or

other balancing function in the international system (Taylor 2001; Van der Westhuizen 1998). The concept of middlepowermanship has been applied to Japan by Cox (1989) who argues that that country's increased utilization of international organizations as diplomatic instruments, its voluminous increase in aid disbursals and its outspokenness on multilateral issues, qualifies Japan as a middle power.

4 In the parlance of Japan's aid bureaucracies, North African states are designated as part of the Middle East region. Aid disbursals to these countries are hence not reflected in official statistics on aid to Africa.

5 The Afro-Asian bloc of the UNGA had its origins in the Bandung Conference of 1955, which saw the establishment of the Non-Aligned Movement.

6 Japan's alliance with the Afro-Asian bloc was one of mutual convenience, for once it became a member of the permanent secretariat in 1957, Japan, as a member of the developed community, provided a useful ally in the decolonization movement which surged in the UN (Ampiah 1996).

7 These were: to reach an 80 per cent completion rate in primary education, to halve illiteracy rates, and to attain gender equality in enrolments in primary and secondary schools by 2005; and by 2015 to eliminate gender disparities in school enrolments, and attain universal primary education. An undertaking was also made to reduce the number of women living in poverty by 66 per cent (MOFA 1998).

8 In 2000, as host of the Kyushu–Okinawa G-8 summit, for example, Japan invited the leaders of South Africa, Nigeria and Algeria to promote their initiative on African development (known initially as the African Renaissance, and later formalized as the New Partnership for Africa's Development (NEPAD)) at the summit meeting.

9 The ODA Charter expounds four principles in accordance with which Japan would disburse its aid. These principles state that recipient countries should commit themselves to the adoption of free market economies and the promotion of democratization and human rights; emphasis should be placed on environmental conservation in developmental efforts; finally, ODA should not be used for military purposes, or towards the aggravation of international conflicts. Relatedly, recipient countries should curtail their military expenditures (MOFA 1996b: 211).

10 This philosophy stems from Japan's own development experience in the nineteenth and early twentieth centuries. It infuses all of Japan's aid and other external economic involvements. As an illustration, since the expansion of the Heavily Indebted Poor Countries (HIPC) Initiative at the G-7 Summit in Cologne in 1999, Japan has been criticized for not fully participating in it. While not opposed to the Enhanced HIPC Initiative, Japan's position is that the promotion of 'ownership' and capacity building in development should be the key elements of debt relief (MOFA 2002). Until the beginning of 2003 it administered its debt relief through its 'Grant Aid for Debt Relief' scheme, which still placed a repayment obligation on debtor countries. The Japanese government had long maintained that it encourages fiscal discipline and a sense of 'self-help' in developing countries (e.g. MOFA 1996b).

11 IDEA was launched by means of a ministerial meeting in August 2002 between the ASEAN states, Japan, the People's Republic of China and the Republic of Korea. It is primarily geared towards developing a new development agenda for the East Asian region that is partly based on challenges in the present economic and political environment, but also draws from previous development efforts (MOFA 2003b).

12 For instance, the promotion of the IDEA formed part of Japan's contribution at the 2002 G-8 Summit held in Kananaskis, Canada, and the World Summit on Sustainable Development in Johannesburg in August 2002, and will also form

part of the TICAD III. This externalization of IDEA aims at making a 'joint intellectual input based on [East Asia's] development expertise ... to the international discussion on development' (MOFA 2003b).

13 Economic cooperation is the Japanese state's denotation of its particular form of aid provision. It refers both to ODA – comprised of grants, loans and technical assistance – which is characterized by its concessional nature, and the non-concessional loans extended by the Japanese government. However, private investment flows may also be included under the rubric of economic cooperation, and in official Japanese aid circles these are all incorporated under the umbrella designation of ODA (Koppel and Orr 1993; Ueda 1995). This terminology contrasts sharply with that of the Development Assistance Committee which stringently delineates ODA to refer only to those resource flows provided by the public sector of a developed country to that of an eligible developing country.

14 As an illustration, although Japan's cumulative foreign investment in the period 1993–5 reached US$75.8 billion, only 3 per cent of this was directed towards SSA countries (figures calculated from statistics from the International Finance Bureau of Japan Ministry of Finance). Japan's trade statistics with SSA are commensurately low (between 1990 and 1994 only 1.2 per cent of Japanese exports found their way to African markets).

15 Information was obtained from the South Africa Department of Finance, *Status Report: Japanese Assistance Package: February 1998*.

16 Personal communication with official from South African Department of Finance, May 1998.

17 Approximately US$3.3bn. In 1992 the South African currency was valued at approximately R3.00 to the US dollar. The rand has seen a steady depreciation throughout the 1990s. In 2001 it traded at R12.00 to the dollar, while in 2003 it was valued at R8.00.

18 The largest joint venture that a Japanese company is involved in is in fact not in South Africa, but in Mozambique. Mozal is an aluminium smelter plant, the largest of its kind in the world. It involves Mitsubishi, which has a 25 per cent stake in the project, the Mozambican government (4 per cent), Billiton, a South African company (47 per cent), and the Industrial Development Corporation of South Africa, which holds 24 per cent of the operation.

19 Until the early 1990s, Toyota SA was wholly owned by a South African family who gradually relinquished their controlling share in the company. In October 1996 the Toyota Motor Corporation increased its share in the South African company from 9.7 to 37.5 per cent by buying up the shares of one of the largest black empowerment companies in South Africa, Johnnic.

20 Among the most important Japanese companies that have invested in South Africa are the Bank of Japan, Hitachi, Honda, Komatsu, Mitsui, NEC, NGK, Nippon Paper, Sanyo, Sony, Sumitomo and Toshiba.

21 Author's interview with an official from the Japan External Trade Organization, November 2002. JETRO is a state institution with the primary function of promoting Japanese exports by fostering business ties between Japanese and other companies.

22 It brings into question the purported objective of an expansive approach to assist Southern Africa's development. At the same time it should be noted that Japan's 'comprehensive approach' to Southern Africa also always had the potential of transmitting to Southern Africa many of the negative facets of Japan's activities in East Asia, which were largely an extension of the type of state developmentalism practised in Japan (see Hatch and Yamamura 1996 and Pempel 1987).

23 Yasushi Naito, Political Affairs attaché, Embassy of Japan, South Africa.

24 This initial warming of relations was followed up with Prime Minister Mori's visit in January 2001, an official state visit by Thabo Mbeki in October of that year, and a brief visit by Prime Minister Junichiro Koizumi in 2002.
25 Nel *et al.* (2001) note how a high level of activism in multilateral institutions (since 1995 South Africa has for instance assumed the chairmanship of, amongst others, the Non-Aligned Movement, the Southern African Development Community, the Commonwealth, the United Nations Commission on Human Rights, UNCTAD and the African Union) has characterized South Africa's post-apartheid foreign policy. Multilateralism is generally used as a means to attain wider international political objectives, most central of which, in the Mbeki era, is the economic and political revival of the African continent.
26 Japan–South Africa Joint Communiqué, 'Japan–South Africa partnership in the new century,' Japan MOFA, October 2001.

References

Adem, S. (2001) 'Emerging Trends in Japan–Africa relations: An African Perspective,' *African Studies Quarterly*, 5, 2, http://web.africa.ufl.edu/asq/v5/v5i2.htm

Alden, C. (ed.) (2002) *Distant Mirrors: Japan and South Africa in a Globalising World*, London: Ashgate.

Ampiah, K. (1996) 'Japanese Aid to Tanzania: A Study of the Political Marketing of Japan in Africa', *African Affairs*, 95: 107–24.

—— (1997) *The Dynamics of Japan's Relations with Africa – South Africa, Tanzania and Nigeria*, London: Routledge.

—— (2002a) 'Japanese investments in South Africa, 1992–1996: The state, private enterprise and strategic minerals,' in C. Alden (ed.) *Distant Mirrors: Japan and South Africa in a Globalising World*, London: Ashgate, pp. 59–82.

—— (2002b) *Japan and ODA: Emerging Trends in Japanese Official Development Assistance to Africa*, London: The Daiwa Anglo-Japanese Foundation.

Bernard, M. and J. Ravenhill (1995) 'Beyond Product Cycles and Flying Geese – Regionalization, Hierarchy, and the Industrialization of East Asia', *World Politics*, 47: 171–209.

Carim, X. and H. Solomon (1994) 'A Short History of South African–Japanese Relations and Prospects for the Future', *Politeia*, 13: 32–49.

Cornelissen, S. and I. Taylor (2000) 'The Political Economy of Chinese and Japanese Linkages with Africa: A Comparative Perspective', *Pacific Review*, 13: 615–33.

Cox, R. (1989) 'Middlepowermanship, Japan and Future World Order', *International Journal*, 44: 823–62.

Development Assistance Committee (2003) *Aid and Debt Statistics, Donor Aid Charts*, http://www.oecd.org/dac

Draper, P. (1998) *The Impact of Japanese Investment on South Africa Viewed through East Asian Lenses*, Johannesburg: South African Network for Economic Research working paper, mimeo.

Embassy of Japan, South Africa (no date) 'Japan's Policy towards Africa'.

—— (1998) 'Bilateral Relations between Japan and the Republic of South Africa', 6 March.

Enoki, Y. (2001) 'Japan's African Policy: Beyond the Japanese Prime Minister's First Visit to Africa,' speech of 24 July, Pretoria, Embassy of Japan, South Africa.

Hanabusa, M. (1991) 'A Japanese Perspective on Aid and Development', in S. Islam (ed.) *Yen for Development – Japanese Foreign Aid and the Politics of Burden-Sharing*, New York: Council on Foreign Relations, pp. 88–104.

Hatch, W. and K. Yamamura (1996) *Asia in Japan's Embrace – Building a Regional Production Alliance*, Cambridge: Cambridge University Press.

Inukai, I. (1993) 'Why Aid and Why Not? Japan and Sub-Saharan Africa', in B. M. Koppel and R. M. Orr (eds) *Japan's Foreign Aid – Power and Policy in a New Era*, Boulder: Westview Press, pp. 252–74.

Islam, S. (ed.) (1991) *Yen for Development: Japanese Foreign Aid and the Politics of Burden-Sharing*, New York: Council on Foreign Relations.

JICA (Japan International Cooperation Agency) (2000) *The Study on Japan's Official Development Assistance to Southern African Countries, Volume 1*, Tokyo: JICA.

Koppel, B. M. and R. M. Orr (eds) (1993) *Japan's Foreign Aid – Power and Policy in a New Era*, Boulder: Westview Press.

(MOFA) Ministry of Foreign Affairs of Japan (1993) *The Tokyo Conference on African Development*, Tokyo: MOFA.

—— (1996a) *Official Development Assistance Summary, 1996*, Tokyo: MOFA.

—— (1996b) *ODA Annual Report, 1996*, Tokyo: MOFA.

—— (1997) *ODA Summary, 1997*, Tokyo: MOFA.

—— (1998) *TICAD II Tokyo Agenda for Action for African Development towards the 21st Century*, Tokyo: MOFA.

—— (2002) *Japan's Development Policy*, Tokyo: MOFA.

—— (2003a) *Development Issues in Developing Countries and Official Development Assistance*, http://www.mofa.go.jp

—— (2003b) *Initiative for Development in East Asia Ministerial Meeting – Outline and Evaluation*, http://www.mofa.go.jp

Morikawa, J. (1997) *Japan and Africa: Big Business and Diplomacy*, London: Hurst.

Moss, J. and J. Ravenhill (1985) *Emerging Japanese Aid and Economic Influence in Africa: Implications for the United States*, University of California, Berkeley: Institute of International Studies.

Nel, P., I. Taylor and J. Van der Westhuizen (eds) (2001) *South Africa's Multilateral Diplomacy and Global Change: The Limits of Reformism*, Aldershot: Ashgate.

Nester, W. R. (1991) 'Japanese Neomercantilism toward Sub-Saharan Africa', *Africa Today*, 3rd Quarter: 31–51.

—— (1992) *Japan and the Third World: Patterns, Power, Prospects*, Basingstoke: Macmillan.

Orr, R. (1990) *The Emergence of Japanese Aid Power*, Columbia: Columbia University Press.

Osada, M. (1997) 'Sanctions and Honorary Whites: Diplomatic Policies and Economic Realities in Japan–South Africa Relations', MA dissertation, Johannesburg: University of the Witwatersrand.

—— (2001) 'South Africa's Relations with Japan', in J. Broderick, G. Burford and G. Freer (eds) *South Africa's Foreign Policy: Dilemmas of a New Democracy*, New York: Palgrave, pp. 99–117.

Pempel, T. J. (1987) 'The Unbundling of "Japan Inc.": The Changing Dynamics of Japanese Policy Formation', *Journal of Japanese Studies*, 13: 271–306.

Rix, A. (1993) *Japan's Foreign Aid Challenge*, London: Routledge.

Söderberg, M. (ed.) (1996) *The Business of Japanese Foreign Aid – Five Case Studies from Asia*, London: Routledge.

Taylor, I. (2001) *Stuck in Middle GEAR: South Africa's Post-Apartheid Foreign Relations*, Westport, Connecticut: Praeger.

Taylor, I. and P. Nel (2002) ' "Getting the Rhetoric Right", Getting the Strategy Wrong: "New Africa", Globalisation and the Confines of Elite Reformism', *Third World Quarterly*, 23: 163–80.

Ueda, H. (1995) 'Japan's aid policies and institutions', *Journal of International Development*, 7: 245–51.

Ueki, Y. (1993) 'Japan's UN Diplomacy: Sources of Passivism and Activism', in G. L. Curtis (ed.) *Japan's Foreign Policy after the Cold War: Coping with Change*, New York: M. E. Sharpe, pp. 347–70.

Van der Westhuizen, J. (1998) 'South Africa's Emergence as a Middle Power', *Third World Quarterly*, 19: 435–55.

Yasutomo, D. T. (1995) *The New Multilateralism in Japan's Foreign Policy*, London: Macmillan.

7 Canada and Africa

Activist aspirations in straitened circumstances

David Black

From a traditional realist perspective, emphasizing instrumental rationality, one of the enduring mysteries of post-1960 Canadian foreign policy has been the prominence of Africa within it. Through a series of controversies and challenges, ranging from South Africa's departure/expulsion from the Commonwealth in 1960 through to the G-7/8's efforts to craft a collective response to African leaders' New Partnership for Africa's Development (NEPAD) initiative at the 2003 Summit in Kananaskis, Canadian politicians and makers of foreign policy have played leading roles. Their engagement with Africa has resonated in the Canadian mass media and among the country's attentive public, notably including a wide range of non-state actors in civil society.

What makes this preoccupation with Africa somewhat mysterious is that it persists despite the absence of many of the sinews that bind most of the other external powers treated in this volume to the continent. Canada, itself a settler Dominion within the British Empire, was never a colonial power in Africa. Partly because of this, Canadian trade and investment links with the continent are relatively shallow, and constitute a tiny share of its global trade and investment flows. Given the continent's geographic remoteness from Canadian territory, as well as Canada's relative lack of global strategic importance or interests, it has never had the direct geopolitical motivations for engagement with Africa that have moved policy-makers elsewhere.

It is not surprising, in this context, that during the first half of the 1990s Africa appeared destined for steady marginalization among Canadian foreign policy priorities. By the latter half of the decade, however, this trend had been reversed; and by the early years of the new millennium the continent was, if only intermittently, close to the top of the Canadian government's discursive and visible priorities, at least. One purpose of this chapter, therefore, is to provide an explanation for the continuing prominence of Africa within Canada – an explanation that rests, to a considerable extent, on the degree to which the former has helped define a compelling self-image of the latter.

Second, and illustrating the elements of this explanation, I will sketch and assess four key aspects of Canada's continental engagement: multilateral diplomacy and (within it) elite political leadership; the rise and implications of the 'human security agenda'; development assistance (ODA); and the role of Canadian corporate investment and debates concerning Corporate Social Responsibility (CSR). This discussion will lead to an overall assessment of Canada's impact on Africa, and the politics surrounding it. In short, this country's persistent, if somewhat inconstant, activist aspirations have been marked by some success in terms of agenda setting and normative and institutional innovation. However, they have been constrained by the limited and diminishing range of 'hard' policy resources it has been able to 'bring to the table' (developmental, diplomatic and military) and, in this context, the absence of sustained followership towards its leadership efforts. Canada's role has also been largely consistent with Western hegemonic aspirations in Africa, in terms of political and economic restructuring.

The trajectory of the 1990s: towards, and then away from, marginalization

As noted above, the early/mid-1990s were marked by apparent signs of the long-term marginalization of African issues among Canadian foreign policy priorities. Like most countries and more severely than many within the OECD, Canada was afflicted with a deep economic malaise during these years, marked by slow growth, relatively high unemployment and large fiscal deficits. In the prevailing neo-liberal mood of the time, the Liberal government that came to power under Prime Minister Jean Chrétien in 1993 embarked upon a combined austerity and trade- and investment-promotion effort that bode ill for Africa.

In the absence of robust trade and investment relations,[1] Canada's links with African countries had depended on aid-based relationships for much of their substance. However, in the austerity years of the 1990s, Canadian aid spending suffered draconian cuts, even by comparative international standards. ODA is estimated to have decreased by 33 per cent in real terms between 1988–9 and 1997–8, compared with a 22 per cent decline in defence spending and cuts of 5 per cent to all other programmes in the same period (see Morrison 1998: 413). The aid to GNP ratio declined from 0.49 per cent in 1991–2 to 0.25 per cent in 2000, dropping Canada well down the OECD donor 'league table' (sixteenth of twenty-two states in 2000). Moreover, aid to Africa was hit hardest of all, with declines in bilateral aid between 1990 and 2000 of 7.2 per cent for Africa, 3.5 per cent for the Americas, and 5.3 per cent for Asia (NSI 2003: 78). The disarray caused by these cuts to Canadian aid programming throughout the continent was considerable, and seemed to indicate a lack of commitment to long-term relationships.

At the same time, the government pushed aggressively to enhance Canadian links with both Latin America and the Asia–Pacific region. Much of the push was commercial, since both regions were viewed as holding considerable promise for trade and investment growth. The clearest sign of this priority was the mounting of several high-profile 'Team Canada' trade missions to both regions, involving a broad cross-section of political and business leaders and led by the Prime Minister himself. Africa, by contrast, has received only much smaller and lower-level delegations, such as that led by the Minister of International Trade to South Africa, Nigeria and Senegal in November 2002 (DFAIT 2002). But enhanced political and diplomatic links were also pursued, through Canada's accession to and activism within the Organization of American States from 1990 onwards, for example, and its hosting of the APEC forum in Vancouver in 1997 (Canada's 'Year of the Asia Pacific', as declared by the Department of Foreign Affairs and International Trade [DFAIT]).

However, Africa never threatened to disappear from the Canadian public imaginary, principally because of the riveting disasters in Somalia and Rwanda.[2] By the latter part of the 1990s, African issues were routinely rising towards the top of the visible foreign policy agenda,[3] culminating in the Prime Minister's vigorous and sustained diplomatic effort to focus the attention of the G-7 on Africa at the 2002 Summit. What accounts for this return to prominence?

Underpinning Africa's (re)prioritization is the persistence, and perhaps even limited resurgence, of what Cranford Pratt has termed 'humane internationalism' as a key element of the Canadian political culture (and, Pratt argues, that of several other traditional northern 'middle powers' – see Pratt 1989; also Munton 2002/3). This he defines as a sense of ethical obligation to 'those beyond our borders who are severely oppressed or who live in conditions of unremitting poverty' (Pratt 2000: 37). While the relative strength of this impulse is open to question, it means that activism in response to suffering, of which there has been all too much in Africa over the past decade, continues to resonate in Canada. Government initiatives in Africa have therefore been widely supported, indeed expected – even if they have usually been inadequately resourced and sustained. There is, of course, a troubling side to this impulse. Laura MacDonald, drawing on postcolonial insights and assumptions, has argued compellingly that there is a clear connection between the moral impulse in post-Second World War Canadian foreign policy (as manifested in aid policies and other policies towards Africa, for example) and the 'paternalistic and universalizing beliefs', frequently tinged with racism, that underpinned Canadian missionary activity prior to this (MacDonald 1995: 130). Regardless of whether one stresses this 'dark side' or the more genuinely solidaristic motives that co-exist in this tradition, however, the general point is that Canadian policy towards Africa is arguably as much about *us* – about our own moral self-affirmation and sense of collective identity and purpose – as it is about the African countries and people Canadians have engaged.

In this context, organizational and political imperatives have emerged which tend to buttress an activist Canadian role in Africa. From 'below', a relatively large and robust community of internationally oriented NGOs has developed over the past four decades, with a shared emphasis on justice and human rights in foreign policy, and a long-standing interest in Africa (see Tomlinson 2002). This community was battered and weakened through the 1990s, both financially and intellectually, but remains a vital source of pressure for engagement with Africa and, in some cases, a vehicle through which initiatives have been undertaken.

From 'above', the persistence of humane internationalism has meant that a succession of political leaders have been inclined towards 'initiativemanship' on high-profile moral issues, many of which have been directly or indirectly concerned with Africa. This tendency is not confined to Canadian foreign policy: a similar dynamic is apparent among other 'like-minded' middle powers (Black 1997: 119–20). Nevertheless, it clearly played a role in the approaches of both former Foreign Minister Axworthy and Prime Minister Chrétien, giving high-level impetus to a renewed emphasis on Africa.

Beyond these domestic organizational and idiosyncratic influences, the sustenance and renewal of emphasis on Africa have been strongly conditioned by the Canadian government's deep multilateralist proclivities. The range and depth of this country's multilateral engagements has been widely noted (former Foreign Minister Joe Clark once remarked that Canada was the best-connected country in the world). And the simple fact is, one cannot be a 'good multilateral citizen' in, for example, the United Nations (UN), the Commonwealth, *la Francophonie* and the IFIs without being drawn towards involvement with Africa. This is as true today as it was in 1960, at the dawn of the decolonization era.

More particularly, former Foreign Minister Axworthy's championing of a new 'human security agenda', particularly in various multilateral forums, both resonated with the humane internationalist tradition in Canada and in effect demanded a greater level of engagement with Africa (see Brown 2001). It is in this domain that some of the Canadian government's most prominent recent initiatives have occurred. It is also here, ironically enough, that the gap between the country's expansive ethical aspirations and its increasingly limited means has been most stark, and has most threatened to compromise its reputation and capacity to lead.

Finally, notwithstanding the economic marginality of Africa as a whole, trade and investment links have grown considerably in the liberalized context of the post-adjustment era. More to the point, Canadian resource multinationals – some of the country's strongest corporate players – have become very active on the continent, sometimes in the context of protracted civil/regional conflicts. The activities of these corporate adventurers are deeply unsettling, particularly in a society marked by a strong humane internationalist self-image. Thus, Corporate Social Responsibility has emerged as a significant and controversial issue in Canadian foreign policy, notably as it pertains to Africa.

These factors and forces help to explain the resurgence of interest in Africa at both official and societal levels in Canada. By examining several of these issues further, along with the shifting fortunes of the aid programme as a cross-cutting theme, one can arrive at a clearer assessment of the means, strengths, limitations and implications of this renewed engagement with African countries and peoples.

Multilateralism and elite political leadership

As noted above, Canada's membership of, and commitment to, a wide range of multilateral organizations has been a hallmark of its post-Second World War foreign policy.[4] These organizations include, first and foremost, the UN, and indeed Canada's wide-ranging involvement with this organization has provided both incentive and opportunity to engage in African debates and issues. Similarly, Canada's active and supportive role within both the Commonwealth and *la Francophonie* has almost inevitably compelled the government to become closely involved in African issues given the large number of African members of each. With regard to the latter, Canada's membership has been a means of signalling its bilingual identity and managing its relationship with the more-or-less nationalist governments of the province of Quebec. It has also enabled the government to broaden and reinforce its links with francophone Africa. In both cases, but particularly within the Commonwealth, these organizations have provided venues in which Canada is undeniably important, and have therefore enabled Canadian leaders to (in the Australian formulation) 'strut the world stage'.

Historically, Canada's role within these organizations on African issues was often that of sympathetic 'honest broker' between their newer African members and the former colonial power.[5] More recently, however, they have provided venues for more proactive leadership attempts. Thus, for example, the government of former Prime Minister Brian Mulroney strongly advocated the incorporation of formal commitments to the promotion of (liberal) human rights and democracy in both organizations, resulting in the Commonwealth's Harare Declaration (1991) but meeting with less success in the *Francophonie* summit of the same year (Keating 1997). Prior to this, again under Mulroney, the Canadian government significantly enhanced its reputation in Africa by confronting the British government of Margaret Thatcher over her resistance to sanctions against apartheid South Africa. Indeed, this case came to be widely seen as something of a personal crusade for the Prime Minister. While the significance of Canadian leadership in the struggle against apartheid has frequently been exaggerated (see Freeman 1997; Black 2001a), its activism on this issue during the mid- to late-1980s strongly resonated with the humane internationalist tradition in Canada, and has been virtually mythologized in this country.

During the mid-1990s, the Commonwealth (and to a lesser extent *la Francophonie*) once again provided the crucial venue for a sustained attempt to bring collective pressure to bear on the repressive military regime of Sani

Abacha in Nigeria. Canada was the leading voice on the Commonwealth Ministerial Action Group (CMAG) for stronger measures against the Abacha regime. While the Commonwealth did suspend the regime from its Councils, however, in this case the Chrétien government (and its Foreign Minister, Lloyd Axworthy) found it was pushing beyond where the organization's 'Third World' majority – notably including its African membership – was prepared to go. This was in sharp and disconcerting contrast to the prevailing dynamics on the earlier South African issue, when the Commonwealth majority had if anything pushed for a stronger stand by the Canadian government (see Black 2001b). The Nigerian case serves to illustrate the broader point that, while Canada has had a prominent diplomatic and agenda-setting role within these organizations, its attempts to lead on key issues have sometimes suffered from an absence of followers.

If a case is to be made for Canada as a 'great power', it surely rests to a significant degree on its status as a member of the G-7/8 – the Summit of the world's wealthiest and most powerful states (with the notable exclusion of China). The opportunity to engineer a consensus amongst this heady group is widely presumed to be one of the Canadian government's greatest diplomatic assets. Yet the challenges and risks of doing so highlight, in the end, the care it must take, as the weakest of the strong,[6] in deploying its limited political capital and the difficulty it has in attracting support for its initiatives.

This was a key lesson from Brian Mulroney's efforts to win G-7 support for stronger pressure against apartheid South Africa, focused on the 1987 Summit in Venice. He got very little for his trouble – hardly surprising in a Summit featuring Margaret Thatcher, Ronald Reagan and Helmut Kohl – and caused considerable apprehension amongst his foreign policy officials that he was 'wasting' precious political capital in what was regarded by his fellow summiteers as a naïve and ill-conceived policy (Nossal 1994: 250; Black 2001a: 184).

Despite these sorts of apprehensions and risks, there is some evidence that the Canadian government has become increasingly assertive and effective in the Summit context during the past decade (see Kirton 2002). And Africa became the focus of one of this country's boldest leadership attempts in the context of the 2002 Summit at Kananaskis in the Canadian Rockies. Here, a confluence of factors – being on 'home turf', a legacy-minded Prime Minister anxious to leave a lasting imprint on world affairs in the twilight of his political career, and perhaps most importantly the efforts of a group of savvy African leaders to create a conducive context for Western action by advancing the NEPAD – combined to produce a focus on Africa unprecedented in the nearly thirty years of Summit history.

The Canadian government, and particularly its Prime Minister, worked very hard to achieve this focus. As Robert Fowler, his chief 'Sherpa' for the Summit and Personal Representative for Africa, has somewhat hyperbolically put it:

From Genoa, in July 2001, it was crystal clear that Prime Minister Chrétien would insist that the Canadian Summit he would host in 2002 would feature an all-encompassing effort to end Africa's exclusion from the rest of the world and reverse the downward-spiralling trend in the quality of life of the vast majority of Africans.

(Fowler 2003: 223)[7]

Chrétien, whose political success has been far more the result of pragmatism and 'street smarts' than statesmanship, was strongly supported in this effort at global leadership by Tony Blair of Britain and Jacques Chirac of France. What unfolded was a concerted year-long diplomatic effort involving wide-ranging consultations with G-7 governments, African leaders and NEPAD architects. The result was that a full day of the two-day Summit (shortened from the three-day format of previous years) was devoted to discussions concerning Africa, and that it involved for the first time direct participation by non-G-8 leaders, specifically from Africa. The Summit resulted in the adoption of the Africa Action Plan (AAP), incorporating 'more than a hundred specific commitments' reflecting G-8 consensus on where and how they should 'respond to NEPAD's promise' (Fowler 2003: 228). These commitments spanned the areas of Resource Mobilization, Peace and Security, Governance, and Human Resources among others. The AAP placed particular emphasis on channelling support to 'Enhanced Partnership Countries' that 'demonstrate a political and financial commitment to good governance and the rule of law, investing in their people and pursuing policies that spur economic growth and alleviate poverty' (see Fowler 2003: 239).

Probing the full meaning and implications of these commitments is beyond the scope of this chapter. In part, such an assessment depends on whether one thinks that the Summits, and the documents they issue, are anything more than talking shops and empty rhetoric (for conflicting views see Kirton 2002 and Elliot 2003). In part, it depends on one's interpretation of both the AAP and the NEPAD, which Fowler characterized as a 'realistic' plan 'aimed at making African nations full and equal partners in the global economic and trading system and, above all, at attracting significant levels of foreign investment to that continent' (Fowler 2003: 226). Particularly when inflected by the new emphasis on rewards to Enhanced Partnership Countries, this is a scheme which, whatever its specific provisions and strengths, strongly reinforces Western hegemonic preferences in terms of the political and economic organization of both African countries and world affairs.

For our purposes, however, the evaluation can perhaps be reduced to a twin bottom line. On the one hand, the governments of the richest countries of the world gave more, and more sympathetic, attention to the challenges and opportunities confronting Africa than ever before. For this, the determined efforts of Jean Chrétien and his government deserve much of the credit. On the other hand, the AAP, for all its 'specific commitments', produced virtually no new resources beyond those already announced at the Monterrey Conference on Financing for Development several months previously. In sum, it produced a qualified commitment to devote half (roughly US$6 billion) of the US$12 billion in new development funding committed at Monterrey to Africa – far short of the US$64 billion that the NEPAD document estimated the programme required. This explains the verdict of most NGO and editorial opinion, reflected in such phrases as 'they're offering peanuts to Africa – and recycled peanuts at that', and 'Africa let down by the rich' (*Guardian Weekly*, 4–10 July 2002). Thus, Canada's best efforts could not bring its G-8 partners around to substantially 'putting their money where their mouths were'. The net result indicates the ability of Canadian policy-makers to shape agendas concerning Africa, on the one hand, but their at best limited ability to shape outcomes.

The human security agenda

Human security is another domain in which elite political leadership and multilateralism, in this case strongly supplemented by novel 'partnerships' with non-state actors, converged to produce a renewed emphasis on Africa during the latter half of the 1990s. The principal champion of this agenda, within the government and beyond it, was Lloyd Axworthy, the Foreign Minister from 1996 to 2000. Axworthy brought a strongly activist and indeed idealistic orientation to the Foreign Ministry which was often resisted by his permanent officials, but which proved popular in the country at large where he was widely regarded as the most successful Foreign Minister for some time. This perception (controversial amongst foreign policy analysts) had much to do with several highly visible initiatives pursued under the rubric of the human security agenda. Strongly reinforcing the profile of this agenda was the opportunity presented by Canada's election to a two-year term on the UN Security Council in 1999–2000 – an opportunity which Axworthy and his officials seized with gusto (see Pearson 2001).

Human security is a notoriously broad and slippery concept. The common element is the privileging of *individual*, versus state, security. In the official Canadian formulation, the focus has been on 'freedom from fear' or, as Axworthy (2001: 4) has put it, 'protecting people from acts of violence and helping build a greater sense of security in the personal sphere'.[8] In a key 1999 DFAIT document, five specific government priorities were highlighted under this agenda: the protection of civilians; peace support operations; conflict prevention; governance and accountability; and public safety (DFAIT 1999a). Regardless of specific modalities, however, it is impossible to take the idea of human security seriously without giving careful attention to the plight of the millions of Africans whose human security is threatened by the armed conflicts and more mundane forms of violence that beset substantial chunks of the continent.

Thus it was that the Canadian government, and Canadian non-state actors, took a number of initiatives broadly linked to this agenda. In general, they experienced greatest success at the relatively abstract level of agenda setting, norm building and research; they were less successful, and less consistent, in the face of actual human security crises on the ground, where Canada's lack of 'hard' resources severely constrained its responses.

At the broadest level, Canada's human security activism involved a number of initiatives with potentially significant long-term implications for Africa. Most famously, Axworthy and a core of DFAIT officials played a central role in the Ottawa Process resulting in the Convention Banning Anti-Personnel Landmines. Canadian officials, Axworthy among them, were also key players in the negotiation of the Rome Treaty for the establishment of the International Criminal Court. Axworthy took a particular interest in the plight of war-affected children (notably child soldiers), culminating in the first Global Conference on War-Affected Children, held in his home town of Winnipeg in September 2000. Less successfully, but nevertheless diligently, he and some of his officials tried to advance international efforts to control the global trade in small arms and promote micro-disarmament.[9] These and similar initiatives were in themselves admirable, and hold some potential to facilitate meaningful long-term change. In the short to medium term, however, they are at best promising beginnings to long-term journeys.

Closer to the coal face of particular conflicts on the ground, the Canadian government was a key participant in/supporter of several related initiatives designed to highlight the nature of war economies, sharpen the effectiveness of sanctions, and shed light on the role of private sector actors in situations of conflict. Robert Fowler, who prior to becoming Sherpa for the Kananaskis Summit was Canadian Ambassador to the UN during the 1999–2000 term on the Security Council, served as Chair of the Angola sanctions committee. In this context, he was responsible for the Council's creation of an unprecedented Panel of Experts, including both governmental and non-governmental participants, to evaluate how sanctions against UNITA were being violated, and how they could be made more effective. The Panel's report caused a furore by 'naming names', but also highlighted key features of the Angolan war economy and produced recommendations that helped to choke off UNITA's ability to sustain the conflict (see Fowler 2003). A second report, commissioned by the small NGO Partnership Africa Canada and prepared by a team of three NGO experts, exposed and publicized the role of 'blood diamonds' in the brutal Sierra Leonean conflict, and contributed to the momentum behind the Kimberley Process aiming to end the trade in conflict diamonds (see Smillie *et al.* 2000). Axworthy himself commissioned a third report, on 'Human Security in the Sudan', which illuminated the role of the Canadian oil exploration company Talisman Energy in that country's ongoing civil war. In each case, these reports helped highlight and stimulate action on the underlying sources of some of Africa's most intractable conflicts.

In these initiatives, and the broader ones noted above, a key feature of Canadian diplomacy was close collaboration with a range of non-state actors, especially in civil society. This 'new diplomacy' holds significant risks for non-state participants in particular, whose creative autonomy may be compromised. Nevertheless, it yielded real benefits for a foreign service itself beleaguered by sustained cutbacks and a burgeoning agenda.[10]

Canada's human security agenda has been least successful when faced with the need to respond to immediate security crises on the ground. Two examples will suffice. First, in late 1996, the government responded to signs of a mounting humanitarian disaster in eastern Zaire by undertaking a high-profile effort to mobilize a large multinational force (MNF) to defuse the crisis. Its decision to do so was strongly motivated by the Prime Minister's emotional personal response to the images of suffering he saw unfolding. In the event, however, the mission became something of a fiasco, as the government could not obtain effective cooperation from its partners, could barely sustain its own commitment in light of persistent cuts to the armed forces, was exposed as utterly dependent on the US for intelligence and transport, and could not even get into theatre in the absence of great(er) power *and* African governmental cooperation (see Cooper 2000; Appathurai and Lysyshyn 1998).

More recently, the government has agonized over how to respond to the latest crisis in the ongoing conflict in the Democratic Republic of Congo (DRC), estimated to be responsible for the deaths of more than 4.5 million people. Faced with an urgent request to the 'international community' from the UN Secretary-General to mobilize an emergency force to respond to the killing in Ituri, and a French offer to commit over a thousand combat soldiers to such a mission, the best the Canadian government could ultimately do in response to what the Prime Minister termed a moral obligation was to supply two Hercules C-130 transport aircraft. While undoubtedly welcome, such a contribution falls far short of what could reasonably be expected of a champion of human security. It reflects both the diminished state of the Canadian armed forces, and their overcommitment in more politically compelling operations in the Balkans, Afghanistan and, prospectively, Iraq (*The Globe and Mail* (Toronto), 17 May 2003; also Cohen 2002/3; Hataley and Nossal 2003).

In short, Canadian leadership has been most effective in the more abstract realm of big ideas and long-term consensus building; it has been least effective, or indeed present, when confronted with acute human insecurity on the ground.

Development assistance

The draconian cuts to Canadian ODA through the 1990s, particularly to Africa, have already been noted. Moreover, these cuts were imposed on a programme that the Canadian International Development Agency (CIDA),

Canada's principal vehicle for bilateral aid, has acknowledged is the least concentrated in the world (CIDA 2002: 9). In Africa, for institutional and domestic political reasons (discussed above), there has been an ongoing imperative to disburse aid across both the francophone and anglophone portions of the continent, for starters. The result has been a programme in which, during 2000, Canada was among the top three bilateral donors in only Gabon and Swaziland; and in which during the same year it expended at least some aid funds (bilateral and/or multilateral) in *every* African country except Libya (NSI 2003: 79).

The costs of the cuts to ODA went substantially beyond the programmes foregone or cancelled and the individuals and organizations negatively affected as a result. Clearly, such a diminishing and diffused programme was liable to reduce Canada's accumulated goodwill and political influence with African governments and other key organizations on the continent. It also limited the government's ability to pursue a human security agenda, since aid funds are essential to governmental efforts to enhance people's human security.[11] Finally, the cuts had a negative impact on Canada's relatively limited trade and investment links with Africa since historically these have been heavily aid-fuelled.[12] In short, it is hard to avoid the conclusion that the extent of the cuts imposed on aid to Africa provided a potent indicator of the government's relative lack of commitment towards long-term relationships with the continent – and beyond this the relative indifference of the majority of the electorate, abstract professions of humane internationalism notwithstanding.

As the fiscal situation improved, therefore, and as the various pressures noted above created a conducive context for enhanced interest in Africa, the government's sustained efforts at aid renewal and 'Strengthening Aid Effectiveness' (as a June 2001 policy document was titled) can be understood at least partly as an implicit effort to rebuild credibility amongst both donors and recipients. It pursued this objective in a number of ways. The first and most obvious was with commitments to increase overall aid spending. These were a little slow in coming, but at the March 2002 Monterrey Conference on Development Financing, the Prime Minister (in the company of other major donors) pledged substantial long-term increases. The Canadian commitment was 8 per cent per year, leading to an overall doubling of aid spending by 2010. In line with the commitments at Kananaskis noted above, 50 per cent of this increase was to be committed to Africa. Moreover, in the context of the Prime Minister's pre-Kananaskis diplomacy, the government had previously announced a C$500 million Canada Fund for Africa in its December 2001 budget, which CIDA candidly described as 'a showcase for Canadian leadership in pursuit of effective development through a series of large-scale, flagship initiatives in support of NEPAD and the G8 Africa Action Plan' (CIDA 2002: 26; see also CIDA 2003).

Second, CIDA has made a concerted effort to bring its programming more closely into line with the core elements of an increasingly comprehensive donor consensus. This consensus grew out of the OECD document *Shaping the 21st Century: The Contribution of Development Assistance* and latterly the UN's Millennium Development Goals. The former advanced a set of principles for effective development, including: local ownership; improved donor coordination; stronger partnerships; and a results-based approach. To these have been added good governance, building capacity and engaging civil society. A number of joint programming instruments have been developed in an effort to give effect to these principles, including in particular World Bank-orchestrated Poverty Reduction Strategy Papers (PRSP's) and Sector-Wide Approaches (SWAps) (see CIDA 2002: 4–8).

It is beyond the scope of this chapter to deconstruct the full meaning and implications of these elements of the international aid regime. There is also reason to question CIDA's ability to sustain real programme reform, based on past practice and the diverse range of pressures to which it is subject (see Black and Tiessen forthcoming; Therien and Lloyd 2000). Nevertheless, if it is even halfway serious about and successful in modifying its programme to conform with these principles and instruments, it will be moving to bring its programme more firmly into line with a hegemonic consensus on 'best practices' for developing countries which bears particularly heavily on African states, and which remains (softened edges notwithstanding) neo-liberal at its core.

Similarly, and in line with the G-8's emphasis at Kananaskis on Enhanced Partnership Countries, CIDA gingerly moved to enhance the geographic concentration of its programme at the end of 2002. Specifically, it has proposed 'increasing its aid investments in a select number of priority sectors in nine developing countries' judged to be 'good performers' based on such criteria as having an approved PRSP, regional importance, good governance and 'the ability to use aid effectively' (personal communication with CIDA official, 29 December 2002). Six of the nine countries are African: Ethiopia, Ghana, Mali, Mozambique, Senegal and Tanzania. Significantly, increases to the aid budgets of these countries will be drawn from the overall increases announced at Monterrey; no country programmes are being cut. Once again, it remains to be seen whether these new concentrations will be sustained and 'enhanced partnerships' will result. Nevertheless, the trend is towards rewarding good performers in terms established by the donor consensus, and thus in support of the reformist project embodied in this consensus, reiterated and reinforced by both the AAP and the NEPAD.

Corporate investment and social responsibility

Consistent with this vision, a significant portion of Canadian government effort since the start of the new millennium has been on enhancing trade and investment links. For example, of the C$421 million already allocated from the Canada Fund for Africa, C$120 million has been committed to what is labelled 'Supporting Growth and Innovation'. This includes C$20 million for trade support measures, including market development and technical assistance to African trade negotiators; and a C$100 million Canada Investment Fund for Africa, aimed at stimulating private sector investment of the same amount in areas such as transportation, water supply and energy (CIDA 2003: 7 and 10).

Moreover, despite Africa's small share of Canada's global trade and investment, there has been significant growth in both areas since the mid-1990s. This can be understood partly as a result of the economic liberalization processes that most African governments have undertaken over the past couple of decades under pressure of Structural Adjustment, as well as the unusually promising opportunities available on the continent, particularly in the natural resource sector. Because of the historical development of Canada's own political economy, some of the country's strongest corporations are in resource exploration and exploitation, including mining, oil and gas, and forestry. A number of these companies have become increasingly active in Africa over the past decade. The focus of their activity spans some of the most reputable countries in Africa, including Ghana and South Africa, the two largest recipients of Canadian foreign direct investment (NSI 2003: 102–3); and some of the most conflict-ridden and rights-abusive situations on the continent – notably Sudan and the DRC.

These two cases have placed into stark relief the tension between the Canadian government's human security agenda and the activities of some of the country's major corporate actors. Of the two, the one that until recently garnered by far the most attention was the Sudan, where Calgary-based Talisman Oil had a 25 per cent stake in the Greater Nile Petroleum Operation Company (GNPOC) operating in the war-torn southern part of the country. Its partners were the state-owned oil companies of China (China National Petroleum Corporation – 40 per cent), Malaysia (Petronas – 30 per cent) and the Sudan (Sudapent – 5 per cent). Even before Talisman finalized the purchase of Sudanese concession rights in 1998, it had been contacted by Canadian human rights and humanitarian assistance groups alerting it to the human rights and security implications of operations in the Sudan. Subsequently, a coalition of NGOs tried to negotiate a human rights monitoring plan with the company, and conveyed their concerns to the federal government. With the company eschewing a monitoring plan, it became the target of vigorous criticism that its presence in the country was, on balance,

> detrimental to human rights and a peaceful conclusion to the civil war. Specifically, Talisman's operations [were] said to be prolonging the civil war, both by contributing to conflict over oil fields and by generating, for the Sudanese regime, revenue used to bankroll the war.
>
> (Forcese 2001: 41, 43)

The controversy arose at a time when Foreign Minister Axworthy's human security promotion was approaching its apex. Through 1999, criticism mounted not only from Canadian development and human rights NGOs associated with the Sudan Inter-Agency Reference Group, but from US sources, including then Secretary of State Madeleine Albright. In October of that year, the Canadian government appointed an Assessment Mission chaired by John Harker to investigate the situation on the ground, and threatened to impose sanctions 'if it becomes evident that oil extraction is exacerbating the conflict in Sudan, or resulting in violations of human rights or humanitarian law' (DFAIT 1999b). In early 2000, the Harker Mission presented its findings to the government, confirming that:

> there has been, and probably still is, major displacement of civilian populations related to oil extraction. Sudan is a place of extraordinary suffering and continuing human rights violations, even though some forward progress can be recorded, and the oil operations in which a Canadian company is involved add more suffering.
>
> (Harker 2000: 15)[13]

Similarly, some two years later a Canadian NGO representative asserted, following a fact-finding mission to southern Sudan, that 'the shameful truth is that a Canadian corporation is extracting profits from oil operations at the core of the most destructive conflict in the world today' (Kenny 2002).

The force of these criticisms was exacerbated by the fact that, following the Harker Report in 2000, the government retreated from its threat of sanctions. Ultimately, its response was limited to Axworthy's exhortation of Talisman to 'ensure that their operations do not lead to an increase in tensions or otherwise contribute to the conflict', accompanied by his urging of the company to complete a human rights monitoring agreement with NGOs – negotiations for which quickly foundered (Forcese 2001: 46).

Craig Forcese cites two key (and arguably related) factors explaining the government's retreat from a more forceful response to Talisman's complicity in a situation of profound human insecurity. The first was 'the potentially damaging (domestic political) consequences for the government of taking on, and possibly wounding, a key Canadian company'. The second was a very narrow and restrictive interpretation of the legal basis for sanctions, as embodied in the government's Special Economic Measures Act (SEMA), requiring either a multilateral decision by an organization or association of states to which Canada belongs, or a decision by the Cabinet that a grave breach of international peace and security has occurred, resulting (actually or prospectively) in a serious international crisis (Forcese 2001: 47–51). This extreme governmental reluctance to act decisively to enforce Corporate Social Responsibility is in fact a long-standing tradition in Canadian foreign policy, dating back at least to the controversy over its policy towards apartheid South Africa in the 1970s (see Freeman 1997; Pratt 1997). It reflects a persistently high degree of sensitivity to the needs and interests of Canadian 'corporate citizens' which are, *in extremis*, characteristically given precedence over considerations of human rights and human security. While such sensitivity is arguably common among capitalist 'state formations', it may be that the Canadian government's sense of vulnerability, as a highly trade- and investment-dependent 'middle power', distinguishes it from more truly 'great powers' with more robust corporate sectors and a greater ability to shape, rather than respond to, world affairs.

In November 2002 Talisman, its share value battered by the controversy and facing legal action in the US under the Alien Torts Claims Act (Harker 2003), agreed to sell its stake in the GNPOC to the Indian state-owned company ONGC Videsh Ltd (OVL) for C\$1.2 billion.[14] This did not mark the end of controversy over Canadian corporate involvement in African conflict zones, however. At about the same time as Talisman was finalizing its sale, a UN panel of experts released a report on the sources of conflict in the DRC. Among other pointed findings, the panel accused eight Canadian resource companies of being in violation of the OECD Guidelines for Multinational Enterprises as a result of their association with warlord networks in the conflict-ridden eastern part of the country (Taylor 2002; Drohan 2003). Despite howls of protest from the companies named, the charges in the report highlight the need for serious scrutiny of their roles, at least. The Canadian government has been, if anything, more reticent about acting in this situation than it was in the case of Talisman.

Corporate Social Responsibility is now a focus of ongoing policy debate in Canada, and is not infrequently raised as a priority in government statements. But grasping the nettle of how to make it happen remains a real problem for policy-makers. The result is almost certain to be continued tension with the human security agenda. Effective efforts to reduce this tension will depend on pressure from below, above and around both corporate and governmental decision-makers – through more robust transnational corporate codes of conduct, and through continued scrutiny and pressure to hold both corporations and governments accountable in relation to the standards they increasingly profess to embrace (see Harker 2003).

Conclusion

As Chris Brown has noted, Canada's ties to Africa are in the final analysis comparatively minor, on virtually any tangible criterion one wishes to apply (Brown 2001: 196). This has been both liberating and limiting. On the one hand, as Brown notes, it gives policy-makers an unusual degree of latitude with respect to their Africa policy. Because of this, as well as the obvious humanitarian imperatives emanating from the continent, Africa has become a key focus for the relatively robust ethical tradition in Canadian foreign policy. African policies become, in other words, a means of recapitulating a favourite story about ourselves: as good international citizens and, more broadly, a force for good in the world.

This is not to discount the positive effects that can and sometimes do emanate from such a policy orientation. Nor should it detract from the dedication of those Canadians, inside and outside government, who have tackled African issues with tireless commitment and creativity. It does, however, help to explain the ultimately limited and inconsistent nature of Canada's African endeavours. It suggests that what tends to matter most is the initiative and the intentions, rather than the results – which often escape critical scrutiny beyond the community of internationalist NGOs, interested academics and a few voices in the media. Thus for example, when times were (a little) tough in Canada, aid to the continent was cut with virtual political impunity; and when specific peacekeeping force commitments are called for in response to situations of grave human insecurity, Canada's ability and willingness to respond is increasingly limited. Similarly, when confronted with the potential costs of taking on a successful Canadian corporation in the human security interest of southern Sudanese, the government has responded gingerly at best.

More broadly, Canada's renewed activism towards Africa can be read as the kinder, gentler face of Western hegemonic aspirations towards the continent. Its efforts to prod the G-8 into a more sustained and generous response to the NEPAD, focused particularly on Enhanced Partnership countries, as well as its efforts to reform its once-again growing aid programme to bring it more closely into line with the priorities and instruments of the 'donor consensus', exemplify this tendency. In addition, its lack of colonial baggage and threatening interests on the continent enhance its ability to play this role. Whether this renewed activism towards Africa can and will be sustained, and what the repercussions of the approach it broadly shares with governments such as Britain's will ultimately be for Africans, are questions that bear watching through the first decade of the new millennium.

Notes

1 For example, in 2001, total Canadian trade (exports and imports) with Africa amounted to roughly C$3.82 billion – less than 0.5 per cent of Canada's total foreign trade, at C$716.61 billion. See NSI 2003: 99–101.

2 Canadians featured prominently in the grim narratives of both. In the former, the Canadian Airborne Regiment became embroiled in scandal over the racist-inflected abuse and death in detention of a Somali youth, leading to a controversial inquiry and the disbanding of the Regiment. In the latter, Canadian General Romeo Dallaire was the tragic UN force commander whose pre-genocide warnings and requests for reinforcement were ignored, and who was forced to impotently witness the subsequent slaughter.

3 This visible/vocal foreign policy agenda can be contrasted with the more routine, if not invisible, and far better-resourced agenda tied up with (above all) the management of the Canadian–American relationship, global economic relationships in the context of the WTO and other major economic forums, and strategic relationships managed both bilaterally and through NATO.

4 This propensity towards multilateralism is one of the reasons why many Canadian foreign policy analysts would argue that Canada is more accurately thought of as a 'middle' than a 'great' power (see Keating 2002). For a more critical view of this tradition, see Black and Sjolander 1996.

5 This was the case, for example, in the Canadian role within the Commonwealth over Rhodesia's UDI in 1965, and the controversy over British arms sales to South Africa in 1971.

6 With the qualified exception of Russia.

7 Significantly, Fowler was himself something of an 'Africa hand', as reflected in his comment that 'as I approached the end of my career I would have another – this time unique – opportunity to assist Africa, a continent and a people that have held my fascination and deep affection for all of my adult and professional life' (Fowler 2003: 221).

8 Canadian officials juxtapose their approach with the even broader approach championed by, among others, the government of Japan, and focusing on 'freedom from want'.

9 For a rare account of these and other initiatives from the officials who were key participants in them, see the essays in McRae and Hubert 2001.

10 For a good discussion of the role of these 'mixed actor coalitions' in the human security domain, see MacLean and Shaw 2001.

11 Although ill-considered aid spending can also *increase* human insecurity, as is increasingly recognized. See, among others, Bush 1996 and Duffield 2001.

12 A reflection, in part, of the high percentage of tied aid in the Canadian aid programme. See CIDA 2003: 19–23.

13 These quotes, and much of the information in this section, are drawn from the excellent article by Craig Forcese (2001).

14 It is worth noting that the human security implications of this divestment are ambiguous at best; see Seymour 2002.

References

Appathurai, J. and R. Lysyshyn (1998) 'Lessons Learned from the Zaire Mission', *Canadian Foreign Policy*, 5, 2: 93–106.

Axworthy, L. (2001) 'Introduction', in R. Macrae and D. Hubert (eds) *Human Security and the New Diplomacy*, Montreal: McGill-Queen's University Press, pp. 3–13.

Black, D. (1997) 'Addressing Apartheid: Lessons from Australian, Canadian, and Swedish Policies in Southern Africa', in A. Cooper (ed.) *Niche Diplomacy: Middle Powers after the Cold War*, London: Macmillan, pp. 100–28.

—— (2001a) 'How Exceptional? Reassessing the Mulroney Government's Anti-Apartheid "Crusade"', in N. Michaud and K. Nossal (eds) *Diplomatic Departures: The Conservative Era in Canadian Foreign Policy*, Vancouver: UBC Press, pp. 173–93.

—— (2001b) 'Echoes of Apartheid? Canada, Nigeria, and the Politics of Norms', in R. Irwin (ed.) *Ethics and Security in Canadian Foreign Policy*, Vancouver: UBC Press, pp. 138–59.

Black, D. and Sjolander, C. (1996) 'Multilateralism Re-constituted and the Discourse of Canadian Foreign Policy', *Studies in Political Economy*, 49: 7–36.

Black, D. and Tiessen, R. (forthcoming) 'Canadian Aid Policy: Parameters, Pressures, and Partners', chapter submitted for book manuscript on *The Administration of Foreign Affairs*.

Brown, C. (2001) 'Africa in Canadian Foreign Policy 2000: The Human Security Agenda', in F. Hampson, N. Hillmer and M. A. Molot (eds) *Canada among Nations 2001: The Axworthy Legacy*, Don Mills: Oxford University Press, pp. 192–212.

Bush, K. (1996) 'Beyond Bungee Cord Humanitarianism: Towards a Developmental Agenda for Peacebuilding', *Canadian Journal of Development Studies*, Special Issue: 75–92.

Canadian International Development Agency (CIDA) (2002) 'Canada Making a Difference in the World: A Policy Statement on Strengthening Aid Effectiveness', Hull, Quebec: CIDA.

—— (2003) 'New Vision, New Partnership: Canada Fund for Africa', Hull, Quebec: CIDA.

Cohen, A. (2002/3) 'Seize the Day', *International Journal*, LVIII, 1: 139–54.

Cooper, A. (2000) 'Between Will and Capabilities: Canada and the Zaire/Great Lakes Initiative', in A. Cooper and G. Hayes (eds) *Worthwhile Initiatives? Canadian Mission-Oriented Diplomacy*, Toronto: Irwin Publishing, pp. 64–78.

DFAIT (1999a) 'Freedom from Fear: Canada's Foreign Policy for Human Security', Ottawa: DFAIT.

—— (1999b) Press release 232, 'Canada Announces Support for Sudan Peace Process', Ottawa: DFAIT.

—— (2002) 'Africa and Canada Strengthen Trade Relations', Department of Foreign Affairs and International Trade News Release, 26 November.

Drohan, M. (2003) 'Talisman is Not Alone', *The Globe and Mail* (Toronto), 12 March.

Duffield, M. (2001) *Global Governance and the New Wars: The Merging of Development and Security*, London: Zed Books.

Elliott, L. (2003) 'Do Us All a Favour – Pull the Plug on G8', *Guardian Weekly*, 5–11 June.

Forcese, C. (2001) ' "Militarized Commerce" in Sudan's Oilfields: Lessons for Canadian Foreign Policy', *Canadian Foreign Policy*, 8, 3: 37–56.

Fowler, R. (2003) 'Canadian Leadership and the Kananaskis G-8 Summit: Towards a Less Self-Centred Foreign Policy', in D. Carment, F. Hampson and N. Hillmer (eds) *Canada among Nations 2003: Coping with the American Colossus*, Don Mills: Oxford University Press, pp. 219–41.

Freeman, L. (1997) *The Ambiguous Champion: Canada and South Africa in the Trudeau and Mulroney Years*, Toronto: University of Toronto Press.

Harker, J. (2000) *Human Security in Sudan: The Report of a Canadian Assessment Mission*, Ottawa: DFAIT.

—— (2003) 'Profits, Policy, Power: CSR and Human Security in Africa', unpublished manuscript.

Hataley, T. and K. Nossal (2003) 'Putting People at Risk: The Crisis in East Timor and Canada's Human Security Agenda', paper presented to the annual meeting of the Canadian Political Science Association, Halifax, NS, 31 May.

Keating, T. (1997) 'In Whose Image? Canada and the Promotion of Good Governance', paper presented to the annual meeting of the Canadian Political Science Association, St. John's, NF, 8 June.

—— (2002) *Canada and World Order: The Multilateralist Tradition in Canadian Foreign Policy*, Don Mills: Oxford University Press.

Kenny, G. (2002) 'Canada's silence on Sudan is a Vote for Oppression', *The Globe and Mail* (Toronto), 1 May.

Kirton, J. (2002) 'Canada as a Principal Summit Power: G-7/8 Concert Diplomacy from Halifax 1995 to Kananaskis 2002', in N. Hillmer and M. Molot (eds) *Canada among Nations 2002: A Fading Power*, Don Mills: Oxford University Press, pp. 209–32.

MacDonald, L. (1995) 'Unequal Partnerships: The Politics of Canada's Relations with the Third World', *Studies in Political Economy*, 47: 111–41.

MacLean, S. and T. Shaw (2001) 'Canada and New "Global" Strategic Alliances: Prospects for Human Security at the Start of the Twenty-first Century', *Canadian Foreign Policy*, 8, 3: 17–36.

McRae, R. and D. Hubert (eds) (2001) *Human Security and the New Diplomacy, Protecting People, Promoting Peace*, Montreal: McGill-Queen's University Press.

Morrison, D. (1998) *Aid and Ebb Tide: A History of CIDA and Canadian Development Assistance*. Waterloo: Wilfrid Laurier University Press.

Munton, D. (2002/3) 'Whither Internationalism?', *International Journal*, LVIII, 1: 155–80.

North–South Institute (NSI) (2003) *Canadian Development Report 2003*, Ottawa: North–South Institute.

Nossal, K. (1994) *Rain Dancing: Sanctions in Canadian and Australian Foreign Policy*, Toronto: University of Toronto Press.

Pearson, M. (2001) 'Humanizing the UN Security Council', in F. Hampson, N. Hillmer and M. Molot (eds) *Canada among Nations 2001: The Axworthy Legacy*, Don Mills: Oxford University Press, pp. 127–51.

Pratt, C. (ed.) (1989) *Internationalism under Strain: The North–South Policies of Canada, the Netherlands, Norway and Sweden*, Toronto: University of Toronto Press.

—— (2000) 'Alleviating Global Poverty or Enhancing Security: Competing Rationales for Canadian Development Assistance', in J. Freedman (ed.) *Transforming Development: Foreign Aid in a Changing World*, Toronto: University of Toronto Press, pp. 37–59.

Pratt, R. (1997) *In Good Faith: Canadian Churches against Apartheid*, Waterloo: Wilfrid Laurier University Press.

Seymour, L. (2002) 'Talisman's out … Now What?' *North–South Institute Bulletin*, Ottawa: North–South Institute.

Smillie, Ian, Lansana Gberie and Ralph Hazleton (2000) *The Heart of the Matter: Sierra Leone, Diamonds and Human Security*, Ottawa: Partnership Africa-Canada.

Taylor, M. (2002) 'Law-abiding or Not, Canadian Firms in Congo Contribute to War', *The Globe and Mail* (Toronto), 31 October.

Therien, J.-P. and C. Lloyd (2000) 'Development Assistance on the Brink', *Third World Quarterly*, 21, 1: 21–38.

Tomlinson, B. (2002) 'Defending Humane Internationalism: The Role of Canadian NGOs in a Security-Conscious Era', *International Journal*, LVII, 2: 273–82.

8 The European Union's external relations with Africa after the Cold War

Aspects of continuity and change

Stephen R. Hurt

The focus of this chapter is to critically review the policies of the European Union (EU) towards Africa since the end of the Cold War.[1] In doing so the main themes will be threefold. First, there is an attempt to identify some of the most important areas of both continuity and change that have influenced the development of EU policy towards the continent. Second, parts of the discussion will relate to debates concerning how significant a global actor the EU is in its own right. Third, the framework of the analysis will highlight how, in many areas, the nature and future direction of EU policy towards Africa is very similar to both the bilateral relations of many major states, and the policies of the major international financial institutions (discussed elsewhere in this volume).

It should be noted from the outset that for the purposes of this chapter when I refer to Africa I am not including North Africa, which by academic convention is often discussed as part of the Mediterranean and, incidentally, is how the EU organizes its policies with North Africa: Morocco, Algeria, Tunisia and Egypt are all included in the Euro-Mediterranean Partnership agreement.[2] Another important assumption to highlight is that the focus here is at the institutional level of the EU itself, rather than the individual Member States themselves, which are analysed elsewhere in this book (see Chapters 2 and 3).

The legacies of European colonialism are still evident in many of the crises across Africa and it is the chief contention of this chapter that to date the external policies of the EU, in particular in the realm of development cooperation, have failed to solve many of these problems. Europe must take responsibility for the consequences of its colonial past and should 'collectively assume such responsibilities in cooperation with Africans in an effort to arrest the continent's decline and put it on a progressive course' (Pfaff 1995: 6). This is in direct contrast to the claims made by Commissioner Pinheiro in 1998 who suggested that the relationship between the EU and Africa had moved into a postcolonial phase (Khadiagala 2000: 83).

Theoretical approaches to EU–Africa relations

Within the vast literature concerning formal relations between the EU and Africa, it is possible to distinguish three different theoretical schools of thought that have been employed to interpret the relationship and its evolution. First, there is the approach based on liberal thinking, which explains the relationship in terms of mutually beneficial cooperation (Gruhn 1976; Zartman 1976). This view highlights the widening of issues covered over the years, which is thought to have led to increased interdependence and the improvement of equality between the two parties. This has been especially dominant in the official view of the European Commission. The model of development underlying this view is one that sees mutual benefits resulting from the further integration of African states into the world economy.

Second, another major interpretation of the relationship, especially dominant during the 1970s, was one based on the dependency critique (Galtung 1976; Shaw 1979). This sought to describe the EU–Africa relationship within a much wider core–periphery structure. Particular emphasis was placed on the Lomé Convention and how it maintained primary product exports to the EU via the System for the Stabilization of Export Earnings (STABEX) and the Stabilization Scheme for Mineral Products (SYSMIN), while failing to allow duty-free access for manufactured exports. Hence Lomé was seen as perpetuating the wider dependent relationship between North and South. This approach, although useful in emphasizing structure, has been somewhat discredited over the years. Certainly it fails to explain the motivations of actors and the wider political and economic context of North–South relations.

A number of more recent studies have attempted to explain and evaluate the history of the relationship within the broad context of North–South relations (for example Brown 2002). It is this general approach that I find the most satisfying, although I would also want to emphasize the importance of government and bureaucratic elites on both sides. Without an emphasis on actors, as well as structure, it is hard to understand both why the relationship has persisted for so long, and why it has developed in the particular way that I will outline in this chapter.

The historical context of EU–Africa relations

The EU has a long history of formalized relations with Africa. It is a major aid donor in its own right and the importance it attaches to development policy in general is officially reflected in the Treaty on European Union. This explicitly states in Article 130u that the EU aims to foster 'the sustainable economic and social development of the developing countries, and more particularly the most disadvantaged among them'. Clearly a high proportion of the most disadvantaged developing countries are to be found in Africa. It is evident from some of the other chapters in this volume that we should not understand EU development policy as a unified European approach, but rather as an additional policy that does not prevent Member

States from formulating their own policies to reflect particular development priorities and approaches.

As discussed in the introduction to this volume, there are two important structural considerations that should be considered when analysing external relations to Africa. First, changes in the global economy over approximately the last two decades have resulted in neoliberal ideas achieving a position of dominance. This is significant for EU relations with Africa, not least because when ideas reach such a position they become automatically incorporated into the characterization of particular problems. Second, the end of the Cold War had a negative impact on the geo-strategic importance of Africa and this has also had a major impact on the policies of external powers. External policies towards Africa in the areas of both development and security have altered drastically in this regard. With respect to both these developments the policies of the EU towards Africa are no exception.

The early years of European development policy were influenced most significantly by the context of colonial relations. Of all the original EU Member States it was the colonial interests of France that were most pressing. Due to French negotiating strength, African colonies were given association status within the Treaty of Rome (Whiteman 1998: 30). This meant that both parties enjoyed preferential trade access and the EU also provided aid to the associate states under the first European Development Fund (EDF). During the 1960s a number of these countries became independent African states, and as a consequence this association was renewed in the two Yaoundé Conventions of 1963 and 1969. By establishing joint institutions such as an association council and a parliamentary assembly, these new agreements did include limited recognition of the independence of these states. Economically little changed, with continued reciprocal trade access coupled with a Second EDF. By the end of the 1960s the EU began to appear more interested in other developing countries, and in 1971 it introduced its Generalized System of Preferences (GSP) that reduced the external European tariff for all developing countries, hence weakening the relative benefits for the signatories of the Yaoundé Convention.

When negotiations began for what was to become the Lomé Convention, the global context was highly important and influential in the eventual outcome. The balance of EU development thinking was altered significantly by Britain's entry into the EU in 1973. For reasons associated with Britain's policies towards its ex-colonies, those members of the Commonwealth that were at a similar stage of development as the other association states had to be included. During the negotiations of the Lomé Convention these new countries united with the existing associates to form the African, Caribbean and Pacific States (ACP) group. The global situation at the time was dominated by the increasing assertiveness of states in the South, and the demands of the ACP states during the negotiations were in several respects similar to those within the UN General Assembly for a New International Economic Order (NIEO). As a result the first Lomé Convention represented something of a breakthrough for the ACP states. Whiteman described how this period of commodity politics led to a situation in the West where 'there were fears of a permanent global power shift' (1998: 31).

Lomé I was of particular significance for two key reasons. First, aid allocations, once made, were guaranteed for the full five years and were to be jointly managed. Second, the trade provisions provided for qualified non-reciprocal trade access for ACP states. In reality, Lomé I reflected the difference between rhetoric and reality in North–South relations at the time. Concessions were made to the ACP states but they were heavily qualified and the EU maintained a large measure of control and influence in vital areas. In the trade provisions of Lomé I, the free trade access offered to ACP states was subject to a number of qualifications, including the non-inclusion of products covered by the Common Agricultural Policy (CAP) (Brown 2002: 61). In addition, although the ACP states were given the chance to develop their own priorities for spending funds from the EDF, the final decision to finance projects was left to a committee that only included EU representatives (Brown 2002: 59). The history of European development cooperation from this point onwards can be understood as the steady erosion of these limited concessions, and the increasing adoption of neoliberal thinking.

It is clear that historically the EU, in its relations with developing areas of the world, has been chiefly concerned with Africa. However, this has changed over recent years. Lister (1997: 147–8) suggests this is for three key reasons. First, there has been a shift in focus towards Eastern Europe since the end of the Cold War. Second, there has been a broadening of the external interests of the EU in general. Third, the external interests of the EU in Africa have dwindled in response to the continent's poor economic performance during the 1980s. This shift in emphasis is clearly reflected in the geographical destination of EU aid shown in Table 8.1.

Nevertheless, this relative decline in EU interest in Africa should not be seen as the end of an established policy. In fact, as the rest of this chapter demonstrates, the EU has continued to develop its relationship with Africa, and there have been some significant changes in the last few years.

Development cooperation since 1989

At the beginning of the post-Cold War period a marked shift took place in the political nature of the development cooperation activities of the EU. Lomé IV was signed in 1989 and unlike its predecessors was of ten and not five years' duration, with a mid-term review in 1995. It marked the growing impact of neoliberal thinking in the EU's relationship with the ACP states. Both economic and political conditionalities were increased and made much more explicit. In the realm of economic policy-making in ACP states, a significant proportion of the financial transfers from the EU were directed towards structural adjustment. Meanwhile in the political arena conditionalities were formally attached to aid provision.

One of the major changes central to Lomé IV was the introduction of the use of aid for structural adjustment. By the late 1980s the impact of structural adjustment policies (SAPs) had been far from convincing and substantial criticism had led to two major changes in the approach of the Bretton Woods Institutions. First, criticism of the socio-economic impacts led to donors altering their focus towards poverty reduction. Second, a lack of commitment to the policies within the recipient states had led to claims that there was a need to match economic policy changes with improvements in governance and an increase in the impact of civil society. For example, the World Bank's interest in governance was famously expressed in *Sub-Saharan Africa: From Crisis to Sustainable Growth* (World Bank 1989). Nevertheless, SAPs were still presented as depoliticized economic policies.

The European Commission sought to justify the reasons for the inclusion of structural adjustment during the negotiations in 1988–9. Two senior figures within the Commission gave an early indication of the new line of European thinking in this area. In discussing the history and failures of African economies they argued that 'their only option is ordered, properly managed adjustment or forced adjustment' (Frisch and Boidin 1988: 67). It was suggested that the former option was preferable and that the EU would diverge in its approach from the IMF and World Bank, by engaging in dialogue with ACP states to encourage *self-designed* adjustment programmes.

Table 8.1 Regional destinations of EU aid disbursements as a percentage of total EU aid flows

Regional destination	1989	1992	1995	1998
ACP	63.5	54.9	41.5	29.1
South Africa	0.7	1.4	0.8	1.1
Asia and Latin America	14.9	11.3	11.7	12.3
Mediterranean and Middle East	11.8	9.9	10.5	14.1
Central and East European countries and Newly Independent States	0.6	16.7	28.7	37.3
Unallocable	8.5	5.8	6.8	6.1
Total	100	100	100	100

Source: Adapted from ECDPM 2001 (Part 5): 3

However, Brown disputes the claims made by the Commission regarding the unique nature of the adjustment support in Lomé IV (2000: 374–5). He suggests that in reality the EU was in complete alignment with the neoliberal policies of the World Bank and IMF. Further primary research of the impact of EU-sponsored SAPs on Zimbabwe led Brown to conclude that, rather than develop a separate approach, officials in the adjustment unit of the Commission were in almost permanent dialogue with the Bretton Woods Institutions (2002: 105). Moreover, it was usually the case that to receive funds from the sectoral and general import programmes of the EU, the recipient states had to already be pursuing SAPs with the IMF or World Bank (Parfitt 1996: 55).

On the issue of structural adjustment we see the claims to mutual interdependence, central to the Commission's official portrayal of its development policy. Moreover, many African elites appeared to accept the need for such reforms. As noted by Lister 'at the Lomé IV signing ceremony, the president of the ACP Council of Ministers even mentioned aid to structural adjustment as a positive signal for future cooperation' (1997: 118). This is indicative of the growing consensus of neoliberal thinking within policy-makers. One of the direct consequences of structural adjustment funding was a reduction in the amount of EU aid targeted for long-term development funding.

The global context is also instructive when analysing the increasing attachment of political conditionalities to EU aid destined for Africa.[3] The end of the Cold War altered this global context by exposing previously unmentioned concern about the value and effectiveness of aid (Burnell 1997: 191). The most contentious part of this debate concerning foreign aid has been the issue of aid and political reform, or what have been called conditionalities. The expansion of efforts by most Western donors to use assistance to promote liberal democracy in other countries raised many questions about the forms and function of aid (see Abrahamsen 2000).

This striking departure took place in the early 1990s. Donors increasingly linked their Official Development Assistance (ODA) to a number of aspirations embracing democracy and such properties as accountability, legitimacy, the rule of law, human rights, transparency and good governance. A remarkable consensus was achieved on both the ends and the means that were declared in the policy statements of donors in the immediate post-Cold War period.

The policy approaches to achieve these objectives were twofold:

1   Positive support for specific aid projects and programmes aimed at strengthening respect for human rights and democratic practices. This approach is often labelled 'democracy assistance'.
2   Aid sanctions when there are perceived violations of human rights, lack of progress towards democratization, or state corruption. Here donors exert pressure on recipient governments to implement political reforms via the threat of economic sanctions.

This whole policy area is usually referred to as political conditionality. The EU–ACP relationship was no exception, with the regulations governing aid altered to include a more specific emphasis on political reform.

A resolution taken at an EU Council of Ministers meeting in 1991 set the framework for the adoption of political criteria. These criteria were used to suspend aid to a number of African states during the 1990s, including The Gambia (in 1994, in protest at the military coup that deposed President Dawda Jawara); Liberia (in 1998, in protest at Charles Taylor's support for the Revolutionary United Front rebels in Sierra Leone); and Togo (in 1998, in protest at the fraudulent presidential elections). ACP states were to go on record in condemning the unilateral imposition of sanctions on aid, given the institutional framework that was available. The ACP–EU Joint Assembly was not consulted when political conditionalities were used as a means of suspending aid.

The 1995 mid-term review of Lomé IV took place in the context of the EU, like other aid donors, being increasingly sceptical about the potential of aid to have positive impacts (Lister 1997: 132). Moreover, given the EU's desire to exert more control over its relationship with the ACP states, thoughts were already turning to a fundamental reformulation of EU development policy. The review led to alterations in the Convention to bring it into line with the 1991 resolution. Article 5 of the Convention was amended to make respect for human rights, democratic principles and the rule of law essential elements of cooperation. This meant suspension of the agreement could be invoked when violation of these conditions took place.

It is important to note that the EU did not devise a clear set of definitions of how Article 5 was to be interpreted. The Commission suggested this would allow the EU to apply political conditionality in a flexible way. However, there is a clear problem here, in that the possibility is for such political criteria to be interpreted in a way that could lead to inconsistencies with different ACP states (Parfitt 1996: 57).

The possibility of political conditionalities was further increased by another controversial aspect of the mid-term review. Previously aid from the EU was dispersed for the entire duration of each Lomé Convention. However, this was altered in 1995 with the introduction of phased programming. This meant that funds would be allocated in two tranches with the second subject to a successful review of progress. The ACP also opposed this idea during the negotiations on the grounds that it represented a mechanism for the imposition of conditionalities. As Crawford suggested, it sent 'the message that it is possible to re-allocate the second tranche to other countries that do perform well and take more account of EU priorities' (1996: 509).

In summary, these notable changes in EU–ACP development cooperation during the late 1980s and 1990s mirrored wider changes in North–South relations. Both the key areas of change outlined above moved EU policy further away from the original ideal of the Lomé Convention. Rather than allow the ACP states to exercise their state sovereignty by defining their own development policies, economic and political conditions severely constrained the policy options for Africa. This approach is defended by the EU, both in terms of the need to satisfy the concerns of European taxpayers who wish to see that resources are not used to support authoritarian regimes, and also by the belief that democracy and good governance are prerequisites for development. However, this threatens any claims to partnership and is a process open to problems of uneven implementation. During the 1990s a number of African states were subject to the imposition of sanctions based on political conditionalities, whereas many Asian countries, notably China, where human rights abuses are well documented, have escaped EU action due to their greater economic significance (Holland 2002: 134–5). More recent developments and the negotiation of a brand new agreement have continued this process in a number of significant ways.

The EU–South Africa Trade, Development and Cooperation Agreement

Before discussing the new agreement between the EU and the ACP states it is worth mentioning the bilateral arrangement with South Africa. Negotiations towards a new relationship between the EU and South Africa began soon after the end of apartheid in 1994. With hindsight it is now possible to see how this agreement was to prove indicative of wider changes in European development policy.

The detail of the Trade, Development and Cooperation Agreement (TDCA) between the EU and South Africa may provide us with a model to help understand the future direction of EU relations with Africa. The proposal that the EU made contained three different parts. First, they would accept South Africa as a qualified member of the Lomé Convention. It was argued that the South African economy was superior to most ACP states and that this meant only a special restricted status should be granted. The major financial plus was that South Africa would be allowed to tender for finance from the Eighth EDF. Second, a number of agreements for specific fields of cooperation were proposed. The first such agreement to be signed covered science and technology and others followed in the areas of wine and spirits, and fisheries.

The third and most important part of the proposal was the creation, after a transitional period to allow for adjustment, of a Free Trade Area (FTA) between the EU and South Africa. This gave an early indication of how the EU was going to interpret the wider context of multilateral trade liberalization and specifically the new requirements of the World Trade Organization (WTO). The rules of the WTO relating to the negotiation of FTAs state that they should cover 'substantially all' trade, and that they should be completed within a 'reasonable length of time'. The EU interpreted the 'substantially all' as an average of 90 per cent of the items traded between the two parties. One of the major disputes that repeatedly stalled the negotiations was the fact that a large proportion of South Africa's agricultural exports would be excluded from the FTA. France, together with the southern European states, were particularly concerned about the possible impact of these products, and one sector that made its own concerns public was the canned fruit industry (Hurt 2000: 75). What this discussion highlights is the degree of flexibility of the WTO regulations.

After four years of negotiations the final agreement was reached in October 1999. As we will see below, the mixture of aid and a free trade agreement, described as necessary to deal with the unique nature of the South African position, actually served as an indicator of the future direction of the relationship between the EU and Africa as a whole. This is ironic given that the European Council, in its negotiating directives to the Commission, had argued in regard to South Africa's membership of the Lomé Convention that 'given the strength of certain sectors of South Africa's economy ... certain Articles of the Convention would not be applicable to South Africa' (European Commission 1997: 23). Botswana, Lesotho, Namibia and Swaziland (BLNS) have expressed concerns over the bilateral nature of the agreement between the EU and South Africa. As members of the Southern African Customs Union (SACU) they stand to lose customs revenue and are also threatened by the tariff-free export of EU products, which may threaten the productive sectors in the BLNS countries (Hurt 2000: 77–8).

Cotonou and the future of EU development cooperation

Throughout the 1990s the Lomé Convention came under increasing pressure for a number of reasons. First, as I have already shown, there was a decline in the common interests between the EU and ACP states, with the priorities of the EU appearing to lie elsewhere. Second, the relationship had become increasingly politicized, which posed a direct threat to the claims to 'partnership'. Third, the completion of the Uruguay Round of the General Agreement on Tariffs and Trade (GATT) and the creation of the WTO increased the pressures for multilateral trade liberalization. Finally, there was a feeling within the Commission that the Lomé Convention had become overly complex and that this was harming its effectiveness. This was a view that was shared by the majority of ACP states, who welcomed the eventual rationalization of the relationship (interview, ACP Secretariat, November 2001). In response to these pressures the European Commission published a Green Paper in 1996, which made a detailed case for significant reform of the EU–ACP relationship (European Commission 1996).

The Green Paper offered four alternative scenarios for the future of the Lomé Convention (European Commission 1996: 43–4). Two of these four proposals would see little change beyond increasing differentiation at a bilateral level. The third option was to split the relationship up into a number of regional agreements and the fourth was to establish a new agreement with the least developed countries (LDCs) that could be extended beyond the geographical limits of the ACP group. The general thrust of the document was that significant change to the Lomé Convention was both desirable and unavoidable. The Commission presented two major arguments in defence of these proposed changes.

The most significant argument was the need to conform to the rules of the WTO. Previous Lomé Conventions needed to be granted waivers by the GATT for two reasons. First, because they offered non-reciprocal trade preferences with no plan to ultimately remove such preferences. Second, the differential treatment offered to ACP states did not include a further eight non-ACP states who should also be included, based on their comparable levels of development (Hurt 2003: 164–5). The second major reason given for the need for change was the historical record of the Lomé Convention. It was argued that the aid part of the EU–ACP relationship had achieved patchy results, the ethos of partnership had been consistently undermined, and the impact of trade preferences had failed to halt the decline in the export performance in most ACP states (European Commission 1996: 11–18).

The new agreement that was eventually reached between the EU and ACP states reflected both the desire to arrange separate regional agreements and the proposal to differentiate between LDCs and non-LDCs. The Cotonou Agreement was signed on 23 June 2000 and was the culmination of eighteen months of negotiations. It entered into force on 1 April 2003. This new agreement can partly be seen as a continuation of some of the changes that took place during Lomé IV. However, it also marks a substantial shift in the development policy of the EU with its increasing adoption of neoliberal values. Moreover, it sets out the relationship for a minimum of twenty years and will therefore have a lasting impact on EU policy towards Africa.

The neoliberal provisions and conformity with multilateral regulations and trends are evident in both the trade and aid parts of the agreement. The trade provisions of the Cotonou Agreement demonstrate how 'liberalisation, privatisation, and support for the private sector have become as dominant as within the WTO, even though many ACP countries do not have a competitive private sector' (Raffer 2001: 4). The aid provisions of the Ninth EDF include a doubling of the proportion of loans, as opposed to grants, and a movement away from support for raw material exports (both STABEX and SYSMIN have been removed), to the financial backing of regional integration, which the EU argues will help in its overall aim of assisting in the integration of the ACP states into the world economy (interview, ACP Secretariat, November 2001).

The implications of the Cotonou agreement can be grouped into three main categories: trade and the related issues regarding regionalization within the ACP group, aid, and the future role of non-state actors and local government. Each of these will now be discussed.

Trade

The proposed solution to the perceived problems of WTO-compatibility (discussed above) is to radically overhaul the EU–ACP trade regime. A new arrangement is due to be agreed by 2008, which will signal an end to the principle of non-reciprocity for all ACP states that had been one of the defining features of the Lomé Convention. The ACP states will be divided into two different groups: LDCs and non-LDCs. The actual composition of these groups throws up a number of anomalies if the Human Development Index of each state is compared (Hurt 2003: 167).

For the thirty-nine LDCs there is the possibility of maintaining a trade relationship with the EU based on non-reciprocity. In Article 37 of the Cotonou Agreement the provision is made for 'essentially all' products to be given duty-free access to the EU for these ACP states. The Member States have agreed that this should be understood as 'everything but arms'. This refers to the fact that all products except the arms trade will be included. This relationship will also include the eight LDCs that are not members of the ACP group.[4] Given the Commission's negative assessment of the impact of the Lomé Convention on the trade performance of ACP states, the EU has created a paradox by offering the *status quo* to the LDCs (Holland 2002: 221).

The non-LDCs have been offered reciprocal Economic Partnership Agreements (EPAs) to be negotiated on a regional level. In essence these are FTAs and many of the issues of contention surrounding these are similar to those encountered during the negotiations between the EU and South Africa (see Hurt 2000). The inclusion of EPAs will thus curtail the preferential access afforded to these ACP states. Their inclusion has been described as a clear attempt by EU Member States to improve their own potential for exports to the ACP states, thus giving themselves an advantage over other developed countries (Raffer 2001: 4). The impact of EPAs will be to cement the neoliberal approach of openly integrating the economies of ACP states into the world economy. In November 1997, before the Cotonou Agreement was negotiated, the ACP Heads of State and Government showed their concerns with regard to the inclusion of reciprocal trade relations. They argued that 'at this initial stage in the transition of our economies, more appropriate mechanisms of cooperation are needed ... we therefore call on the EU to maintain non-reciprocal trade preferences and market access in a successor agreement' (ACP Heads of State and Government 1997: 7).

There are also clear implementation problems relating to the introduction of EPAs and their impact on regionalization within the ACP group. All the potential regional organizations within Africa would be likely to have capacity problems in negotiating with the EU. Moreover, although the ACP states classified as LDCs are not required to sign EPAs with the EU, each region currently has a mix of LDCs and non-LDCs. This is demonstrated by the case of southern Africa, where the Southern African Development Community (SADC) is composed of six non-LDCs, seven LDCs and South Africa, which, as already discussed, has its own arrangement with the EU.

This is likely to result in fragmentation of the process of regional integration in Africa and will also necessitate strict control of intra-SADC trade movements that may not be easily enforceable (Hurt 2003: 173). It has also been suggested that the division of the ACP states into regional groups will enable the EU to target its trade restrictions more effectively on products that it chooses not to liberalize (Raffer 2001: 5).

Aid

The claims to partnership in the Cotonou Agreement are further undermined by the introduction of 'rolling' programming within the aid pillar. This has been introduced to allow regular assessment of ACP states and their use of EDF resources. A tension between ownership and conditionality is especially evident in European aid. The EU has attempted to distance itself from the conditionality of other donors by frequent reference to this concept of partnership. However, this may 'be lost on governments who will not fail to notice that the Commission is increasing its interference in their internal decision-making' (Van de Walle 1999: 348).

Of key concern are the inclusion of human rights, democratic principles and the rule of law as essential elements. This means that if a Party fails to respect these principles, after a period of political dialogue, a partial or full suspension of the agreement may take place. The Cotonou Agreement differs from the Lomé Convention in its 'relatively explicit and ambitious definitions of democracy and the rule of law' (Martenczuk 2000: 470). We can expect liberal interpretations of these terms to be adopted by the EU if the historical experience of the Lomé Convention is continued. The inclusion of good governance as a fundamental element is also significant as it is the first time the EU has used this issue as a negative conditionality (Martenczuk 2000: 472).

A recent example of such sanctions came in Zimbabwe in early 2002. Concerns about political violence and human rights abuses led the EU to send a mission, led by Pierre Schori, to observe the country's parliamentary elections in May 2000. The mission concluded that 'violence and intimidation in the run-up to the campaign and during the election period marred the final result' and that the Zimbabwean 'government failed to uphold the rule of law' (EU 2000: ch. 7). Consequently, the EU declared its intention to deploy observers for the presidential elections scheduled to take place in 2002. From 29 October 2001, EU foreign ministers unanimously agreed to apply political pressure on Zimbabwe under Article 96 of the Cotonou Agreement. This Article had previously been invoked in the EU's relations with Haiti (which led to sanctions) and Côte d'Ivoire (which did not). Article 96 regulates EU relations with the ACP states and stipulates that if there is no progress on human rights issues within seventy-five days after formal consultations began, 'appropriate measures', including sanctions, may be implemented. In line with these mechanisms, the EU sent a letter to Zimbabwe seeking political consultations, but in response the Zimbabwean government rejected the EU's request to allow its officials to monitor the presidential elections. The EU's dilemma was that both its ministers and Zimbabwe's President Robert Mugabe knew that stopping its £7.35m of development aid would only harm the poorest Zimbabweans (*Financial Times*, 11 January 2002). The final straw in EU–Zimbabwe relations came when Mugabe expelled Schori from the country. The EU's subsequent sanctions entered into effect on 18 February 2002 and entailed a travel ban on President Robert Mugabe and nineteen members of his inner circle (in July the number was increased to fifty-two), an asset freeze affecting those same individuals, an embargo on the sale of arms and technical and training assistance relating to arms, and an embargo on the sale or supply of equipment that might be used for internal repression in Zimbabwe. Throughout the sanctions regime, the EU continued to deliver food aid to Zimbabwe as part of the World Food Programme's emergency initiative.

Use of EDF resources for structural adjustment is continued from the last Lomé Convention but no extra provisions are included with regard to the continuing problem of the indebtedness of many ACP states. This position maintains the approach previously adopted by the EU, which plays down the significance of debt in ACP states, while delegating chief responsibility to the World Bank and IMF.

Non-state actors and local government

Another of the key changes in the Cotonou Agreement is the desire of the EU to shift the emphasis of its development policy away from a relationship that is formed only with central governments. The role of non-state actors is included in Articles 6 and 7 of the Cotonou Agreement. They are defined as 'the private sector, economic and social partners including trade union organizations, and civil society in all its forms'. It is anticipated that non-state actors will play an important role in both the formulation and implementation of the National Indicative Programmes (NIPs), which outline in detail how each ACP state intends to use finance from the EDF (Hurt 2003: 172). However, Martenczuk suggests that 'this role is only weakly reflected in the other parts of the Agreement, which essentially remains an intergovernmental cooperation agreement' (2000: 467). Moreover, there is a clear tension here between the overt claims to partnership and ACP states having ownership of their own development strategies, and an increase in the role of non-state actors. The claims to *ownership* are also not unique to the EU, and this is evident in the approach of most major aid donors. It seems obvious that governments receiving aid that is increasingly decentralized to non-state actors are unlikely to feel an increasing sense of ownership over their development programmes (Van de Walle 1999: 346).

Another aspect of the increasing adoption of neoliberal values in the Cotonou Agreement is the role assigned to the private sector. The inclusion of non-state actors is rather ambiguous and it is highly significant which actors are given priority. Article 22 of the Cotonou Agreement states that support will be provided for those ACP states which are working towards 'Macro-economic growth and stabilisation through disciplined fiscal and monetary policies ... [and] structural policies designed to reinforce the role of the different actors, especially the private sector'. Often the official reason given for the inclusion of non-state actors is to improve the effectiveness of development cooperation by targeting the needs of the poorest sections of society. However, given the emphasis on the private sector there is a strong possibility that their inclusion will merely serve to shift the balance between state and market further towards the market and the private provision of vital public services in ACP states (Hurt 2003: 173).

Common foreign and security policy

In contrast to the EU's development policy, attempts at developing a common EU foreign policy have historically remained weak and uncoordinated. Both changes in the global context and institutional changes within the EU mean that in the post-Cold War era the EU has made some progress, albeit limited, towards developing an effective Common Foreign and Security Policy (CFSP). This section explores the consequences this has had for EU external relations towards Africa since 1989, and whether more recent developments in the area of security hold any clues as to the future impact of EU policies towards the continent.

Cooperation in the realm of European foreign policy dates back to the Hague Summit of 1969 when the process of European Political Cooperation (EPC) was created. The dominant view regarding EPC is that although it led to increased consultations between Member States, it achieved only a negligible impact in harmonizing their foreign policies (Lister 1997: 11). This system of EPC remained in place until the Treaty on European Union in 1992, when it became clear that the EU did not have an effective framework for reaching common positions on many of the new post-Cold War foreign policy issues.

An early EU position in relation to Africa was taken when Gaston Thom, the President of the Council of Ministers, made a statement condemning the policy of apartheid in South Africa on 23 February 1976 (Holland 1988: 31). This resulted in the implementation of a foreign policy initiative by the EU. This was a Code of Conduct for European firms operating in South Africa, which was an adaptation of an existing UK Code of Practice (Holland 1985: 411). The aim was to reconcile the difficulties between the political rhetoric of opposition to apartheid while justifying the continuing high levels of European trade and investment. The Code had limited success and was seen as the lowest common denominator of European opinion.

During the 1990s a number of crises occurred in Africa, and the response of the EU was far from impressive. In response to the Rwandan genocide of 1994 the EU issued several condemnatory statements but little in the way of concrete action, although it did offer support to the second UN Assistance Mission to Rwanda (UNAMIR II) operation after the genocide was over. The EU subsequently adopted CFSP common positions condemning the ethnic violence in Burundi and providing humanitarian aid to Rwanda, despatched a special envoy, Aldo Ajello, to the region in 1996, and adopted a joint action aimed at helping Rwandan refugees to return home. EU ministers also produced several statements outlining their support for democracy promotion (especially in South Africa) and conflict resolution initiatives (in relation to Angola, Liberia, Mozambique and Sudan), and denounced the lack of progress towards democratization in the then Zaire and Nigeria. In May 1998, the Council approved a common position (reviewed regularly) on human rights, democratic principles, the rule of law, and good governance in Africa (see Hill and Smith 2000).

The defence components of the CFSP did not begin to be addressed by the EU until 1998. In 1999 the EU agreed at a summit in Helsinki to develop a common security and defence policy including the creation of a European rapid reaction force. A target was set for 2003, by which time the EU should be able to deploy a military force of up to 60,000 troops within sixty days and sustain such a force for at least one year. In December 2001 at the EU summit in Laeken, this European rapid reaction force was declared partially operational and able to conduct some crisis-management operations.[5]

As this chapter has demonstrated, for years the most significant part of the link between the EU and Africa has been the policy of development cooperation. However, these developments during the 1990s have begun to bring other parts of this relationship to the fore. It has been suggested 'that using the rapid reaction force can contribute to giving the EU a long-aspired role as a significant international actor' (Olsen 2002: 88).

With regard to Africa, the question remains whether these developments will have an impact on the continent. There is certainly a case to be made that during the post-Cold War period European policy-makers have become increasingly disillusioned with the performance of development cooperation (European Commission 1996: 9–20). Again, this is not a situation unique to the EU but a much wider trend, where 'policy elites themselves are more sceptical about aid than ever before' (Van de Walle 1999: 339). Although it would be a fallacy to claim that Africa is top of the list of foreign policy priorities of the EU, there is enough evidence to suggest that such developments may have a direct impact on the continent in the future. Former Commissioner for EU development policy Joao de Deus Pinheiro recently argued that the significant increase during the 1990s of violent conflict kept Africa as a major focus for the EU (Olsen 2002: 90). During the 1990s the EU did adopt the approach of trying to provide support for African states to improve their capacity for conflict management; however, these attempts have so far proved unsuccessful. It is therefore likely that this will put a prime responsibility on the more recent moves towards a European rapid reaction force and its use in Africa (Olsen 2002: 95). More recently, the potential for European rapid reaction forces to participate in crisis management operations on the African continent has not been ruled out.

It is important to highlight that development policy should not be seen as divorced from the CFSP or the possibility of a European rapid reaction force. Poverty reduction is now the overall stated objective of EU development cooperation, yet the EU is more than just a development agency and is a political actor in its own right. It seems clear that there are links between political and economic instability and poverty. However, the EU has yet to develop an integrated approach to poverty reduction to take account of these. The Danish Foreign Minister, during their recent Presidency of the EU, called for policies related to migration and conflict prevention to be brought into the debate over poverty reduction (ECDPM 2002).

One reason for this lack of coordination is that a liberal division between the external economic relations of the EU and its 'political' foreign policy has existed both in numerous treaties and also in the design of the European Commission. The existence of two distinct bureaucracies in the Commission, responsible for development and external affairs respectively, 'has resulted in duplication of effort and extraordinary difficulty in achieving overall coordination and coherence of external policy' (Bretherton and Vogler 1999: 170). There have been recent examples of a limited appreciation of this problem. First, a new body within the Commission, Europeaid, was created at the beginning of 2001 to help improve the management and implementation of the EU's aid programmes. Although this organization is not set the task of overcoming the problems of coordination, it has been suggested that it marks a first step on the road to a more integrated approach that may culminate in a single External Relations Directorate-General (Forwood 2001: 440). Second, the Africa–Europe Summit held in Cairo in April 2000 did acknowledge in its final declaration that both peace and security are vital to making progress in socio-economic development.

Nevertheless there remains a clear tension between the different policy approaches of the EU towards Africa. As I have demonstrated in this chapter, the development policy of the EU has increasingly adopted neoliberal values. We should conclude that this is likely to increase the need for conflict prevention, rather than contribute to peace and security as Article 1 of the Cotonou Agreement suggests. Greater appreciation of the direct relationship between EU development policy and the CFSP is needed, especially with respect to Africa.

Conclusions

The Cotonou Agreement reflects the long-held wishes of the EU that actually date back to the early 1970s and the negotiations prior to Lomé I. The desire to create a number of non-preferential trade agreements with smaller regional groups of developing countries was the EU's preference, but this was prevented by both the global context at the time and the creation of the

ACP group itself (Raffer 2001: 1). This approach is now justified by depicting the WTO rules as both fixed and external to the EU. One of the examples often cited as evidence of the incompatibility of the Lomé Convention and the WTO was 'the WTO's repeated condemnation of the Community's banana regime, through which the Community intended to provide preferential access to bananas originating in ACP countries' (Martenczuk 2000: 464). This represents a deliberate attempt by the EU to absolve itself of responsibility for its own policy decisions (Hurt 2003: 174).

The concept of partnership, in line with other development agencies, has been fully embraced by the EU in the language of the Cotonou Agreement. However, the genuine equality of the relationship has been criticized by a number of commentators who have described this use of the term 'partnership' as merely rhetorical (Hurt 2003; Raffer 2001; Van de Walle 1999).

In summary, the evolution of EU relations with Africa continues to be dominated by its policy of development cooperation. The idea of a strong European CFSP is still very much in its infancy. The EU has the potential to overcome its self-perceived problem of not being a dominant political player in world politics by developing a unique policy that targets Africa's long-term needs. However, as this chapter has suggested, it has not been able to achieve this and the Cotonou Agreement is reflective of this failure. This must be understood within the context of the global trends of both bilateral and multilateral aid donors. The current dominance of neoliberal ideas is broadly compatible with the interests of political elites and the outward-orientated fraction of the capitalist class within the EU and, to a lesser extent, African states. It is this international environment that has made it far more difficult for Africa, as a whole, to redefine its relations with Europe in a positive way (Khadiagala 2000: 103).

Notes

1   I use EU throughout this chapter to represent both the European Union and the organization, pre-Maastricht Treaty, officially referred to as the European Community.
2   Libya currently has observer status at certain meetings and may become a future partner in the Barcelona Process.
3   In 1992 the European Community Humanitarian Office (ECHO) was created in an attempt to distinguish between development aid and humanitarian assistance. ECHO provides funds for humanitarian aid, emergency food aid and disaster relief and prevention, to any non-EU state. It is important to note that ECHO assistance, in contrast to development aid administered through the EDF, does not employ either economic or political conditionalities.
4   The other LDCs are Afghanistan, Bangladesh, Bhutan, Cambodia, Laos, Maldives, Nepal and Yemen. Myanmar would also qualify as an LDC but all its EU trade preferences are currently suspended.
5   The EU launched its first military operation in March 2003 when it took over the job of a NATO peacekeeping mission in Macedonia. This is a modest 300-strong force but is nevertheless an important testing ground for more complex operations in the future.

References

Abrahamsen, R. (2000) *Disciplining Democracy: Development Discourse and Good Governance in Africa*, London: Zed Books.

ACP Heads of State and Government (1997) *The Libreville Declaration*, http://www.acpsec.org

Bretherton, C. and J. Vogler (1999) *The European Union as a Global Actor*, London: Routledge.

Brown, W. (2000) 'Restructuring North–South Relations: ACP–EU Development Co-operation in a Liberal International Order', *Review of African Political Economy*, 27: 367–83.

—— (2002) *The European Union and Africa: The Restructuring of North–South Relations*, London: I. B. Tauris.

Burnell, P. (1997) *Foreign Aid in a Changing World*, Buckingham: Open University Press.

Crawford, G. (1996) 'Whither Lomé? The Mid-term Review and the Decline of Partnership', *Journal of Modern African Studies*, 34: 503–18.

ECDPM (2001) *Cotonou Infokit: The New ACP–EU Partnership Agreement*, Maastricht: ECDPM.

—— (2002) *Cotonou Newsletter No. 5: Global Responsibility for Development: The Priorities of the Danish EU Presidency*, Maastricht: ECDPM.

EU (2000) *Report of the EU Election Observer Mission on the Parliamentary Elections in Zimbabwe, 24–25 June 2000*, http://www.europa.eu.int

European Commission (1996) *Green Paper on Relations between the European Union and the ACP Countries on the Eve of the 21st Century: Challenges and Options for a New Partnership*, Luxembourg: Office for Official Publications of the European Communities.

—— (1997) *The European Union and South Africa: Building a Framework for Long Term Co-operation*, Brussels: European Commission.

Forwood, G. (2001) 'The Road to Cotonou: Negotiating a Successor to Lomé', *Journal of Common Market Studies*, 39: 423–42.

Frisch, D. and J. C. Boidin (1988) 'Adjustment, Development and Equity', *The Courier*, 111: 67–72.

Galtung, J. (1976) 'The Lomé Convention and Neo-Capitalism', *African Review*, 6: 33–42.

Gruhn, I. (1976) 'The Lomé Convention: Inching towards Interdependence', *International Organization*, 30: 241–62.

Hill, C. and K. E. Smith (eds) (2000) *European Foreign Policy Documents*, London: Routledge.

Holland, M. (1985) 'The European Community and South Africa: Economic Reality or Political Rhetoric?', *Political Studies*, 33: 399–417.

—— (1988) *The European Community and South Africa: European Political Co-operation under Strain*, London: Pinter.

—— (2002) *The European Union and the Third World*, Basingstoke: Palgrave.

Hurt, S. R. (2000) 'A Case of Economic Pragmatism? The European Union's Trade and Development Agreement with South Africa', *International Relations*, 15: 67–83.

—— (2003) 'Co-operation and Coercion? The Cotonou Agreement between the European Union and ACP States and the End of the Lomé Convention', *Third World Quarterly*, 24: 161–76.

Khadiagala, G. M. (2000) 'Europe in Africa's Renewal: Beyond Postcolonialism?' in J. W. Harberson and D. Rothchild (eds) *Africa in World Politics: The African State System in Flux*, Boulder: Westview Press, pp. 83–109.

Lister, M. (1997) *The European Union and the South: Relations with Developing Countries*, London: Routledge.

Martenczuk, B. (2000) 'From Lomé to Cotonou: The ACP–EC Partnership Agreement in a Legal Perspective', *European Foreign Affairs Review*, 5: 461–87.

Olsen, G. R. (2002) 'The EU and Conflict Management in African Emergencies', *International Peacekeeping*, 9: 87–102.

Parfitt, T. (1996) 'The Decline of Eurafrica? Lomé's Mid-Term Review', *Review of African Political Economy*, 23: 53–66.

Pfaff, W. (1995) 'A New Colonialism? Europe Must Go Back into Africa', *Foreign Affairs*, 74: 2–6.

Raffer, K. (2001) 'Cotonou: Slowly Undoing Lomé's Concept of Partnership', *DSA Discussion Paper No. 20*, Manchester: DSA.

Shaw, T. M. (1979) 'EEC–ACP Interaction and Images as Redefinitions of Eurafrica: Exemplary, Exclusive and/or Exploitative?' *Journal of Common Market Studies*, 18: 135–58.

Van de Walle, N. (1999) 'Aid's Crisis of Legitimacy: Current Proposals and Future Prospects', *African Affairs*, 98: 337–52.

Whiteman, K. (1998) 'Africa, the ACP and Europe: The Lessons of 25 Years', *Development Policy Review*, 16: 29–37.

World Bank (1989) *Sub-Saharan Africa: From Crisis to Sustainable Growth*, Washington, DC: World Bank.

Zartman, I. W. (1976) 'Europe and Africa: Decolonisation or Dependency?' *Foreign Affairs*, 30: 241–62.

9 The international financial institutions' relations with Africa

Insights from the issue of representation and voice

Caroline Thomas

Since the mid-1990s the governance and policies of the international financial institutions (IFIs, i.e. the IMF and the World Bank) have come under close scrutiny. The IFIs have played a central role in promoting global economic integration, and they have acted far beyond their original mandates. Yet the results have been disappointing. This has prompted a consideration of their need of reform, transformation or even closure. Certainly the governments and peoples of sub-Saharan Africa (SSA) have cause for concern with their relationship with the IFIs. The region has undergone the most intense and continuous application of IFI policies over an expanding range of areas for over two decades, with deeply unsatisfactory economic and social results. Yet SSA suffers from a significant lack of voice and representation in the IFIs.

Sensitive to the intensifying public gaze, the IFIs suggest that the form of their engagement with the countries and peoples of SSA is changing from dominance to partnership, and their policy recommendations from growth to pro-poor growth and poverty reduction. The Poverty Reduction Strategy Papers (PRSPs) are presented as the flagship of new policy ownership by SSA states and new, pro-poor policies. However, many people both within and beyond SSA question this interpretation. For them, the relationship bears the hallmarks of continuity: it remains unequal at core, with no substantive change for SSA states either as members or as clients of the IFIs. Also these critics point to the continuity in the IFIs' fundamental understanding of the African development challenge: impediments to development are understood primarily in terms of domestic shortcomings, rather than external/structural factors associated with Africa's place in the global economy, or indeed a balanced combination of both.

This chapter analyses and evaluates the scope and depth of changes in the IFI–Africa relationship, by using the issue of representation and voice as an indicator. The issue is explored in two contexts: first, for SSA states as *members* of the IFIs – representation and voice at the fundamental structural level; and second, for SSA states as *clients* of the IFIs – representation and voice in the process of borrowing. To this end, the chapter begins with a note on SSA's development challenge, as the backdrop against which to appreciate the importance of the IFI–SSA relationship, and the significance of voice for SSA. Thereafter the chapter is divided into two main parts. The first part focuses on the *structure of power and influence which operates within, through and around the IFIs*. Who do these institutions represent? What are the mechanisms by which SSA is represented and how effective are these? To what extent is the issue of representation for Africa recognized as problematic within the IFIs? How is this matter being addressed, why, by whom, and with what effect? The second part of the chapter explores evidence regarding SSA voice, in terms of IFI dealings with client states as borrowers. Why are the IFIs concerned to characterize their relationship with African clients as changing? How far do PRSPs represent a change in ownership of development policy in favour of African governments and poor people? What are the implications for development policy? Finally, the conclusion suggests not only that the IFI relationship with SSA is characterized more by continuity than change, but that the IFIs have appropriated the language of change without substantially altering the form of their engagement with SSA, or their policy framework. The result has been to mask the growing control which the IFIs, and those interests which they characteristically represent, exercise over development in SSA. When cast against past experience of the IFI–SSA relationship and future challenges, this is worrying.

A note on the development challenge in SSA

Recent IFI statistics on SSA make grave reading. World Bank figures show that over the 1990s there were improvements globally in reducing the number living on less than $1 a day, yet the situation in Africa deteriorated (Tables 9.1, 9.2). An estimated 49 per cent of the population lives in extreme poverty. Even if projected growth remains on track globally – a questionable assumption – the figure in extreme poverty in SSA is expected to rise to 404 million by 2015 (World Bank 2003).

Measuring poverty is not a precise art. An UNCTAD study (2002a) used the World Bank definition of poverty, but a different methodology; the

Table 9.1 Extreme poverty in sub-Saharan Africa

	Million people < $1 a day			Share of people on < $1 a day (%)		
	1990	1999	2015	1990	1999	2015
SS Africa	241	315	404	47.4	49.0	46.0
Global total	1,292	1,169	809	29.6	23.2	13.3
Excluding China	917	945	735	28.5	25.0	15.7

Source: Adapted from World Bank 2003: ch.1, p. 5

Table 9.2 Poverty in sub-Saharan Africa

	Million people < $2 a day			Share of people on < $2 a day (%)		
	1990	*1999*	*2015*	*1990*	*1999*	*2015*
SS Africa	386	480	618	76.0	74.7	70.4
Global total	2,712	2,802	2,320	62.1	55.6	38.1
Excluding China	1,892	2,173	2,101	58.7	57.5	44.7

Source: Adapted from World Bank 2003: ch. 1, p. 5

result gave estimates of extreme poverty at 64.9 per cent for the late 1990s. Recent studies point to fundamental flaws in the assumptions on which the World Bank measures poverty. If valid, then the extent of poverty has been underestimated by the IFIs (Reddy and Pogge 2003).

SSA is not on course to meet the Millennium Development Goals (MDG) by 2015. Reviewing achievements to date, Sahn and Stifel (2003: 23) note that 'the problem of faltering social progress is especially acute in Africa ... [where] realizing the MDG ... will be a particularly challenging task'. Projections suggest that the required annual growth of at least 7 per cent which SSA needs to meet poverty alleviation targets will not be achieved (World Bank 2000: 2).

Given the multiplicity of major problems facing the continent – such as huge debt, declining aid, declining commodity prices, conflict, corruption, HIV/AIDS, the weather, population growth – it would be unreasonable to lay the blame for lack of achievement in development solely at the door of the IFIs. It would be equally unreasonable, however, not to put the IFI–SSA relationship under the microscope, given its poor history, continuing intensity and expanding reach. It is to that task that we turn.

The IFIs: whose institutions? Representation and voice for SSA as member states

African states were still colonies at the founding of the IFIs, therefore their interests were not directly represented. Following independence, their experience in these institutions was marred by the unequal distribution of voting power within the IFIs' decision-making structures. African governments sought greater influence on the global economic stage via the discursive UN system, where the more congenial principle of one state, one vote operated. They pursued collective representation in the G-77, and argued successfully for the creation of the UN Conference on Trade and Development (UNCTAD) to deal with economic matters. The Western powers did not object, secure in the knowledge that funding and economic policies would be determined through the IMF and the World Bank where weighted voting operated in their favour.

SSA voice in the IFIs: NGOs make a noise

It was not until the mid to late 1990s that the issue of African representation and voice in the IFIs made an impact in the global political arena. This was largely due to efforts by Northern and Southern advocacy groups and networks such as Christian Aid, 50 Years is Enough, Jubilee 2000 and SEATINI, with some input from agencies such as UNDP. By the turn of the new century, the issue had reached the agenda of the IFIs. Why did this occur?

Over the 1980s, economic crisis and the debt burden had forced SSA countries to look to the IFIs for financial support. But help was conditional on the acceptance of structural adjustment programmes designed not by Africans but by IFI officials. Economic sovereignty, previously weak, was further undermined. Doubts grew particularly in the 1990s about the legitimacy, economic efficacy and social impact of these adjustment policies. By then, the IFIs were intimately involved in promoting an agenda for good governance, as well as economic reform, in Africa. Yet in the democratic spirit of the decade, they found their own governance being scrutinized and exposed by a transnational alliance of NGOs. The Center of Concern in Washington DC was particularly effective in engaging the IFIs in a dialogue. Key issues included general transparency of the institutions, accountability and leadership selections. More recently, the spotlight has shifted to the composition of, and voting rights on, the IFIs' Executive Boards (EBs), the different capacities of Executive Directors (EDs) and the transparency of the Boards themselves.

Structural power: impediment to voice

Those advocating increased voice for SSA in the IFIs face significant obstacles, not least existing decision-making structures. Decision-making in the IFIs takes place through their Boards, each comprised of twenty-four EDs. The five largest vote holders are guaranteed one seat each on the Boards: US, Britain, France, Germany, and Japan. Saudi Arabia, China and Russia, as large constituencies, have one seat each also. The remaining 176 states are in sixteen multi-constituency groupings, with each group represented by one ED. Forty-six SSA states are represented by two EDs.

While decisions on the Boards are taken on the basis of consensus rather than voting, the number of votes which each ED commands is crucial for the potential influence s/he can exercise. For each ED, the number reflects the combined votes of the states s/he represents. Initially, when the IFIs were established, every member state was given 250 basic votes, with additional votes – quota for the IMF, or capital subscription for the World Bank – being added to reflect economic standing in the world economy. Over time, the significance of the basic vote has diminished, as the formula to attribute votes has increasingly favoured economically strong countries on the basis that they meet capital requirements. Thus in the IMF, for example, by 1999 basic votes as a share of total votes stood at 2.1 per cent, compared with

11.3 per cent in 1944 (Development Committee 2003a: 8). Yet it is note-worthy both that the increased economic power of Asian countries has not been reflected in their share of votes, and also that the increased share of IFI funding via loan repayments, arrangement fees, etc., has not been reflected in changed voting distribution.

Weighted voting privileges the G-7 countries, particularly the US. The latter, with over 16 per cent of the votes in the IMF and World Bank, is the only state which can unilaterally exercise veto power on important decisions requiring an 85 per cent majority. Arguably, an equally big distortion is that fifteen states of the EU have 29.9 per cent of the votes at the IMF, and eight seats on its Board.

The task of representing forty-six SSA states falls largely to the two dedi-cated African EDs. When we consider that most or all of these SSA states are likely to be borrowing from the IFIs, the relative workload of these two people is clearly unmanageable. Therefore the situation regarding represen-tation is unfair on multiple levels (Christian Aid 2003: 4).

In addition to the two dedicated African EDs, African interests are cham-pioned within the IFIs by the G-24, a sub group of the G-77, mandated since 1971 to ensure that the interests of the developing countries are adequately represented in respect of financial matters. The G-24 is made up of representatives of three regional groupings: Africa, Asia and Latin America. In general terms, the G-24 is true to this mandate. In 2002, for example, it argued that: 'The participation of developing countries in the decision-making structure of the Bretton Woods institutions should be strengthened – particularly for SSA.' In 2003, the G-24 argued that:

> in order to enhance the legitimacy of the IMF and the World Bank, the voice, participation, and voting power of developing countries in the decision-making processes of these institutions should be significantly strengthened through: (i) a quota distribution that reflects correctly the relative economic position of these countries in the world economy; (ii) a substantial increase in basic votes to restore their role in relation to total voting power at the inception of the IMF and the World Bank.

However, the G-24 constituency is made up of very divergent interests: oil producers, heavily indebted countries and emerging economies. A more effective mechanism is needed to ensure that SSA's interests are canvassed and protected.

Sometimes, ad hoc opportunities to present African interests may arise. For example, South African Finance Minister Trevor Manuel was Chair of the IFI Boards in 2000. The issue of representation was raised during his tenure, but without noticeable vigour (Bond 2001) and the IFIs chose to interpret the issue in terms of their need for greater listening skills.

The preponderance of power within the IFIs leaves these institutions open to the charge of being the vehicles for the exercise of G-7 economic priorities, or even for the pursuit of US foreign policy (Houtven 2002: 42). In the words of Christian Aid (2003: 2): 'This small group of countries can agree policies outside of the IFIs and implement these policies through them.' These countries then pursue their national foreign policy objectives through the IFIs. Effectively, SSA states are the recipients of policies made for them and not necessarily with their interests as the primary concern. In addition, the preponderance of power poses important obstacles to change in the governance of the IFIs, not least that significant amendments of the IFI Articles of Agreement are dependent on large majorities of total voting power on their Boards.

New international commitments to voice: but how deep do they go?

The political profile of the issue of representation and voice in the IFIs grew rapidly at the turn of the new century. In March 2002, a potentially important development occurred in the context of the UN Monterrey Conference on Financing for Development, where a new partnership compact between developed and developing countries, based on mutual accountability, was launched. It was agreed there that the IMF and World Bank should 'continue to enhance the participation of all developing countries ... in their decision-making' (Monterrey Report 2002: point 63).

This commitment has elicited multiple interpretations, ranging from adherence to the status quo, to reform of various hues, to transformation, and even closure. The fault line lies along approaches to change: whether it is best delivered through formal changes in voting strength, more effective exploitation of existing opportunities for representation (i.e. capacity building), a combination of both, or abolition.

Many IFI career staff adopt a fairly conservative stance. Following Monterrey, the IFIs' Development Committee asked their own technical staff to prepare a document on ways of broadening and strengthening voice for developing countries in the IFIs for consideration at the spring meetings in 2003. The tone of the document (IMF/World Bank 2003) was conservative. It identified two types of participation: 'voting' and 'the use of opportunities for articulation of views' (p. 3). The document favoured the latter, claiming that a broad degree of consensus exists among members that 'the principle underlying the distribution of quotas, shares and voting rights – that these should in large measure reflect the relative importance of member countries in the global economy – remains appropriate' (p. 3) and therefore needs no further discussion. Moreover, it claimed that the 'distribution of Fund quotas – and related governance issues – are part of the work program ... on which the Fund Executive Board is expected to provide a status report ... [in] September 2003' (p. 8), the implication being that prior discussion was unnecessary or inappropriate.

The US and most European countries have adopted a minimalist reformist perspective, geared towards incrementally enhancing the capacity/effectiveness of the two EDs representing SSA within the existing governance structure. Reform measures would include increasing the number of support staff in the African EDs' offices, increasing the African EDs' communications links with national capitals via videoconferencing, etc., and developing African national capacity for engagement with EDs. They argue that such measures are underway, for example through the IMF's African Capacity Building Initiative and associated African Regional Technical Assistance Centres (AFRITACs). The latter will train Africans locally in the core competencies of the IMF. A further suggestion is the creation of a trust fund to provide research and technical support to individual EDs and to the G-24. These reformists argue against the creation of new seats on the Boards (or reallocating existing ones), not on the basis of legitimacy issues, but rather speed and efficiency of decision-making (IMF/World Bank 2003: 6, note 7).

Further along the spectrum, the developing countries, joined by the Nordic states and Britain, have sought a more deep-rooted amendment of Board structure in addition to African capacity-building. They have found champions within the UN system, such as UNDP (2002) which has argued that 'the IMF and the World Bank will not be able to do their job effectively if they remain tied to structures that reflect the balance of power of the Second World War'. For this group, crucial changes would include increased votes and increased voice on the Boards of the IFIs, and their oversight committees – the Development Committee and the International Monetary and Financial Committee (IMFC). Even within this grouping, however, the structural proposals forthcoming so far are not radical. For example, these might involve creating an extra one or two additional ED posts for African states.

Deeper reforms are sought by a collection of civil society organizations in the North and South, several of which loosely coordinate their advocacy around the Bretton Woods Project. They are putting pressure on the IFIs and their member governments to make substantive, rather than cosmetic changes. For example, they advocate a reallocation of Board seats to ensure that all member states can fairly represent themselves, and so that creditors and borrowers have an equal allocation of votes; the removal of the veto power from a single country; and a limitation on ten countries per constituency represented by one ED.

However, there are other representatives of civil society, such as Pan African Jubilee South, which call for the closure of the IFIs, believing them to be inherently oppressive and exploitative of SSA people. Instead they want space for the articulation of national, regional and continental alternatives and they do not believe this is possible within the existing organizational structure.

The joint IFI spring meetings in 2003 provided the opportunity to address the Monterrey commitment to enhanced participation in the IFIs . While the Communiqué of the IMFC (2003) merely referred to this under 'Other Issues', the issue of voice received more attention in the Development

Committee meeting. There, the two African EDs – Mr Famara Yatta of Gambia, representing the Group 1 African countries, and Mr Bohoun Bouabre, of Côte d'Ivoire, representing the twenty-five Group 11 African countries, made important contributions. Bouabre applauded the capacity-building measures already agreed by the IFIs to increase staff of the African offices, but he added: 'for us, the question of the developing countries' "voice" does not hinge solely on building office capacity ... it is also important to introduce changes in the level of representation on the Boards, as well as voting rights' (Bouabre 2003). Yatta made similar points, suggesting a restoration of the value of the basic votes. (As noted above, the issue of raising basic votes in order to restore their value in terms of voting power was also championed by the G-24 in their communiqué to the spring meetings.) Anxious not to alienate the G-7, Yatta (2003) reiterated that 'we are definitely not in favour of a system of governance based on the "1 country, 1 vote" principle'. From his perspective, the political implications of reform required the matter to be handled cautiously, lest all hope of change be lost.

The spring meetings did not result in any improvements in representation for African countries at a structural level. The IMF continues to present the issue of representation for SSA in terms of the Fund's own need for better 'listening skills', rather than structural change. However, the meetings did result in a restatement of commitments to capacity building, and importantly they contributed to a momentum which it will be difficult for the G-7 and the IFIs to stop or ultimately ignore. In this context, it will be necessary to scrutinize the upcoming Fund Review of Quota and review its implications for SSA representation and voice. It is cautionary to note that fifteen years ago a committee to examine and make recommendations on the voting strength of small countries came to no agreement, and deliberations were quietly dropped (IMF/World Bank 2003: 13).

The IFI/donor 'Coherence Agenda': a moving target for SSA representation and voice?

Increasingly the G-7 bypass the IFIs and use their summits and other venues to set policies. Indeed, there is growing disquiet both among members and media that 'the international financial agenda appears to be increasingly set in the annual summits of the major industrialized countries' (Houtven 2002: 32). Indeed, the G-7 have established exclusive discussion forums on economic and financial matters, involving themselves and a select group of those developing/emerging countries whose economies they consider the most important, with representation from the IFIs. For example, in 1999 they created the G-20, in fulfilment of their commitment at the June G-7 Summit at Cologne 'to establish an informal mechanism for dialogue among systemically important countries within the framework of the Bretton Woods institutional system'. The only SSA country to be represented is South Africa.

Yet while the political framing of the global policy agenda at the most fundamental level may lie outside of the IFIs, those institutions are intimately involved in policy discussions and, through conditionality, implementation. The IFIs occupy a central place in the emerging global governance network of public and private actors which oversees and implements development policy. The urgent need for, and growing obstacles to, effective African voice and representation is clear when we consider key aspects of this network. One such feature is the rapidly growing collaboration and convergence between the IFIs and other institutions, especially the WTO. Indeed, since 1996 these three institutions have been developing a dedicated 'coherence agenda', even though only the World Bank is charged explicitly with development as a primary task. In April 2002, the World Bank President James Wolfensohn (2002) commented on the 'common strategic direction', in other words the general policy framework, shared by these institutions. He remarked that: 'Together with other Multilateral Development Banks (and bilateral donors, through the OECD Development Assistance Committee), we are implementing the agreed action plan to harmonize donor operational policies, procedures and practices.' This convergence further strengthens the already overwhelming influence of the IFIs in global development policy, as bilateral donors line up behind IFI policies.

The problem of lack of representation and voice for African states as members of the IFIs is historical and structural. However, the depth of the problem has increased over the past twenty years, and recently has reached new levels as the IFIs have become central players in the emerging global governance network. The concentration of power and influence represented in the increased collaboration and convergence within this network works against effective voice for SSA. Despite the enhanced political profile of the issue of voice for SSA members of the IFIs since the late 1990s, largely due to the campaigning of NGOs, this trend shows no signs of abating in the near future; but for the same reason, it will surely not go away.

SSA as clients of the IFIs: what place for African ownership?

The foregoing examination suggests that continuity rather than change characterizes the IFI relationship with SSA *member states*. But what of the IFIs' claim that their relationship with SSA states as *clients* has changed? To interrogate this claim, this section explores briefly why the apparent change of heart occurred in the IFIs in the late 1990s, and then assesses the nature and scope of the change, focusing on ownership and related policy matters through the lens of the PRSPs.

Why the change of heart in the IFIs?

By the late 1990s, especially after the Asian crisis, the IFIs and their universal blueprint of export-led growth for development were under pressure from a number of sources, both external and internal. With respect to SSA, the IFIs' growth strategies had failed to deliver. Economic growth remained under 2.5 per cent during the 1980s and the 1990s (UNCTAD 2001). In twelve states, GDP per capita remained below the level for 1960; and in twenty-four countries, it was below the level for 1975 (Milanovic 2003). The thirty-three SSA HIPC countries were more heavily indebted than two decades earlier (Easterly 2002). SSA was becoming increasingly marginalized in the global economy, and within African states poverty was mounting. The public antagonism between certain African governments and the IFIs – for example, Mozambique over the cashew nut trade liberalization question – was bitter, and lent weight to long-standing concerns that their Washington Consensus model was being externally imposed on needy, vulnerable client states in violation of national sovereignty and expressed policy preferences not only of governments but of local people (Hanlon 2000). Popular unease with the IFI relationship was mounting, with privatization being a rallying point. In addition, an extremely vocal and effective transnational alliance of NGOs canvassed for debt cancellation through the Jubilee 2000 campaign (Birdsall and Williamson 2002). Civil society groups also campaigned hard on the adverse impact of IFI policies on the poor: for example, the general destruction of Africa's health infrastructure, user fees for medicines and water, and the links between poverty and the spread of HIV/AIDS.

With the Bank under scrutiny, President Wolfensohn responded to a civil society challenge by agreeing to the establishment of a joint multiyear World Bank/civil society/government participatory review (SAPRI). The experience of ten countries in structural adjustment, four of which were African (Uganda, Mali, Zimbabwe and Ghana), would be assessed, based on an agreed methodology emphasizing participatory techniques. The aim was to give voice to civil society constituencies, and bring them into the national and global economic decision-making process. Yet what began as a joint learning exercise, based on extensive joint field research and consultations, eventually ended with two separate final reports, one produced by the Bank (World Bank 2001b), the other by civil society groups (SAPRIN 2000). Key Bank staff and NGOs interpreted the findings of the review quite differently. The status of the initiative within the Bank was lowered, and trust broke down. Civil society groups felt that the Bank was not seriously interested in learning from local people, and in particular that it was unwilling to address the links as experienced by people on the ground between core economic policies such as trade liberalization and poverty.

IFI prescriptions: from growth to pro-poor growth

The IFIs adhered to the belief that growth is good for the poor (Dollar and Kray 2000), and they were unwilling to explore the relationship between macroeconomic policy and poverty generation. However, they did concede some problems regarding the export-oriented growth model to which they had subjected SSA for twenty years. First, despite the temporary upturn in growth in SSA in the mid to late 1990s, that growth was not consistent and strong enough to deliver the needed social gains. Second, the policies used to promote growth (budgetary cuts, deregulation, trade liberalization, privatization, financial liberalization, etc.) did sometimes hurt some poor people and erode the middle classes. Third, the relatively minor modifications made in policy to attend to the needs of the poor, such as safety nets, micro-credit or user fee exemption, were insufficient. These concessions did not, however, prompt a reassessment of the basic strategy; rather, the Bank took the view that adjustment was a difficult process, and it needed to be locally owned rather than imposed by the IFIs (World Bank 2001b).

Thus the Post Washington Consensus (PWC) emerged, based on the belief that growth, while necessary, was not sufficient for development – it had to be made 'pro-poor'; that targeted poverty reduction was crucial; and that a better balance had to be achieved between economic growth and other values such as equity and sustainability. The PWC also stressed the role of national governments in owning development strategies, and of civil society's participation in their formulation. Good governance – already featuring in IFI policies in the 1990s – was critical to the PWC: tackling corruption, developing and enforcing property rights and contracts, and building national capacity for policy ownership.

A series of frameworks and policies reinforced these ideas. In 1999, President Wolfensohn launched the Comprehensive Development Framework, which, in contrast to the Washington Consensus, claimed to put the recipient country 'in the driver's seat' (World Bank 2001) and provide 'a compass, not a blueprint' for development (World Bank 2001a). The donor/creditor relationship looked set to change, as the language of *partnership* between donors and recipients permeated development discourse. Also in 1999 the *Enhanced* Heavily Indebted Poor Country Initiative (HIPC) was launched, which moved away from the original (1996) HIPC's emphasis on debt sustainability, to a new emphasis on deeper, faster, broader relief linked directly to poverty reduction. Once a country qualified for debt relief under the Enhanced HIPC, *access* to relief would depend on acceptance by the IFI Boards of the country's national Poverty Reduction Strategy Paper.

The birth of the Poverty Reduction Strategy Papers (PRSPs) concept

At its September 1999 meeting, the IFIs' joint Development Committee endorsed proposals that all low-income countries receiving support from the World Bank's International Development Agency (IDA) and through the Enhanced Structural Adjustment Facility (ESAF) should develop national PRSPs. Henceforth, these papers would be used by multilateral and bilateral funders as the litmus test of a country's suitability for debt relief and new funds. Debt relief and poverty reduction would be directly linked, as would poverty reduction and new funds. Hence, they would play a crucial role in the IFI–SSA relationship.

The Development Committee emphasized that PRSPs should

> be country-driven, be developed transparently with broad participation of elected institutions, stakeholders including civil society, key donors and regional development banks, and have a clear link with the agreed international development goals – principles that are embedded in the Comprehensive Development Framework.
>
> (Development Committee 1999)

In theory, whereas the WC promoted *policy conditions*, the PWC was to promote *process conditions*.

The idea of the PRSP was rapidly adopted by the official aid community, and it is now the centrepiece for policy dialogue in all countries seeking concessional funds. In April 2002, Wolfensohn's first recommendation, in setting out a post-Monterrey action plan to the Development Committee, was the use of PRSPs as 'anchors for securing fresh donor support' (World Bank 2002). From the points of view of debtors and creditors, these papers are assuming crucial significance in development policy and funding. The IMF has replaced the ESAF with a Poverty Reduction with Growth (PRG) facility, and the World Bank has established Poverty Reduction Support Credits (PRSCs). The EU Commission has noted the 'central place [of the PRSP] in Commission development policy and in the programming of the resources for which the Commission is responsible' (EU Commission 2001).

In a potentially positive move, the World Bank organized a major review of the Poverty Reduction Strategy, beginning in summer 2001 and culminating in January 2002 with a conference involving donors, creditors and civil society representatives. A positive reading might suggest that, given the strategy was barely two years old, the World Bank was keen to ensure real dialogue on the efficacy of its policies more rapidly than it had done in the case of structural adjustment. (The SAPRI did not get going until the policy had been in operation for about a decade and a half). A more critical reading, however, given the experience of the SAPRI, noted above, might be that the Bank was anxious to legitimize this new approach as soon as possible. Following the review, while the Bank felt 'there was no need for major adjustments in the approach' (World Bank 2002b), many NGOs remained dissatisfied, feeling that the PRSP process was not true to the spirit of country ownership. Some of the key issues related to ownership are discussed below.

The issue of ownership

There is a widespread concern over the issue of national sovereignty/ownership of PRSPs. Charles Abugre (2000) of Ghana's Integrated Social Development Centre argues cogently that the concept of the PRS threatens the sovereignty of Third World countries at the *most fundamental* level, because it actually *enables* the IMF and World Bank to assume even more extensive powers over developing countries. The IFIs have the sole authority to give the stamp of approval to an entire *national* development strategy, including its social and political aspects. While the sovereignty of national governments is undermined, the power of the IMF and World Bank is enhanced even though they are only lending or underwriting a very small part of that strategy. In the words of Jubilee South's (2001) Pan African Declaration on PRSPs: 'This reflects the ultimate mockery of the threadbare claim that the PRSPs are based on "national ownership".' A related concern is that the coordination of the entire spectrum of donor activity around the IMF/World Bank-endorsed PRS gives the developing country little room for manoeuvre between different donors, constraining sovereignty further. Without an IFI-approved PRSP, a poor country 'can be virtually cut off from international aid, trade and finance' (Malaluan and Guttal 2003: 3).

A further concern is the context in which the SSA countries are drawing up their PRSPs, and in which PRGF and PRSC loans are being negotiated. Starved of investment resources and crippled with the debt burden, they are desperate for immediate debt reduction to free up resources for the import of essential items without which they cannot function. Therefore they are under intense pressure to develop PRSPs quickly, because without these they cannot receive debt reduction under the Enhanced HIPC or new loans. *They are drawing up these plans, however, in full knowledge that if their plans do not fit with the worldview of the World Bank and Fund, they are unlikely to get approval,* and this knowledge is bound to affect the shape of the plans. Indeed, a key conclusion of the highly detailed study of the Ugandan experience is that real national ownership is impossible while debt relief is linked to the PRSP; any chance of an autonomous national framework is lost (Nyamugasira and Rowden 2002: 71).

The imperative to gain IFI approval may help account for the fact that PRSPs are so similar in essentials, even though local ownership is in theory supposed to militate against the 'one size fits all' approach that characterized the 1980s and 1990s. The macroeconomic framework is taken as given in PRSPs. A South–South inquiry has suggested that:

> In every case examined the most important element of the PSRPs or interim PRSPs devised are the mandatory policy matrices. These orientations detail the now standardized Bank–Fund assortment of policy 'reform' including liberalisation, privatisation, fiscal and administrative reform, assets management.
>
> (Jubilee South *et al.* 2002)

In other words, in important ways they resemble structural adjustment packages.

With one or two notable exceptions (such as the policy reversal on Mozambican cashew nut liberalization in 2002), we have yet to see IFIs walk the talk of policy flexibility. This is very well understood by personnel in African Ministries of Finance, and partly explains why, despite their countries' intensely painful and costly experience of increased openness to trade since the late 1960s (World Bank 2000: 4), they go along with the basic package. Indeed, they receive help and guidance in the drafting of PRSPs, for example via joint IFI staff reviews. However, a further reason may be the intellectual hegemony of the Bank: 'Through its global and national-level studies, and its extensive network of official, journalist and academic contacts, the Bank has a strong influence on policy debates' (Wilks and Lefrancois 2002: 8). The IFIs even provide a thousand-page PRSP Sourcebook. African Ministers of Finance seem comfortable taking the lead from the 'knowledge Bank' (IMF 2003). Again, the study on Uganda by Nyamugasira and Rowden supports this interpretation, as does close examination of Africa's so-called 'home-grown' NEPAD on a broader level (CODESRIA/TWN 2002; Chabal 2002).

There seems to be no discussion of the link between growth-oriented macroeconomic policy and *poverty creation*, or *inequality*, and possible *alternatives* to the orthodoxy. This is evident in the PRSPs for Mauritania, Burkina Faso, Uganda and Tanzania (WEED 2003). Consider the example of trade: PRSPs offer very limited discussion of trade and trade policy, and this 'tends to use the simplistic language of wholesale and rapid liberalization' following the PRSP Sourcebook (Ladd 2003: 1). This is surprising, especially given the cautionary contrary findings even of IFI-funded research in respect of SSA (Milanovic 2002). PRSPs fail to consider the likely impacts of trade liberalization on different social groups, and these will be complex and varied (Ladd 2003). Yet the goal of poverty reduction *requires* a prior analysis of the likely impact on the poor. Moreover, the IFIs have committed to *ex ante* Poverty and Social Impact Analysis as part of macroeconomic reforms, but they have not delivered on this (Joint NGOs 2003).

Within Africa, there is a growing body of knowledge on the poverty and social impact of macroeconomic policies, and a discussion of alternative pathways. This knowledge should be given appropriate consideration. The South–South assessment showed that PRSPs fail to give due consideration to potentially important strategies, such as

> Policy and political measures indispensable in many cases to effective poverty and inequality reduction … land and agrarian reform, progressive taxation, support for domestic markets and protection, food sovereignty, the protection of the environment and labour *vis-à-vis* investors, assurances of social rights and entitlements, and other forms of governmental protection *vis-à-vis* the free market.
>
> (Jubilee South *et al.* 2002: para. 5)

CODESRIA – a key association of African intellectuals – and the advocacy group Third World Network Africa have done important work outlining alternatives (CODESRIA/TWN 2002). If the growth–poverty reduction link is to be truly embedded in IFI lending, this knowledge must be tapped to inform a trade-off between macroeconomic policy and microsocial policy.

The adverse impact of the failure to link macro policies and micro effects is magnified when we consider that PRSPs are the trigger for conditional loans via PRGF and PRCS. Again, the study on Uganda concluded that 'the actual policies in the loans were determined by the IMF and World Bank representatives in consultation with small technical teams within the Ministry of Finance and Central Bank' (Nyamugasira and Rowden 2002: 5). In terms of policy conditionality – which the IFIs claim to be streamlining in support of national ownership (IMF 2002) – a recent review suggests that 'good performers' (i.e. those that are already following IFI prescriptions, such as Tanzania and Uganda) are subject to fewer conditions than countries with a bad track record, such as Zambia (EURODAD 2003). Also, while the IMF is retreating into policy conditions associated more closely with its core mandate, the space is taken up by the World Bank conditions.

Cross conditionality further erodes the possibility of national ownership. In the case of Zambia, for example, the first condition in a HIPC loan was that the country was on track with a PRGF programme. The latter required privatization of the Zambia National Commercial Bank, which had been opposed by civil society groups (EURODAD 2003: 8). Indeed, one analyst believes that HIPC countries face a 'tighter policy straitjacket' even when experiencing fewer conditions from the IFIs (Killick 2002).

The issue of participation

Central to the PRSP concept is broad-based participation by local stakeholders to deepen country ownership. The PRSP process is still at an early stage, and the development of broad genuine participation within a country is a long-term project, particularly where there is little history of this. The World Bank uses the idea of a 'ladder of participation' to describe different levels of participation: information sharing, consultation, joint decision-making and initiation and control by stakeholders.

Participation in PRSPs has been the subject of several studies, most of which conclude that it has been 'patchy, limited to consultation rather than decision-making, and without impact at all in the field of macroeconomic policy' (McGee and Hughes 2002: para 3.3.5). The World Bank's own study of participation in PRSPs found the process to be failing particular groups in SSA, such as poor women (World Bank 2002a). It is clear, however, that where there is political will, proactive governments can exert a powerful influence on civil society participation. In Rwanda, for example, a clear effort was made to involve a wide cross-section of people, including those from the poorest communities (Bugingo 2002). However, consulting does not amount to involving people in participatory decision-making. For the PRSP process to gain legitimacy, governments and the IFIs must support the development of *genuine participation*, and this means that *policy frameworks* must be up for negotiation.

To date, the practical outcomes of the PRSP process seem to be at odds with the theory in terms of ownership. A G-24 briefing paper on the PRSPs (2003: 4) concludes that 'the progress made has been limited by a variety of obstacles ... above all lack of ownership'. Regarding participation, many important issues remain, not least the appropriate role for elected parliaments in this process. A study of the Zambian PRSP process, for example, suggested that Members of Parliament were marginalized (Malaluan and Guttal 2003: 3), and the same has been suggested in relation to Ghana (Abugre 2000).

Despite obvious weaknesses in the PRSP process, some commentators believe that continued engagement with the IFIs and donors aimed at reforming the process offers the best hope available both to expand national ownership of economic policy and to make decision-making more inclusive in SSA (e.g. Cheru 2002). If all parties operate in the spirit which was intended, the PRSP process could enhance representation and voice for SSA.

Conclusion

It is difficult to avoid the conclusion that the IFIs' claims of a change in their form of engagement with SSA, as well as in their policies, are unsupported by the evidence. In terms of representation and voice for SSA states, changes in the relationship with the IFIs are limited and soft. Enhancing the effectiveness of the existing two African ED posts is a necessary, but totally insufficient, condition for increasing African representation and voice. Without changing the structure of voting power on the Boards, such actions amount to 'doing something without doing anything'. Similarly, as regards SSA states as clients of the IFIs, the impact of changes to date has been quite shallow. Portrayal of the PRSPs as nationally owned is unconvincing, given that the intellectual hegemony of the IFIs goes unacknowledged, the macroeconomic framework remains unchanged, and the link to poverty goes unexplored. The anticipated change from policy conditions to process conditions has not been achieved. For participation to be meaningful, space must be created for the expression and consideration of a full range of views, and policy frameworks must be up for negotiation.

When considered against the trend towards creditor coherence and harmonization, and the enormity of the SSA development challenge, progress in increasing voice and representation for SSA is wholly inadequate. Donor harmonization may be applauded for attempting to enhance efficiency, reduce waste and overlap, promote a more integrated approach, and generally make aid more effective – especially given its diminishing volume. However, harmonization also raises a number of potential problems for SSA states and peoples. Most important is that they are massively under-represented within this global development governance network, which suffers from an acute democratic deficit. Second, this trend towards policy convergence is closing off possible alternative options for developing countries and their peoples to canvass their views of appropriate development pathways across of range of donors open to different perspectives. Developing countries are losing what little leverage they had previously to move between donors, and they are faced with an increasingly united front. The words of the Development Committee (2003) lend weight to this fear:

> There is a need for donors/IFIs to ensure that their country-based allocations focus aid resources on those countries where there is an international consensus that governments are already proponents of reform ... Alongside this approach, there is a need to analytically support countries which do not appear ready.
>
> (Development Committee 2003a)

But *whose consensus* is this international consensus?

Efforts are underway at the global level to enhance the legitimacy of the coherence/harmonization agenda. For example, the high-level Rome Forum in February 2003 was part of this process, aimed at expanding developing country support for harmonization. The forum brought together representatives of the IFIs, the regional development banks, bilateral donors, plus twenty-eight creditor states, thirteen of which were African. Tanzanian President Benjamin Mkapa – whose country has been applauded as a model of development partnership good practice – opened the forum. In the context of voice for SSA, his remarks bear repeating: 'The debate on harmonization needs to be more comprehensive ... should address wider issues of ... global governance.' In keeping with high-profile IFI reports such as the World Bank's *Can Africa Reclaim the 21st Century?*, such high-profile international forums routinely recommend changes in the methods and institutions of African governance, but rarely do they make recommendations to address the democratic deficit by which the global level governance of development is characterized. The Rome meeting was no exception.

The evidence of the post-Cold War period regarding representation and voice suggests that changes in the IFI–SSA relationship have been more cosmetic than substantive. However, what has changed significantly is the desire of the IFIs to be able to claim greater legitimacy for a policy framework which has failed to deliver in the past and which at the most fundamental level remains unaltered. This is attempted by presenting it as home-grown and home-owned. When it fails to deliver – based as it is on an inappropriate, narrow view which obscures the crucial international dimension of the African development predicament – the blame will be laid squarely on the 'owners', SSA. The IFIs will deem themselves absolved of responsibility for poor policies. But in the context of the new development partnership espoused at Monterrey, accountability cuts both ways.

References

Agubre, C. (2000) 'Who Governs Low Income Countries? An Interview with Charles Abugre on the PRS Initiative', *News and Notices for IMF and World Bank Watchers*, 2, 3. http://attac.org/fra/toil/doc/gci3.htm

Birdsall, N. and J. Williamson (2002) 'Gold for Debt: From Debt to a New Development Architecture', from conf-moderator@coc.org on 27 February.

Bond, P. (2001) 'South Africa's Agenda in 21st Century Global Governance', *Review of African Political Economy*, 89: 415–28.

Bouabre, B. (2003) 'Statement to the Development Committee of the IMF and World Bank', 13 April, DC/S/2003–0029(E), http://wbln0018.worldbank.org/dcs/devcom.nsf/(statementsattachmentweb)/April2003EnglishDCS20030029E/$FILE/DCS2003–0029_E_-bouabre.pdf

Bretton Woods Project (2003) 'Open statement on steps to democratize the World Bank and the IMF', http://www.brettonwoodsproject.org

—— (20003a) 'Window of Opportunity on IFI Governance', http://www.brettonwoodsproject.org

Bugingo, E. (2002) 'Missing the Mark? Participation in the PRSP Process', http://www.christian-aid.org.uk/indepth/0212rwanda/rwanda.pdf

Cammack, P. (2002) 'The Mother of All Governments: The World Bank's Matrix for Global Governance' in R. Wilkinson and S. Hughes (eds) *Global Governance: Critical Perspectives*, Routledge: London, pp. 36–53.

Chabal, P. (2002) 'The Quest for Good Governance and Development in Africa: Is NEPAD the Answer?', *International Affairs*, 78, 3: 447–62.

Cheru, F. (2002) 'Building and Supporting PRSPs: Achievements and Challenges of Participation', a note prepared for World Bank, 12 June, http://www.worldbank.org/poverty/strategies/events/attckpov/presnesnt2.pdf

Christian Aid (2003) 'Options for Democratizing the World Bank and the IMF, Submission to IMF/World Bank Development Committee Annual Meeting', http://www.christianaid.org

CODESRIA/Third World Network – Africa (2002) 'Declaration on Africa's Development Challenges', 26 April, Accra, http://www.50years.org/updates/twn.html

Development Committee (1999) 'Communiqué', IMF/World Bank, 27 September.

—— (2003) 'Communiqué' 13 April. http://wbln0018.worldbank.org/DCS/devcom.nsf/(communiquesm)/15F072E02473F18F85256D0700653045?OpenDocument

—— (2003a) 'Progress Report and Critical Next Steps in Scaling Up: Education for All, Health, HIV/AIDS, Water and Sanitation', 27 March, DC2003–0004, http://Inweb18.worldbank.org/dcs/devcom.nsf

Dollar, D. and A. Kray (2000) 'Growth is Good for the Poor', World Bank, Washington DC, http://www.worldbank.org/research/growth/pdfiles/growthgoodforpoor.pdf

Easterly, W. (2002) 'How Did Heavily Indebted Poor Countries Become Heavily Indebted? Reviewing Two Decades of Debt Relief', *World Development*, 30, 10:1677–96.

EU Commission (2001) PRSP Review: Key Issues 2001, http://www.eurodad.org/2poverty/indexpoverty1.htm

EURODAD (2003) 'Streamlining of Conditionality – What has Happened?' May, http://www.eurodad.org

G-24 (2002) 'G-24 Communiqué' *IMF Survey*, 31, 18, October, http://www.imf.org/external/pubs/ft/survey/2002/100702.pdf

—— (2003) 'Intergovernmental Group of Twenty-Four on International Monetary Affairs and Development: Communiqué', 11 April, http://www.imf.org/external/np/cm/2003/041103.htm

Hanlon, J. (2000) 'Power without Responsibility: the World Bank and Mozambican Cashew Nuts', *Review of African Political Economy*, 27, 83: 29–45.

Houtven, L. van (2002) 'Governance and the IMF: Decision-making, Institutional Oversight, Transparency and Accountability', *IMF Pamphlet Series*, No. 53, http://www.imf.org/external/pubs/ft/pam/pam53/pam53.pdf

IMF (2002) 'IMF Conditionality – A Fact Sheet', 4 December, http://www.imf.org/external/np/exr/facts/conditio.htm

—— (2003) 'Transcript of a Press Conference of African Finance Ministers and Governors of Central Banks' 11 April, http://www.imf.org/external/np/tr/2003/tr030411.htm

IMF/World Bank (2003) 'Voice and Participation of Developing Countries in Decision-Making at the World Bank and IMF. A Technical Note by Bank/Fund Staff for the Development Committee' 27 April, http://http://lnweb18.worldbank.org/dcs/devcom.nsf/(documentsattachmentsweb)/April2003EnglishDC20030002/$FILE/DC2003–0002.pdf

IMFC (2003) 'Communiqué of the International Monetary and Financial Committee of the Board of Governors of the IMF', 12 April, http://www.imf.org/external/np/cm/2003/041203.htm

Joint NGOs (2003) *Where Is the Impact? PSIAs*, Briefing Paper, April, http://www.eurodad.org/articles/default.aspx?id=451=yes

Jubilee South (2001) 'Pan African Declaration on PRSPs', 12 May, Kampala.

Jubilee South, Focus on the Global South–Bangkok, AWEPON (Kampala) and Centro de Estudos Internacionales (Managua) (2002) *The World Bank and the PRSP: Flawed Thinking and Failed Experience*, January, http://www.eurodad.org

Killick, T. (2002) 'The Streamlining of IMF Conditionality: Aspirations, Reality and Repercussions', http://www.eurodad.org/uploadstore/cms/docs/odi_imfconditionalitystreamlining.pdf

Ladd, P. (for Christian Aid) (2003) *Too Hot to Handle? The Absence of Trade Policy from PRSPs*, April, http://www.christian-aid.org/wk/indepth/0304toohot.pdf

McGee, R. and A. Hughes (2002) '*Assessing Participation in PRSPs: A Desk-based Synthesis of Experience in SSA*, An IDS study sponsored by DFID, February, http://www.eurodad.org

Malaluan, J. and S. Guttal (for Focus on the Global South) (2003) 'PRSPs: A Poor Package for Poverty Reduction', http://www.eurodad.org/uploadstore/cms/docs

Milanovic, B. (2002) 'Can We Discern the Effect of Globalization on Income Distribution?' *World Bank Policy Research Working Paper* 2876, April, http://http://econ.worldbank.org/files/17877_wp2876.pdf

—— (2003) 'The Two Faces of Globalization: Against Globalization as We Know It', *World Development*, 31, 4: 667–83.

Mkapa, B. W. (2003) 'Opening Speech at Rome High Level Forum on Development Assistance Harmonization', 24 February, http://www1.worldbank.org/harmonization/romehlf/Documents/mkapa.pdf

Monterrey Report (2002) *Report of the International Conference on Financing for Development*, 18–22 March, Monterrey, http://ods-dds-ny.un.org/doc/UNDOC/GEN/N02/392/67/PDF/N0239267.pdf? OpenElement

Nyamugasira, W. and R. Rowden (2002) *New Strategies, Old Loan Conditions: Do the New IMF and World Bank Loans Support Countries' Poverty Reduction Strategies? The Case of Uganda*, http://www.brettonwoodsproject.org/topic/adjustment/a28ugandaprsp.pdf

Oxfam International (2001) *Are the PRSPs Working?*, December, http://www.eurodad.org/2poverty/indexpoverty1.htm

Reddy, S. and T. Pogge (2003) 'How *Not* to Count the Poor', 26 March, http://www.socialanalyis.org

Sahn, D. and D. Stifel (2003) 'Progress toward the Millennium Development Goals in Africa', *World Development*, 31, 1: 23–52.

SAPRIN (2000) 'The Policy Roots of Economic Crisis and Poverty: A Multi-country Participatory Assessment of Structural Adjustment', http://www.saprin.org/global_rpt.htm

UNCTAD (2000) *The Least Developed Countries 2000 Report*, http://www.unctad.org

—— (2001) *Economic Development in Africa: Performance, Prospects and Policy Issues* (UNCTAD/GDS/AFRICA/1), New York and Geneva: UN.

—— (2002) *Trade and Development Report*, Geneva: UNCTAD, http://www.unctad.org

—— (2002a) *The Least Developed Countries Report*, Geneva: UNCTAD, http://www.unctad/org/en/pubs/ps1ldc02.en.htm

UNDP (2002) *Human Development Report: Deepening Democracy in a Fragmented World*, http://www.undp.org/hdr2002/complete.pdf

WEED (2003) 'Lessons from the Analysis of the First Five Full PRSPs', http://www.eurodad.org/uploadstore/cms/docs/WEEDsAnalysisoffivePRSPs.pdf

Wilks, A. and F. Lefrancois (for Bretton Woods Project and World Vision) (2002) *Blinding with Science or Encouraging Debate? How World Bank Analysis Determines PRSP Policies*, http://www.brettonwoodsproject.org/briefings

Wolfensohn, J. (2002) 'President's Revised Note to the Development Committee of the IMF and World Bank', DC2002–0007/Rev1, 12 April, Annex on Multilateral Development Bank Collaboration and Reform, Washington DC: World Bank.

World Bank (2000) *Can Africa Reclaim the 21st Century?*, Washington DC: World Bank, http://www.worldbank.org/html/extdr/canafricaclaim.pdf

—— (2001) *Background and Overview to the Comprehensive Development Framework*, http://www.worldbank.org/cdf/overview.htm

—— (2001a) *Comprehensive Development Framework: Questions and Answers*, http://www.worldbank.org/cdf/cdf-faq.htm

—— (2001b) *Adjustment from Within: Lessons from the Structural Adjustment Participatory Review Initiative*, Washington DC: World Bank.

—— (2002) *Daily News*, 16 April, http://www.worldbank.org/developmentnews/stories/html/041602a.htm

—— (2002a) *Participation in PRSPs: A Retrospective Study*, http://www.worldbank.org/participation

—— (2002b) 'Committee of the Whole: Review of the PRSP Approach', 12 March, ref: SecM2002–0155, Washington DC: World Bank.

—— (2003) *World Development Indicators*, http://www.worldbank.org/data/wdi2003.worldview.pdf

—— (2003a) *Rome Declaration on Harmonization*, 24 February, http://www1.world-bank.org/harmonization/romehlf/Documents/mkapa.pdf

Yatta, F. (2003) 'Statement to the Development Committee of the IMF and World Bank', 13 April, DC/S/2003–0033. http://wbln0018.worldbank.org/dcs/devcom.nsf/(statementsattachmentweb)/April2003EnglishDCS20030033/$FILE/DCS2003–0033-jatta.pdf

10 From Congo to Congo

United Nations peacekeeping in Africa after the Cold War[1]

Adekeye Adebajo

The United Nations' (UN) credibility in Africa was badly shaken by its controversial intervention in a turbulent civil war in the former Belgian Congo in the early 1960s. Today, the organization is struggling to keep peace in the same country in another protracted civil war four decades later. The Congo, a huge country at the heart of Africa, is a perfect symbol of the difficulties that the UN has experienced in its peacekeeping efforts in Africa. This chapter assesses six major UN peace operations undertaken in Africa after the end of the Cold War: Mozambique, Angola, Somalia, Rwanda, Sierra Leone and the Democratic Republic of Congo (DRC). All six conflicts examined are cases of civil war, reflecting the changing nature of post-Cold War peacekeeping. The varied cases, most of which have seen the large-scale deployment of troops, have been selected for the significant lessons that they provide for UN peacekeeping in Africa.

This chapter investigates five important questions related to the changing fortunes of UN peacekeeping missions in Africa. What are some of the factors that have determined the success or failure of such missions? What factors account for the seeming resurgence of UN peacekeeping in Africa after 1990? Why did the main actors on the UN Security Council then become disillusioned with Africa after 1993? Does the mandating of three UN peacekeeping missions to Africa after 1999 signify the failure of Africa's regional organizations and a revival of UN peacekeeping in Africa? How can a new division of labour be established between the UN and Africa's regional security organizations to manage conflicts on the continent?

Africa has repeatedly tested the capacity and political resolve of the Security Council. The end of the Cold War raised great expectations that the UN would finally be able to contribute decisively to ending Africa's wars. Under the loose heading of peacekeeping[2] the UN has launched an unprecedented number of missions in the post-Cold War era, and of the forty-two UN operations established since the end of the Cold War, seventeen have been in Africa. But despite expectations that with a more united Security Council the Blue Helmets would fill Africa's post-Cold War security vacuum, disasters in Somalia and Rwanda have scarred the organization and made its most powerful members wary of intervening in an area of (generally) low strategic interest.

Since the UN's peacekeeping successes and failures are often contingent on the domestic, regional and external dynamics of conflict situations, this chapter focuses particularly on these factors in each case. I pay particular attention to the politics of peacekeeping, and focus less on its technical and logistical constraints. Based on a thorough assessment of the selected cases, I identify six factors which have most often contributed to success in UN peacekeeping missions in Africa: the willingness of internal parties to disarm and accept electoral results; the development of an effective strategy to deal with potential 'spoilers' (Stedman 1997); the absence of conflict-fuelling economic resources in war zones; the cooperation of regional players in peace processes; the cessation of military and financial support to local clients by external actors and their provision of financial and diplomatic support to peace processes; and the leadership of peacekeeping missions by capable UN envoys. It is worth noting that the presence or absence of these factors does not automatically determine the outcome of peacekeeping missions. All the factors will clearly not be met in every case of success or failure.

The UN mission in Mozambique met all the criteria for success: the internal parties were willing to cooperate with the peace process and accept electoral results – an outcome helped by the end of the Cold War, which facilitated the successful exertion of external pressure on the warring parties. Regional and external players provided crucial diplomatic and financial support to the peace process and stopped arming Mozambique's warring factions, and the UN had an effective Special Representative in Aldo Ajello. In stark contrast, Angola lacked most of the criteria for success: until his death in February 2002, Jonas Savimbi proved to be a successful 'spoiler' who refused to disarm or abide by election results. Savimbi had the economic resources to frustrate the UN whilst continued American support for Savimbi obstructed UN efforts to win the cooperation of the warlord. In addition, the UN mission sent to Angola in 1991 was grossly under-funded and under-staffed.

Rwanda was tragically tarred with the Somali brush of failure. The UN missions in both countries were, in a sense, contrasts in failure. Somalia was a well-funded mission that had some of the best-equipped soldiers in the world. The UN, Ethiopia and external actors provided support for diplomatic efforts to end the conflict, but Somalia also lacked a peace accord among the parties before the UN intervened in 1992, and Mohammed Farah Aideed, the most powerful warlord, was unprepared to share power with other factions. The aggressive military approach adopted by the UN Special Representative, Admiral Jonathan Howe, contributed to the confrontation with Aideed that led to the loss of political support for, and the eventual termination of, the mission. In contrast, Rwanda was, from the start, a mission based largely on ill-equipped armies from developing countries which lacked strong political and financial backing from the powerful members of the Security Council. This weakness encouraged Rwanda's extremist factions to force the withdrawal of the UN by killing its peace-keepers. France, which had trained members of and provided military support to the genocidal regime, was considered a partisan and compromised intervener, while the UN Special Representative, Jacques-Roger Booh-Booh, did not enjoy the confidence of many of Rwanda's parties.

The fate of the UN peacekeeping missions in Sierra Leone and the DRC underlined the importance of our criteria for success. The mission in Sierra Leone eventually enjoyed strong regional and external support, and Britain was able to use its permanent membership of the Security Council to convince the US to support the establishment of the largest peacekeeping mission in the world in Sierra Leone in 2000. With support from British troops, the UN mission in Sierra Leone (UNAMSIL) was also prepared to act against the Revolutionary United Front (RUF) leader, Foday Sankoh, and his sponsor, Liberia's Charles Taylor, after Sankoh had tried to sabotage the mission in May 2000. This resulted in the emergence of a more cooperative RUF leadership, and UNAMSIL's Special Representative, Olu Adeniji, was eventually able to steer the mission towards success.

The existence of mineral resources in the DRC has been exploited by the warring factions, as well as by Rwanda, Uganda and Zimbabwe. Regional actors involved in the DRC remain deeply divided. Rwanda and Uganda sent troops to support a rebellion against the government in Kinshasa in 1998, which in turn was provided military support by Zimbabwe, Angola and Namibia. Scarred by earlier experiences in Rwanda and Somalia, Security Council members have provided only sporadic and often inadequate assistance to peacekeeping missions in Africa. Western countries have also failed to provide significant troops for these peacekeeping missions, which are largely staffed by poorly equipped soldiers from developing countries.

Wars of liberation: Angola and Mozambique

Liberation movements had emerged in Mozambique and Angola to challenge Portuguese colonialism by the 1960s. In April 1974, a military coup in Lisbon led Portugal to abandon its African colonies but the transitions collapsed in Mozambique and Angola, leading to civil wars in which Washington and Moscow backed different clients. The end of the Cold War made it possible for the installation of UN peacekeeping missions in both countries (see Malaquias 1996). Mozambique and Angola both had 'spoilers' who seemed determined to wreck peace processes, but the presence of economic resources in Angola and the greater cooperation of the warring parties in Mozambique were crucial in explaining the different outcomes in the two cases. The sustained interest and cooperation of the powerful members of the UN Security Council and their contribution of financial, diplomatic and logistical support to the UN mission was important to success in Mozambique, but was mostly lacking in Angola.

Between 1975 and 1990, the Front for the Liberation of Mozambique (FRELIMO) government and the Mozambique National Resistance (RENAMO) rebels were locked in a brutal civil war. For two years, from July 1990, direct meetings were hosted in Rome between FRELIMO and RENAMO by the Italian government and the Community of Sant' Egidio (Bartoli 1999). Significantly, the meetings were assisted by four important Western states (US, Portugal, France and Britain). This gained early donor interest and potential support for an eventual peace settlement. In October 1992, President Joaquim Chissano and RENAMO leader Afonso Dhlakama signed a General Peace Agreement calling for the deployment of UN peace-keepers within a few weeks; the demobilization of 80,000 FRELIMO and RENAMO troops within a few months; and the organization of elections within a year. This unrealistic timetable was unsurprisingly not met and reflected the 'euphoric planning' of the mediators.

In December 1992, the Security Council approved the UN Operation in Mozambique (ONUMOZ). The mission's military and civilian staff totalled 7,000, and it cost nearly $1 million a day. ONUMOZ's most important body was the Supervision and Monitoring Commission (CSC), which took over some of the FRELIMO government's powers in areas relevant to imple-menting the peace accord. Members of the UN-chaired commission included the two parties, the Organization of African Unity (OAU), Britain, France, Germany, Italy, Portugal and the US. Other commissions were established to oversee the cease-fire, the reintegration and demobilization of soldiers, the creation of a new 30,000-strong army, and the conducting of elections. Three other commissions dealt with issues related to police, intelli-gence and administration.

ONUMOZ had five military battalions and 350 military observers who were tasked to supervise the assembly and demobilization of FRELIMO and RENAMO troops, investigate cease-fire violations, and provide security to humanitarian relief convoys and returning refugees. The mission was also mandated to repatriate two million refugees from neighbouring countries and oversee the coordination of humanitarian assistance. Despite its common reputation for being a glowing success, ONUMOZ experienced several diffi-culties. In late 1992, RENAMO broke the cease-fire by capturing several towns, and the crisis required speedy UN diplomatic intervention before it was defused. ONUMOZ's deployment took seven months. Demobilization of troops took place between March and August 1994, and the UN had to set up a Trust Fund to provide soldiers with an additional eighteen months' wages. The elections themselves took two years to organize.

Furthermore, Dhlakama's 'spoiler' tactics nearly wrecked the mission. In March 1993, the warlord recalled his officials from Maputo and refused to cooperate with the UN's commissions. He also refused to demobilize his troops unless more funds were provided for transforming his guerrilla movement into a political party. $17.5 million was eventually provided to RENAMO for this purpose, much of it by the Italian government. On the eve of elections in

October 1994, Dhlakama threatened a boycott of the polls, citing evidence of government-organized fraud. The mediation role played by the UN's Special Representative, Aldo Ajello, combined with external pressure, was crucial in convincing the RENAMO leader to implement the peace agreement. The Italian diplomat interpreted his mandate with flexible dexterity. He effectively used the CSC to resolve military issues, tirelessly lobbied donors to provide funds for implementing the agreement, and skilfully co-ordinated the political mission with the humanitarian activities (Ajello 1999). Twelve hundred UN electoral observers oversaw elections in October 1994, which FRELIMO won. RENAMO had lost the support of its South African patron, and unlike the belligerents in Angola had no access to domestic natural resources – oil and diamonds – with which to fund continued war.

In relation to Angola, in August 1988, US-brokered talks were held in Geneva involving South Africa, Cuba and Angola. A cease-fire was reached, and South African troops withdrew from Angola. With the involvement of the UN, two peace agreements were signed in New York in December 1988, linking Namibia's independence to the withdrawal of 50,000 Cuban troops from Angola within thirty-one months. The first United Nations Angola Verification Mission (UMAVEM I), involving about seventy unarmed military observers, was established in December 1988 to verify the withdrawal of Cuban troops by 1 July 1991. The mission cost $18.8 million, and completed its tasks early, with Cuban troops withdrawing by 25 May 1991, over a month ahead of schedule (Fortna 1994).

The success of UNAVEM I provided the impetus for the ruling *Movimento Popular de Libertacao de Angola* (MPLA) and *Uniao Nacional para a Independencia Total de Angola* (UNITA) rebels to sign the Bicesse peace accords in May 1991 after a year of arduous negotiations. The agreement was negotiated by the Troika of the US, the Soviet Union and Portugal. Similar to the deal that had ended Mozambique's war, Bicesse called for a cease-fire, the demobilization of 200,000 MPLA and UNITA troops, the creation of a new unified 50,000 army, the extension of a central administration to the entire country, the development of a neutral police force, and the holding of elections by November 1992. The accord also created a Joint Political–Military Commission, consisting of MPLA and UNITA representatives, as well as Troika observers. Unlike the CSC in Mozambique which the UN had chaired, Angola's parties took turns in chairing this commission, and the UN played only a marginal role on it.

The UN mission to Angola (UNAVEM II) was established in May 1991, and had only a limited observation and verification role. Not until December 1991 was a civilian component added to the mission to oversee the electoral process. Margaret Anstee, the UN Special Representative, arrived in Luanda only in March 1992, six months before the elections. UNAVEM II had 350 unarmed military observers, 126 civilian police, and 400 electoral observers to monitor a country the combined size of Germany, France and Spain. Its seventeen-month budget was a paltry $118,000. This was peacekeeping on a shoestring. UNAVEM II clearly lacked the human and financial resources to execute its mandate effectively. Its peacekeepers proved to be too few for their demobilization tasks and the parties did not cooperate with its security sector reform mandate (Anstee 1999; Sibanda 1999).

Angola's elections were held in September 1992. The presidential election was won narrowly by incumbent president José Eduardo dos Santos, but required a run-off. However, Savimbi refused to conclude the electoral process and to disarm his fighters. He openly defied the peacekeepers and instead continued to rebuild his army. The warlord returned to armed conflict assisted by the sale of diamonds. UNITA's erstwhile patron, the US, offered diplomatic recognition to the MPLA government in May 1993, and four months later the UN Security Council imposed sanctions on the sale of arms and oil to UNITA. In November 1994, the Lusaka Protocol was signed, establishing the third UN mission in Angola (UNAVEM III) headed by Alioune Blondin Beye. UNAVEM III was a deliberate effort to correct the flaws of Bicesse by giving the UN a central role in its implementation, providing 7,000 peacekeepers, and bringing UNITA representatives into a transitional government in Luanda. But neither side was serious about implementing the agreement, and in October 1997 the UN Security Council imposed sanctions on UNITA's diamond exports. By 1998, full-scale war had returned to Angola.

The killing of Savimbi by government troops in February 2002 led to the signing of a Memorandum of Understanding between the government and UNITA. Both sides then undertook to implement the Lusaka Protocol with the assistance of the UN mission in Angola (UNMA), created in August 2002 under the leadership of Ibrahim Gambari. A government of national unity has now been created and some UNITA elements reintegrated into the national army and police. But problems remain. As of February 2003, 105,000 ex-combatants and their family members still required reintegration assistance, about 20 per cent of ex-combatants remained outside the government's payroll, uncertainty remained about the timing of new elections, and 400,000 Angolan refugees still awaited repatriation from neighbouring countries (Gambari 2003; Annan 2003a).

Of warlords and *génocidaires*: Somalia and Rwanda

Somalia and Rwanda were orphans of the Cold War in the era of intervention by external powers in Africa. Somalia had been fought over by the superpowers, while Rwanda was entangled in French efforts to maintain a sphere of influence in Africa. The UN Security Council erroneously treated both conflicts as humanitarian disasters, and the political will for stronger military action was lacking after Western peacekeepers were killed in both countries. Political support for the UN missions in Somalia and Rwanda simply crumbled in the Security Council, and rather than bolster the UN presence, its peacekeepers were instead withdrawn.

Somalia's civil war erupted in full force in January 1991 after Siad Barre – backed by Washington until 1988 – fled Mogadishu (Adam 1995). The central government collapsed and Somalia joined the growing ranks of 'failed states' as two powerful warlords, Mohamed Farah Aideed and Ali Mahdi Mohamed, battled for control of the capital. With growing starvation in Somalia, the Security Council established the UN Operation in Somalia (UNOSOM I), deploying 500 peacekeepers to protect food convoys. As Somalia's warlords continued to blockade food convoys and with UNOSOM I's unarmed military observers unable to stop them, 300,000 deaths resulted. Amid a worsening situation, 38,000 peacekeepers, led by 25,000 Americans, entered Somalia from December 1992 as part of the United Nations Task Force (UNITAF). Operation Restore Hope was mandated to facilitate the delivery of humanitarian goods to Somalia. The mission started well enough, with the presence of the peacekeepers ensuring the delivery of food, reducing looting and banditry, rebuilding roads and bridges, and facilitating the repatriation of Somali refugees from neighbouring countries. Between December 1992 and October 1993 a staggering $2 billion was spent on the international effort.

But Washington had quixotically assumed that it could deploy its troops and feed Somalis while avoiding any confrontation with the country's warlords. It refused UN Secretary-General Boutros Boutros-Ghali's frequent requests to disarm Somalia's factions. However, Aideed, who had been consolidating his military position before the UN's arrival, felt that the entry of the peacekeepers would deprive him of the presidency. The mere presence of the UN force changed the military balance on the ground. While Aideed reluctantly accepted the peacekeepers, his less powerful rival, Ali Mahdi, enthusiastically supported their presence. Further complicating the UN's tasks, Aideed distrusted Boutros-Ghali, whom he had considered pro-Barre since the latter's tenure as Deputy Foreign Minister of Egypt.

US Special Envoy Robert Oakley, a former Ambassador to Somalia, arranged reconciliation meetings between Aideed and Mahdi as well as regular security meetings between their factions. Two UN-led peace conferences were also held in Addis Ababa with fourteen Somali factions in January and March 1993, with Ethiopia playing a strong mediation role. An agreement was eventually signed, calling for a two-year Transitional National Council (TNC) with a parliament, rotating presidency, and regional and district councils (Lyons and Samatar 1995: 49–51). But the accord was never implemented and Aideed in particular did much to subvert the functioning of the councils.

In May 1993, UNITAF was transformed into UNOSOM II, including 4,000 American troops. The new UN 'nation-building' mandate was ambitious in calling for the revival of national and regional institutions and the establishment of civil administration throughout Somalia. Growing human rights abuses by UN peacekeepers, involving the killing of Somali civilians, soon resulted in the civilian population turning against the UN. After the killing of twenty-four Pakistani peacekeepers by Aideed's fighters in June 1993, Washington successfully championed a Security Council resolution calling for the warlord's capture and trial. It was within this context that Admiral Howe virtually declared war on Aideed, sending US helicopters to kill or capture his supporters and putting a $25,000 bounty on Aideed's head. The mission went disastrously wrong when American Rangers became caught in a firefight with Aideed's men, resulting in the death of eighteen American soldiers and about a thousand Somalis, mostly civilians. In order to deflect the strong domestic backlash at the sight of a dead American soldier being dragged through the streets of Mogadishu by enraged Somalis, Bill Clinton's administration and much of the US media inaccurately blamed the botched mission – planned entirely under American command – on the UN. In early 1995, the UN withdrew all its peacekeepers from Somalia, leaving the country as anarchic as it had found it.

Following Somalia, Washington placed severe restrictions on the approval of future UN missions through the heavy-handed Presidential Decision Directive 25. Boutros-Ghali's requests for new UN peacekeeping missions in Burundi and Liberia met with silence, even as the West continued to employ the UN for 'rich men's wars'[3] in places that it considered of more strategic value, like Bosnia and Haiti. Six months after the Somalia debacle, Washington led the opposition to a UN response to the genocide in Rwanda, in a situation that was tragically and erroneously viewed through a tainted Somali prism. The Rwandese Patriotic Front (RPF), which had invaded Rwanda from Uganda in October 1990, were mostly the vengeful progenitors of Rwanda's Tutsi minority who had been forced out of their homeland and denied the right to return by the Hutu-dominated government of Juvenal Habyarimana. Uganda backed the RPF, while France and Zaire supported Habyarimana. The OAU arranged peace talks in Arusha, which resulted in a comprehensive peace settlement by August 1993. Arusha called for a transitional government involving the country's political groups, a power-sharing arrangement, establishing a new army composed equally of Hutu and Tutsi, and the demobilization of the remaining fighters.

The 2,500-strong and $120 million a year UN Assistance Mission in Rwanda (UNAMIR) was mandated to implement the agreement. The Security Council resolution establishing UNAMIR, however, made two crucial changes which weakened the peacekeeping force before its deployment. Arusha had called for the peacekeepers to guarantee the overall security of Rwanda and to confiscate illegal arms. The UN resolution mandated the force only to contribute to security in Kigali and its environs and did not sanction a seizure of arms. The UN peacekeepers arrived in Rwanda two months behind schedule and without the armoured unit and helicopters that had been authorized by the Security Council. General Roméo Dallaire, the UN Force Commander, had also called for a contingent that was twice the size of the one deployed. The force, consisting largely of soldiers from Belgium, Bangladesh, Ghana and Tunisia, lacked an intelligence unit; it had a small civilian police unit and no human rights cell, limiting its ability to monitor abuses (Suhrke 1997: 107–8). To make matters worse, the situation in Kigali was scarcely conducive to peacekeeping: the transitional government was not installed, Rwanda's soldiers were not demobilized, and arms were flooding illegally into the capital. Jacques-Roger Booh-Booh, the UN Special Representative, was seen by many to be out of his depth.

On 6 April 1994, Habyarimana's plane was shot down over Kigali, signalling the start of a genocide against the Tutsi minority and moderate Hutus. The genocide had been planned by a group of extremists within the Habyarimana regime including members of the ruling party, officers of the Presidential Guard, the *interahamwe* and *impuzamugambi* militias, and members of the *Comité pour la Défense de la République* (CDR). These groups saw power-sharing as not only a betrayal but a threat to their own positions and privileges. They also feared that the RPF's presence in a new national army would facilitate the launching of a Tutsi military coup.

Over the next three months, the *génocidaires* eliminated 800,000 mostly Tutsi people. The killing of ten Belgian peacekeepers led to the irresponsible withdrawal of its entire contingent, the backbone of the UN force, from Rwanda on 12 April 1994. The slaughter ended only with an RPF military victory on 17 July 1994. The genocidal militias and Rwandan army retreated into eastern Zaire with a hostage Hutu population of about one million people. This retreat was facilitated by the controversial UN-sanctioned French intervention, Opération Turquoise, which had ostensibly been launched to save lives. However, revelations that France had trained and continued to arm many of Rwanda's death squads raised troubling questions (Prunier 1995: 287).

Led by strong American and British demands (Boutros-Ghali 1999: 138), the UN Security Council withdrew most of its peacekeepers from Rwanda, leaving a token force. It pursued an utterly inappropriate diplomatic posture in search of an elusive cease-fire. Many observers, including General Dallaire and his Ghanaian deputy, General Henry Anyidoho, have since convincingly argued that a strengthened UN force could have prevented many of the civilian deaths, which were mostly carried out by gangs using machetes, clubs, knives and spears. Much controversy remains over the failure of the UN's Department of Peacekeeping, led at the time by the current Secretary-General, Kofi Annan, to report the contents of a fax from Dallaire, warning of the impending genocide, to Boutros-Ghali and the Security Council. A month later, the Council reversed its earlier decision and authorized the dispatch of 5,500 peacekeepers (UNAMIR II) to Rwanda, who arrived too late to save victims of genocide. The world had fiddled while Rwanda burned (UN 1999; Melvern 2000; OAU 2000).

Wars of misrule and plunder: Sierra Leone and Congo

In the aftermath of efforts by Africa's sub-regional organizations to step into the vacuum created by the departure of UN peacekeepers from the continent after debacles in Somalia and Rwanda, the lack of logistical and financial support for interventions in Africa's civil wars was epitomized by the travails of a Nigerian-led West African peacekeeping force, the Economic Community of West African States Cease-fire Monitoring Group (ECOMOG), which attempted, for over eight years, to bring peace to Liberia and Sierra Leone. A South African-led effort to restore order to Lesotho in 1998 was similarly embroiled in military and political difficulties. Regional actors in Africa often became entangled in parochial political and economic agendas, even as neighbours complained about the bullying instincts of local hegemons like Nigeria and South Africa (Adebajo and Landsberg 2003). These difficulties eventually resulted in the return of UN peacekeepers to Africa with missions in Sierra Leone, DRC and Ethiopia/Eritrea.

In both Sierra Leone and the DRC, decades of bad governance eventually resulted in state collapse and civil war. During peace negotiations, internal parties failed to demonstrate a genuine commitment to implementing peace agreements, and used their access to economic resources to fund military campaigns. Despite the destabilizing regional consequences of these conflicts, key regional actors provided military support to the warring parties. The permanent members of the Security Council, with the notable exception of Britain in Sierra Leone, did not show the political commitment to end these conflicts.

Sierra Leone's civil war erupted in 1991. By the end of 1998, about 13,000 ECOMOG peacekeepers had intervened to try to end the war. Following a rebel invasion of Freetown in January 1999, ECOMOG eventually forced the rebels to withdraw from the capital with heavy civilian and ECOMOG losses. But it was difficult for ECOWAS to turn its back on a conflict with such devastating effects on its own sub-region. Sierra Leone's RUF rebels were consistently backed by Liberia's Charles Taylor, and during the war both Liberia and Burkina Faso provided the RUF with arms and rear bases in return for a cut in Sierra Leone's lucrative diamond trade. Not surprisingly, the conflict spilled over into Liberia and Guinea.

The Lomé peace agreement, spearheaded by the UN and ECOWAS, was signed on 7 July 1999. The accord called for the RUF to be transformed into a political party and gave RUF leader Foday Sankoh the vice-presidency as well as the chairmanship of a Commission for the Management of Strategic Resources. A controversial amnesty was offered for war crimes committed during the conflict (though the UN entered an exception for egregious crimes against humanity), and the UN agreed to contribute personnel to help oversee disarmament and elections. A Joint Implementation Committee was to meet every three months to oversee the agreement's implementation (Annan 1999: 1–3).

Shortly after being installed as Nigeria's president in May 1999, Olusegun Obasanjo announced the phased withdrawal of 8,500 of Nigeria's 12,000 troops from Sierra Leone. With enormous domestic problems, the new civilian regime was not prepared to continue the sacrifices, involving costs of $1 million a day, which Nigeria's former military junta had incurred. In order to fill the void left by the departure of Nigerian peacekeepers, a UN mission in Sierra Leone was established. Oluyemi Adeniji, a Nigerian diplomat who had served as the UN Special Representative in Central African Republic, was appointed Special Representative to Sierra Leone. UNAMSIL's largest contingents came from India, Nigeria, Jordan, Kenya and Bangladesh.

UNAMSIL faced tremendous problems, as Sankoh, despite having signed a peace accord, acted as a 'spoiler'. The RUF continued to fight the Armed Forces Revolutionary Council (AFRC) and Civil Defence Forces in the countryside, prevented the deployment of UN peacekeepers to the diamond-rich eastern provinces, and, from May 2000, attacked UN peacekeepers, killing some of them, holding about 500 hostage, and seizing their heavy weapons and vehicles. A UN assessment mission sent to Sierra Leone in June 2000 cited serious management problems in UNAMSIL and a lack of common understanding by peacekeepers of their mandate and rules of engagement. The report also noted that some of UNAMSIL's military units lacked proper training and equipment (UN 2000: 9). There were constant allegations of tension between the UN's political and military leadership even before a confidential report, written by General Vijay Jetley, was leaked and published in the international press in September 2000. In the report, UNAMSIL's Indian Force Commander accused senior Nigerian officials of attempting to sabotage the UN mission in Sierra Leone by colluding with RUF rebels to prolong the conflict in order to benefit from the country's illicit diamond trade. Consequently, Nigeria refused to put its peacekeepers under Jetley's command and India announced the withdrawal of its entire 3,000-strong contingent from Sierra Leone in September 2000.

A British military intervention between May and June 2000 helped stabilize the situation in Freetown and its environs. A small British contingent that remained outside the UN military command stayed behind to help rebuild a new Sierra Leonean army. Following UNAMSIL's baptism of fire, ECOWAS agreed to send a US-trained 3,000-strong rapid reaction force to bolster the peacekeeping mission. The number of UN peacekeepers was eventually increased to 20,000 in a bid to avoid the fate of logistically ill-equipped peacekeepers in Angola and Rwanda. In recognition of the role of the illicit diamond trade in fuelling this conflict, the Security Council prohibited the global importation of rough diamonds from Sierra Leone in July 2000, and the Council later imposed diamond sanctions on Liberia in May 2001 for its support of RUF rebels.

Following the debacle in May 2000, UNAMSIL devised a new strategy to restore confidence in the flagging peacekeeping mission. Adeniji convinced ECOWAS leaders to replace Sankoh as head of the RUF, and the young RUF battlefield commander, Issa Sesay, eventually co-operated with the UN in its disarmament tasks. UNAMSIL then created a high-level consultative group, under the chairmanship of President Kabbah, to discuss the UN's implementation of its tasks with the RUF. The third leg of the UN strategy was the little-noticed Abuja agreement of November 2000 between the government and the RUF. Since UNAMSIL could not openly repudiate Lomé – an accord the RUF continued to criticize – Abuja was described as a cease-fire agreement. It was, however, in reality the third peace accord in Sierra Leone's civil war, following Abidjan in 1996 and Lomé in 1999. Abuja was a comprehensive agreement that tackled the political, military and socio-economic obstacles to establishing peace in Sierra Leone. Within a week after the signing of the Abuja agreement, all sides started to implement its provisions: disarmament, demobilization, release of prisoners, and opening of roads. Eight months after the signing of Abuja, Kabbah was able to declare an end to Sierra Leone's decade-long conflict.

Despite the remarkable progress of the UN mission in Sierra Leone, which had been on the brink of a catastrophic collapse, many problems remain that could still lead to a reversal of the sacrifices made by ECOMOG and UNAMSIL. The UN must actively promote security sector reform, building on the British-led efforts. UNAMSIL must also avoid a premature withdrawal of its peacekeeping force before a durable peace has been established in Sierra Leone. Many of Sierra Leone's 45,000 ex-combatants have yet to be reintegrated into local communities. Finally, the decision by the Special Court for Sierra Leone to indict Foday Sankoh, Issa Sesay, Johnny Paul Koromah (a former military junta leader) and Kabbah's popular deputy defence minister, Sam Hinga Norman, on charges of war crimes in March 2003 could destroy Sierra Leone's fragile peace. In June 2003, Charles Taylor was also indicted for war crimes by the Special Court. Instability in the Ivory Coast could yet threaten Sierra Leone, with fighters from Sierra Leone and Liberia having joined that country's civil war.

The UN faces an even more difficult and complicated mission in the DRC than it does in Sierra Leone. In early 1997, Laurent Kabila's Alliance of Democratic Forces for the Liberation of Congo-Zaire (AFDL) launched a rebellion against Mobutu Sese Seko, who had been abandoned by most of his Western patrons after the end of the Cold War. With help from Uganda, Rwanda and Angola, the revolt succeeded in toppling Mobutu in May 1997. In August 1998, Kabila's former allies, Uganda and Rwanda, invaded the DRC in support of anti-Kabila rebels (Lemarchand 2001; Nzongola-Ntalaja 2002: 227–40). Burundi also sent in troops on the side of Kigali and Kampala. Rwanda was particularly angered by Kabila's ousting of Rwandan-supplied Tutsi officers from his army. In response to the invasion by Uganda and Rwanda, the leaders of Zimbabwe, Angola, Namibia and Chad sent troops to the DRC to prop up Kabila's regime. Foreign armies in the DRC have plundered the country's rich mineral wealth, and Uganda and Rwanda clashed militarily in mineral-rich Kisangani in 1999 and 2000. Not until June 2000 (nearly two years after the outbreak of the conflict) did the UN Security Council criticize Kigali and Kampala's invasion of a sovereign country, asking them to withdraw from the DRC (Nzongola-Ntalaja 2002: 232). Washington, particularly under the Clinton administration, was a close ally of Kigali, providing it with counter-insurgency training.

The OAU led mediation efforts in the DRC. At a meeting in Lusaka in July 1999, Angola, DRC, Namibia, Rwanda, Uganda and Zimbabwe signed a peace accord. The Lusaka accord called for a cease-fire and redeployment of troops to specified positions; the release of prisoners of war; the withdrawal of all foreign troops from the DRC; a national dialogue between Kabila, the armed opposition groups – the Rally for a Democratic Congo (RCD) and the Movement for the Liberation of Congo (MLC) – and the unarmed civilian opposition; the disarming of all militias and 'armed groups'[4]; the re-establishment of state administration throughout the country; and the creation of a new national army. The UN was asked to deploy a peacekeeping force to the DRC, in collaboration with the OAU. Lusaka also called on the OAU to nominate a chair for a Joint Military Commission (JMC) and to designate a neutral facilitator for the inter-Congolese dialogue. The JMC was mandated to verify the disengagement of forces and the quartering and disarmament of armed groups, as well as to monitor the withdrawal of foreign troops from the DRC. Sir Ketumile Masire, the former president of Botswana, was nominated as the facilitator of the Inter-Congolese dialogue (Mwanasali 2003: 213–15).

In November 1999, the Security Council established the UN Organization Mission in the Democratic Republic of the Congo (MONUC). After deploying ninety military liaison officers to the DRC by the end of 1999, MONUC's military observers were increased to 4,386 by February 2003. If the implementation of the accord is judged to be proceeding well, MONUC's numbers could rise to 15,000 or more. SADC ambassadors in New York have continually lobbied the UN Secretary-General and Security Council, accusing the Council of neglect and over-cautiousness in expecting more stable conditions in the Congo than required elsewhere before deploying a substantial UN force (Annan 2000: 2–3).

On 16 January 2001, Laurent Kabila was shot by one of his presidential bodyguards. Kabila's son, Joseph, then assumed power in Kinshasa. By October 2001, sporadic fighting continued, particularly in Oriental province and the Kivu region. The Inter-Congolese dialogue met in South Africa's Sun City between 25 February and 18 April 2002 and a power-sharing agreement was negotiated between the main parties (though the Rwandan-backed RCD declined to sign). In July 2002, Kofi Annan appointed Ibrahima Fall as his Special Representative to the Great Lakes region. Fall was mandated to organize an international conference on the Great Lakes involving regional governments, civil society actors and foreign donors. The work of the Special Representative is expected to culminate in a conference in 2004 that aims to craft a regional settlement of the conflicts in the Great Lakes and muster donor support for the economic reconstruction of the region.[5]

Energetic South African diplomacy eventually produced results, and Pretoria also promised to provide a substantial force to a strengthened MONUC. On 30 July 2002, Thabo Mbeki brokered the Pretoria accord between Kinshasa and Kigali, in which Rwanda agreed to withdraw from the DRC in exchange for Kabila's tracking down and disarming of *interahamwe* and ex-FAR militias. Rwandan troops withdrew from the DRC by the autumn of 2002. US pressure was said to have played an important part in Kigali's withdrawal. The UN has, however, since received reports that Rwandan forces may have re-entered areas in the DRC, particularly around Bukavu (Annan 2002: 3). Namibia had already withdrawn its troops from the DRC. Zimbabwe, Angola and Burundi started withdrawing the rest of their contingents in 2002.

A month after South Africa's diplomatic triumph, Angola brokered the Luanda accord between Kinshasa and Kampala, in which Uganda agreed to withdraw from the Congo. In December 2002, the Global and All-Inclusive Agreement on the Transition in the Democratic Republic of the Congo was signed in Pretoria by all the parties that had participated in the Inter-Congolese Dialogue. The accord called for a two-year transition period, during which Joseph Kabila would remain president of the DRC and run the country with four vice-presidents nominated by the government, RCD-Goma, the MLC and a member of the unarmed opposition.

In May 2003, Kofi Annan called for the increase of MONUC's forces to 10,800, and urged a strengthening of the UN's mandate to enable the mission to contribute more effectively to conflict resolution efforts and to provide greater political support to the transition government (Annan 2003b: 9, 28). MONUC's current $581 million annual cost will rise significantly if the Security Council approves this troop increase. But despite progress on the diplomatic front, instability continued in the Kivu region, while the situation in Bunia deteriorated sharply following the withdrawal of Uganda's troops from the north-eastern town by 6 May 2003. The departure of Ugandan soldiers left a security vacuum which ethnic-based militias rushed in to fill, slaughtering hundreds of civilians and threatening the beleaguered UN compound. A 720-strong MONUC contingent of Uruguayan peacekeepers was unable to stop the fighting in Bunia due to its lack of a strong mandate and military equipment.

With increasing concern about genocide in Bunia, Annan called on the Security Council to deploy a well-equipped peace-enforcement force to Bunia to protect the town's 20,000 civilians, UN staff and key installations. In early June 2003, France responded by deploying the first soldiers of a 1,400-strong largely European force which was mandated to protect civilians in Bunia until the arrival of 3,000 Bangladeshi peacekeepers by September 2003 (*Economist*, 14 June 2003: 43). At the time of writing, it remains unclear whether the UN Security Council can muster the political will and provide the resources to help sustain efforts to end a five-year war that has claimed an estimated 3 million lives.

Conclusion

The cases of UN peacekeeping in Africa surveyed in this chapter offer important lessons for the future. There remains an urgent need for Western donors to demonstrate a similar generosity to Africa as they have done in Bosnia, Kosovo and East Timor. For example, in early 2000, while $2 billion was pledged for the reconstruction of the Balkans, barely $150 million was pledged for Sierra Leone. There is also a pressing need to establish a proper division of labour between the UN and Africa's fledgling security organizations, which need to be greatly strengthened. Rwanda's Arusha agreement and the DRC's Lusaka accord clearly revealed the military weakness of the OAU – now the African Union – whose members lacked the resources to implement agreements they had negotiated without UN peacekeepers. In Sierra Leone, the UN also had to take over peacekeeping duties from ECOMOG. The UN must work more closely with Africa's regional organizations to strengthen their security mechanisms (IPA 2002; Muyangwa and Vogt 2000).

The Security Council has not done much to strengthen the capacity of regional peacekeepers and to collaborate effectively with them in the field. The Brahimi Report on reforming UN peacekeeping of August 2000 was curiously and disappointingly short of details on the subject of establishing an effective division of labour between the UN and regional organizations. The willingness of Western peacekeepers, possessing both the equipment and resources, to continue to contribute to UN missions in Africa remains important. The limited British intervention in Sierra Leone in 2000 demonstrated that, even if only to provide logistical support, the involvement of such armies is crucial in filling gaps created by the deficiencies of armies from developing countries. Despite the presumed domestic political risks of participating in such missions, it is important that a new aristocracy of death not be established where the lives of Western soldiers are worth more than those of non-Western peacekeepers and African civilians.

The missions in Sierra Leone and the DRC could signify an innovative approach to UN peacekeeping in Africa based on regional pillars supported by local hegemons like Nigeria and South Africa, whose political dominance of such missions is diluted by multinational peacekeepers from outside their regions. By placing regional forces under the UN flag, the hope is that the peacekeepers will enjoy the legitimacy and impartiality that the UN's universal membership often provides, while some of the financial and logistical problems of regional peacekeepers can be alleviated through greater burden sharing. These missions should also be more accountable, since the peacekeepers will have to report regularly to the UN Security Council. This might also force the Council to focus more attention on African conflicts.

The commitment of important members of the Security Council to UN peacekeeping in Africa and the politics surrounding their interactions within the Council are often vital to the outcome of these missions. The US role in Somalia and Britain's role in Sierra Leone were crucial to the establishment of UN missions in these countries. Washington played a critical role in preventing UN action during the genocide in Rwanda in 1994. The decision to send a UN peacekeeping force to Rwanda in 1993 was pushed strongly in the Security Council by France, which hoped to use the peacekeepers for its own parochial national interests of keeping Habyarimana in power and blunting the RPF's growing military strength (Suhrke 1997: 105).

The Somalia case underlines the importance of impartiality to UN peace-keeping. In Somalia, Aideed distrusted Boutros-Ghali while Admiral Howe's military tactics led to further questioning of the UN's neutrality. The quality of diplomats serving as UN Special Representatives can also be important to the success of a mission, as the example of Ajello in Mozambique, and eventually Adeniji in Sierra Leone, demonstrated. Less skilful Special Representatives can, on the other hand, make a difficult situa-tion worse, as appears to have been the case with Howe in Somalia and Booh-Booh in Rwanda. But it is important to note that adroit diplomacy alone is insufficient to achieve success. While personalities do matter in peacekeeping, it should be stressed that the will of the parties to implement agreements, the consistent support of regional and external actors, and the availability of resources with which to work, appear to be the most impor-tant factors in determining success.

There is a strong case to be made for developing strategies to deal with 'spoilers' like Aideed, Sankoh, Savimbi and Rwanda's *génocidaires*, who are determined to see the UN fail and attempt to ensure its withdrawal by attacking its peacekeepers. The economic, political and legal sanctions of the sort that were imposed on the RUF in Sierra Leone and UNITA in Angola would seem appropriate in such cases. The recent innovation of establishing UN panels to 'name and shame' states and leaders that are supporting rebels could also be a useful tool for the UN to achieve compli-ance with peace accords, as long as such reports are based on meticulous research and information. The economic sanctions imposed on Savimbi and Taylor by the Security Council appear to have made a significant contribu-tion to ending the wars in Angola and Sierra Leone.

Peace remains fragile in Sierra Leone and the DRC. The UN will need a substantial increase and better-equipped troops, as well as more logistical support from Western armies. Certainly, Sierra Leone's fragile peace will require consistent attention in light of the instability in Liberia and the Ivory Coast. If the UN is to avoid a repeat of the debacles in Angola, Somalia and Rwanda, and achieve success as it did in Mozambique, the Security Council will have to continue to strongly support peace efforts in Africa. Only through such sustained action will Africans be able to bid a final farewell to arms.

Notes

1 This chapter builds on an earlier article, Adekeye Adebajo and Chris Landsberg (2001) 'Back to the Future: UN Peacekeeping in Africa', in A. Adebajo and C. L. Sriram (eds) *Managing Armed Conflicts in the 21st Century*, London: Frank Cass, pp. 161–88.
2 For most of the post-Cold War era, the UN's distinctions between peacekeeping, peacemaking, peace-enforcement and peacebuilding were based on Boutros-Ghali (1992).
3 This expression was coined by Boutros Boutros-Ghali.
4 These groups included: the *interahamwe*, the ex-FAR, the Allied Democratic Front (ADF), the Lord's Resistance Army (LRA), the Forces for the Defence of Democracy (FDD), the former Ugandan National Army, the Uganda National Rescue Front II, the West Nile Bank Front and UNITA.
5 Author's discussions with Ibrahima Fall, New York, 7 May 2003.

References

Adam, H. (1995) 'Somalia: A Terrible Beauty Being Born?' in I. W. Zartman (ed.) *Collapsed States: The Disintegration and Restoration of Legitimate Authority*, Boulder: Lynne Rienner, pp. 69–78.

Adebajo, A. and C. Landsberg (2003) 'South Africa and Nigeria as Regional Hegemons', in M. Baregu and C. Landsberg (eds) (2003) *From Cape to Congo: Southern Africa's Evolving Security Challenges*, Boulder: Lynne Rienner, pp. 171–203.

Ajello, A. (1999) 'Mozambique: Implementation of the 1992 Agreement', in C. Crocker, F. O. Hampson and P. Aall (eds) (1999) *Herding Cats: Multiparty Mediation in a Complex World*, Washington DC: United States Institute of Peace, pp. 619–42.

Annan, K. (1999) *Seventh Report of the Secretary-General on the United Nations Observer Mission in Sierra Leone*, 30 July, S/1999/836.

—— (2000) *Fifth Report of the Secretary-General on the United Nations Organization Mission in the Democratic Republic of the Congo*, S/2000/1156, 6 December.

—— (2002) *Twelfth Report of the Secretary-General on the United Nations Organization Mission in the Democratic Republic of the Congo*, S/2002/1180, 18 October.

—— (2003a) *Report of the Secretary-General on the United Nations Mission in Angola*, S/2003/158, 7 February.

—— (2003b) *Second Special Report of the Secretary-General on the United Nations Organization Mission in the Democratic Republic of the Congo*, S/2003/556, 27 May.

Anstee, M. J. (1999) 'The United Nations in Angola: Post Bicesse Implementation', in C. Crocker, F. O. Hampson and P. Aall (eds) (1999) *Herding Cats: Multiparty Mediation in a Complex World*, Washington DC: United States Institute of Peace, pp. 587–613.

Baregu, M. and C. Landsberg (eds) (2003) *From Cape to Congo: Southern Africa's Evolving Security Challenges*, Boulder: Lynne Rienner.

Bartoli, A. (1999) 'Mediating Peace in Mozambique: The Role of the Community of Sant'Egidio', in C. Crocker, F. O. Hampson and P. Aall (eds) (1999) *Herding Cats: Multiparty Mediation in a Complex World*, Washington DC: United States Institute of Peace, pp. 245–73.

Boutros-Ghali, B. (1992) *An Agenda for Peace*, New York, United Nations.
—— (1999) *Unvanquished: A US-UN Saga*, London: I. B. Tauris.
Crocker, C., F. O. Hampson and P. Aall (eds) (1999) *Herding Cats: Multiparty Mediation in a Complex World*, Washington DC: United States Institute of Peace.
Fortna, V. P. (1994) 'United Nations Angola Verification Mission I', in W. J. Durch (ed.) *The Evolution of UN Peacekeeping*, Basingstoke: Macmillan, pp. 376–87.
Gambari, I. (2003) 'Peacebuilding in Post-Conflict Angola', address at the IPA Policy Forum, New York, 3 June.
International Peace Academy (IPA) (2002) *The Infrastructure of Peace in Africa: Assessing the Peacebuilding Capacity of African Institutions*, New York: IPA, September.
Lemarchand, R. (2001) 'Foreign Policy Making in the Great Lakes Region', in G. Khadiagala and T. Lyons (eds) *African Foreign Policies: Power and Process*, Boulder: Lynne Rienner, pp. 87–106.
Lyons, T. and A. I. Samatar (1995) *Somalia: State Collapse, Multilateral Intervention, and Strategies for Political Reconstruction*, Washington DC: The Brookings Institution.
Malaquias, A. (1996) 'The UN in Mozambique and Angola: Lessons Learned', *International Peacekeeping*, 3, 2: 87–103.
Melvern, L. (2000) *A People Betrayed: The Role of the West in Rwanda's Genocide*, London: Zed Books.
Muyangwa, M. and M. A. Vogt (2000) *An Assessment of the OAU Mechanism for Conflict Prevention, Management and Resolution*, New York: IPA.
Mwanasali, M. (2003) 'From the Organisation of African Unity to the African Union', in M. Baregu and C. Landsberg (eds) *From Cape to Congo: Southern Africa's Evolving Security Challenges*, Boulder: Lynne Rienner, pp. 205–23.
Nzongola-Ntalaja, G. (2002) *The Congo: From Leopold to Kabila*, London: Zed Books, pp. 227–40.
Organization of African Unity (OAU) (2000) *The International Panel of Eminent Persons to Investigate the 1994 Genocide in Rwanda and the Surrounding Events*, July.
Prunier, G. (1995) *The Rwandan Crisis: History of a Genocide*, New York: Columbia University Press.
Sibanda, P. (1999) 'Lessons from UN Peacekeeping in Africa: From UNAVEM to MONUA', in J. Cilliers and G. Mills (eds) *From Peacekeeping to Complex Emergencies: Peace Support Missions in Africa*, Johannesburg and Pretoria: The South African Institute of International Affairs and the Institute for Security Studies, pp. 119–25.
Stedman, S. (1997) 'Spoiler Problems in Peace Processes', *International Security*, 22, 2: 5–53.
Suhrke, A. (1997) 'UN Peacekeeping in Rwanda', in G. Sorbo and P. Vale (eds) *Out of Conflict: From War to Peace in Africa*, Uppsala: Nordiska Afrikainstitutet, pp. 97–113.
UN (1999) *Report of the Independent Inquiry into the Actions of the United Nations during the 1994 Genocide in Rwanda*, 16 December, S/1999/1257.
—— (2000) *Fifth Report on the United Nations Mission in Sierra Leone*, 31 July, S/2000/751.

Index

Lightning Source UK Ltd.
Milton Keynes UK
29 September 2009

144312UK00001B/99/A